EARLY INTERVENTION

SOURCE BOOKS ON EDUCATION
VOLUME 44
GARLAND REFERENCE LIBRARY OF SOCIAL SCIENCE
VOLUME 887

EARLY INTERVENTION
CROSS-CULTURAL EXPERIENCES
WITH A MEDIATIONAL APPROACH

PNINA S. KLEIN
BAR ILAN UNIVERSITY
RAMAT GAN, ISRAEL

IN COLLABORATION WITH:

Karsten Hundeide
Henning Rye
University of Oslo, Norway

Tirussew Teferra
Lakew Wolde Tekle
Addis Ababa University, Ethiopia

Ingrid Pramling
University of Göteborgs, Sweden

Andreas Fuglesang
Dale Chandler
Redd Barna (Save the Children),
Africa

Martha L. Coulter
University of South Florida
Tampa, Fla., United States

Ruth F. Gold
Mary McKnight-Taylor
Hofstra University
Long Island, N.Y., United States

GARLAND PUBLISHING, INC.
NEW YORK AND LONDON
1996

Library of Congress Cataloging-in-Publication Data

Klein, Pnina S.
    Early intervention : cross-cultural experiences with a mediational ap-
proach / Pnina S. Klein.
        p.   cm. — (Garland reference library of social science ; v. 887.
Source books on education ; v. 44)
        Includes bibliographical references (p.   ) and index.
        ISBN 0-8153-1244-X (alk. paper)
        1. Child development—Cross-cultural studies.   2. Exceptional chil-
dren—Services for—Cross-cultural studies.   3. Early childhood education—
Cross-cultural studies.   I. Klein, Pnina S.   II. Series: Garland reference library of social science ; v. 887.   III. Series: Garland reference library of social science.   Source books on education ; vol. 44.
HQ767.9.E254   1996
305.23'1—dc20   95–39963
                                                                    CIP

Printed on acid-free, 250-year-life paper
Manufactured in the United States of America

Contents

v

LIST OF ABBREVIATIONS

AGA	Appropriate for Gestational Age
ASM	Auditory Sequential Memory
CCYC	Cognitive Curriculum for Young Children
COGNET	Cognitive Enrichment Network
ECSE	Early Childhood Special Education
HIPPY	Home Instruction Program for Preschool Youngsters
ITPA	Illinois Tests of Psycholinguistic Abilities
MIL	Mediational Intervention for Literacy
MISC	Mediational Intervention for Sensitizing Caregivers
MISC	More Intelligent and Sensitive Child
MLE	Mediated Learning Experience
NGO	Nongovernmental Organization
OMI	Observing Mediational Interaction
PAR	Participatory Action Research
PPVT	Peabody Picture Vocabulary Test
RBSL	Redd Barna Sri Lanka
SGA	Small for Gestational Age
SES	Socioeconomic Status
VLBW	Very Low Birth Weight
WISCR	Wechsler Intelligence Scale for Children-Revised
WHO	World Health Organization

Introduction

This book presents a new theoretical and practical model for early intervention: the Mediational Intervention for Sensitizing Caregivers (MISC). Aid agencies including the World Health Organization (WHO), UNICEF, and Redd Barna supported research projects on the implementation of this approach with poor, high-risk children in various countries. This book presents reasons for implementation, processes of intervention, and some outcomes of the MISC approach in six countries: Israel, Sweden, USA, Ethiopia, Sri Lanka, and Indonesia.

The current book describes a model for understanding specific components or "criteria" within adult–child interaction affecting *flexibility* or *plasticity* of mind in young children. Through the suggested approach one can identify a series of factors that may turn an adult–child interaction into an enriching learning experience for a child. The proposed approach is particularly suitable for cross-cultural adaptation because these factors may be identified within existing childrearing practices, and parents or caregivers could be helped to identify and increase them within interactions with their children. The program focuses on cultural resensitization and on establishing "emotional literacy" as a prerequisite for cognitive development. Whereas most commonly known interventions are designed to enhance children's skills or abilities, the MISC is primarily concerned with affecting children's need systems and creating dispositions that are essential for future learning, that is, to focus on things; to seek meaning; to inquire about and associate past, present, and future experiences; to seek success or approval; to evaluate one's own actions; and to plan before doing.

Variability in the intervention objectives, processes, and outcome creates a most interesting network of variables that should be considered prior to intervention with young children in various cultures. In addition, the use of the intervention with populations of children with special needs, that is, children born with very low birth weight, children with Down's syndrome, and gifted children, are discussed in the book as possible models for the application of the mediational approach in early intervention programs designed for these children and others requiring special mediation to enable their future learning and development.

Pnina S. Klein

PART 1
MEDIATION AND INTERVENTION

1 A MEDIATIONAL APPROACH TO EARLY INTERVENTION

INTRODUCTION

Why Is an Educational Early Intervention Needed?

There are considerable differences between cultures in the world with regard to what is perceived as an ideal child, a good parent, or a good teacher, and educational philosophies and goals vary. These factors contribute to the formation of differences in childrearing objectives and practices. Still, in the rapidly changing world of today, one can hardly predict the situations that a child will be required to cope with in the future. Under such conditions, preparing young children for future development must include provisions for creating in them *flexibility of mind*, a predisposition for learning from new experiences that they may encounter within their traditional cultural setting or confront as changes introduced by "modernity." *Flexibility of mind* cannot be defined merely by the quantity or variety of content areas acquired by children, but by the needs or "appetites" they acquire for modes of perception, elaboration, and expression that will enable them to learn from new experiences and become more sensitive and socially adjusted.

What these children will learn—in other words, the content and means through which the objective of promoting flexibility of mind will be achieved—is determined by each adult caregiver, and may differ from family to family and from culture to culture.

The respect for cultural differences and the belief in their equal, potential impact on flexibility of mind should not cast a shadow over the needs of millions of individual children across various cultures, who suffer starvation of any cultural transmission or mediation from adult caregivers. This type of deprivation may appear together with actual physical deprivation as well as independent of it. Adults may see to it that infants' basic physical needs are met without thinking of the need to "mediate," to focus and expand their experience of the world to the infant. Furthermore, better medical care leads to the survival of infants who require specialized care and specialized mediation to develop their potential. Lacking such mediation, they will join all other children who are starved for an enriching interaction with a sensitive, human caregiver. World care agencies have made remarkable progress in sustaining life, reducing infant mortality, and improving nutritional conditions of young children. There is still, however, a growing need to focus on the mental type of starvation which, if not dealt with, may lead to retardation and to waste of human potential that is almost as painful and tragic to humanity as the loss of lives.

We are currently in the position to prevent this tragedy by helping and guiding caregivers to recognize these factors in their interactions with children that may promote flexibility of mind. The MISC approach fits in with the cultural background of the family and does not depend upon the import of external methods, ideas, and tools, because it operates inside the existing childrearing practices.

Why Do Things That Have Been Done Naturally in Past Generations Require Special Intervention Now?

In many families infants and young children are still well prepared for future learning. Their mothers, fathers, and other members of the society in which they live provide them with the kind of mediated learning experiences they need, either through the Western type of analytical mediation or through the more traditional non-Western approach of storytelling and other forms of cultural sharing. However, there are many whose normal lives have been interrupted by external economic and social conditions that affect childrearing practices in most dramatic ways, for example, moving from a rural to an urban way of life; mothers joining the workforce outside the home (which may increase their workload and level of stress); war, poverty, and undernutrition; family mobility; breakdown of extended family structures; the growing rate of divorce or single-parent families in some countries. Parents in a rapidly changing world may feel pressured by growing economic needs, alienated from the "new" or core culture, unfamiliar with it, and yet unsure whether the "old" culture is worth transmitting to their young. The young child, growing up under such conditions, may lack the guidance necessary to form relations between past, present, and future, and to benefit from future learning.

Although love is certainly very important for adequate psychological development, love alone will not guarantee a child's intellectual development. This is not to say that children do not need to feel secure, loved, and accepted in order to ensure healthy intellectual development. Quite the contrary, in order to satisfy their curiosity, explore their environment, and relate to others, children need to have a sense of security and a warm, stable, and secure relationship with at least one other person (usually one of their parents). If they do not have this secure relationship, they will not have the courage or peace of mind to explore and investigate new environments and relationships, or the optimistic orientation that something good may be there for them if they try harder.

In a way, one can say that the affectionate bond between a child and its caregiver opens the gate to the child's mental development, but does not, in itself, determine what will pass through the gate.

One of the objectives of the MISC program is to help parents or other caregivers to identify and understand the process through which they affect their child's development and, it is hoped, to improve the quality of the relationship between them and the babies or young children they care for. These changes may consequently promote the chances for mental and emotional development of their children.

Stimulation and Mediation

Parents, especially those in middle-class, modern Western countries, become increasingly aware of the need to help their children race ahead and learn to adjust to the rapidly changing world. In the past decade, scientists in the field of child development have succeeded in demonstrating that immediately following birth (or even *in utero*) babies are able to perceive, process perceptions, and respond far more than we have ever been aware of. Parents are led to believe that these early capacities should be "exercised" and that the way to do it is through stimulation of all the senses. Despite the fact that the concept has become an overused and criticized cliché, many parents and educators still advocate "stimulation." Bombarding infants with visual, auditory, or tactual experiences cannot contribute to the babies' development. In fact, it may even hurt them, leading infants to develop defenses against such intrusion. These defenses may become generalized in the form of dislike for new experiences and contact with others. Mediation presents a sane alternative to stimulation. Parental objectives of mediating the world to the child are achieved through the process of matching what they intend to mediate to the baby with the baby's response. It is the baby's response that regulates the amount of "stimulation" responding to the baby's communication, reading his/her intentions, needs, and preferences and responding to the baby's initiatives. Furthermore, through mediation the complex world is organized for the child, channeled by a network of cultural transmission into a world in which things have meaning, importance, and relevance to future as well as past experiences.

In a competitive, industrialized society, one cannot expect parents to be held back from "stimulating" their young children, especially when they know that others around them are doing it for their children. The MISC approach presents an alternative, helping parents realize that improving their mediational interaction with their children can make a real difference in their lives. It may help them relax and enjoy their children more, become more critical consumers of educational programs and materials, and rest from driving children from one extracurricular activity to the next.

How Do Children Who Are Deprived of Proper Mediation Behave?

Many differences among children in their capacity to benefit from new experiences are linked to the type of interactions they have had with the adults who care for them. These differences are apparent in the way these children approach new experiences, in the way they integrate them with other experiences, and in the way they express themselves. Many of these children lack the enthusiasm or need to explore their environment, to seek out "newness." They are satisfied with a blurred, undifferentiated picture of their environment. Their eyes and ears are not tuned to detect fine differences between various things they perceive through their senses. In cases of extreme deprivation, they grow up to be uninterested, apathetic, and uninvolved. They do not have the need to seek meaning, to make spontaneous comparisons, to compare and contrast things (e.g., "This is a dog, I was once bitten by one . . . so I should be careful now"). Many of these deprived children live in a reality that is constructed from bits and pieces rather than from a continuous flow of experiences. They do not have the need to form a link between cause and effect, between past, present, and future experiences. It is clear that fragmentation in time and space limits one's capacity to benefit from experience, because each experience is "boxed in" in one's mind in isolation from all others. Many of these children have difficulties in bearing in mind a goal or setting a goal for their behavior, especially if such a goal requires several steps for its attainment. They have no need to adjust or plan their behavior in line with the requirements of the task, and, in general, they have no need to control or regulate their own behavior.

Many of these children have no need to express themselves verbally or communicate in a way that will be clearly understood by others. They think and speak in an egocentric manner and are frequently unaware of the need to modify their behavior so that others can better relate to it.

Many of these children are not aware of the fact that they can obtain information from adults or from other sources beyond what meets their eyes or their other senses. Lacking experiences in which someone related events for them or pointed out information about objects or people beyond what can be perceived directly through the senses, these children are not aware that something meaningful may be obtained through questioning or exploration.

Lacking experiences in which adults associate various objects, people, and behaviors with meaning or excitement, these children may feel excitement in relation to very few experiences or objects, in a limited range that is primarily associated with the satisfaction of basic physiological needs. Most of these behaviors have been identified by Feuerstein (1979, 1980) as deficient cognitive processes related to poor mediation experiences. Children who have these limitations may be considered as lacking in flexibility of mind or as having difficulties in benefiting from new experiences.

In an even more serious condition are the children who have been deprived not only of meaningful and challenging interactions with adults, but who have also been deprived of human contact in general, closed off in institutions in which only their physical needs were cared for. Such children have been described by many researchers, including the early writing of Spitz (1946). When these infants were separated from their mothers, they were unhappy and depressed, sometimes to the point of panic. Some of these children showed symptoms such as prolonged screaming, crying, and convulsive trembling. After prolonged periods of separation and isolation, they showed symptoms of either apathy and withdrawal from all human contact, or restlessness, hyperactivity, inability to concentrate, and craving for affection.

In contrast to the children who have suffered from severe maternal deprivation, children who have benefited from proper affectionate care and mediation are basically secure and interested both in people and in the world around them. They have developed the need to interact and to share experiences with the caregiver; to focus and perceive clearly; to associate and form links between perceptions, ideas, and behaviors; to choose an objective; to plan and organize their behavior; to seek information, to ask, to explore, and to take different components of reality into consideration. These children are better equipped to learn from other people and from new experiences and to adjust to their human and general environment in any given culture.

At What Age Is Flexibility of Mind Best Achieved?

One of the most typical of all human traits is the capacity to be modified as a result of new learning. This capacity is characteristic of human beings throughout their entire life cycle (Feuerstein, 1979, 1980). Even adults or old people change following various life experiences. Yet, in infancy and in early childhood, children are most susceptible to environmental effects. They learn several generalized expectations that have the potential of affecting most of their later experiences. Children learn that it pays to be active, that someone out there responds to their demands; alternatively, they learn that they should stay passive, because there is no response to their activity. Children develop a need to explore and share meanings; they seek more information about their environment, or they refrain from it and stick to the minimum obtained through their senses. Children develop the need for active elaboration, comparing, contrasting, summarizing their experiences. Their behaviors clearly affect new experiences that in turn affect others. The younger children are when they develop these various needs and "appetites," the more opportunities they have to benefit from them.

A school-age child who has no flexibility of mind, in the sense defined previously, may be confronted with a wealth of information but will most likely be left unaffected by it unless a "mediator" actively places him/herself between the particular child and the environment, and guides the child step-by-step, so that needs, capacities, and interests are matched with specific components of the subject matter to be learned. At this time the child may have already experienced the feeling of frustration and failure. Although it is possible to affect children's behavior even at a later age, it is probably more pleasant, easier, and more economical in terms of time and effort to begin early in infancy, to prevent difficulties rather than engage in correcting them.

Can We Affect the Development of Infants and Young Children?

It appears that across most cultures, young children begin to sit, walk, and even talk at about the same time. There seems to be an almost universal, sequential timetable of infant development. Is it possible to affect the development of infants?

There is now a great deal of evidence that it is possible to affect motor development as well as cognitive and emotional development.

Many early intervention programs claim success, but their work is often hard to assess. Criteria used to define success and to define which children are needy differ (Scarr & McCartney, 1988). There is, however, a general consensus supporting the idea that early intervention can have lasting and valuable effects (Lazar, Darlington, Murray, Royce, & Snipper, 1982), but there is no guarantee that any given program with any given group of children is sure to work (Ramey, Bryant, & Suarez, 1985; Woodhead, 1988).

This chapter describes a model for understanding specific components or "criteria" within adult–child interactions affecting flexibility or plasticity of mind in young children. Through the suggested approach, one can identify a series of factors that may turn any adult–child interaction into an enriching learning experience for that child. This approach is based in part on Feuerstein's theory of "mediated learning experience" (MLE). The proposed approach is particularly suitable for cross-cultural adaptation because these factors may be identified within existing childrearing practices, and parents may be helped to refocus on those aspects of the interaction with their child that are promoting MLE.

We use several simple criteria to help parents understand and activate positive aspects of their own interaction with their children. Recently it has become clear that most basic factors affecting cognitive development depend upon the kind and amount of human interaction to which a child is exposed. Still, it is surprising that little has been known until recently about those factors within the interactive experiences between the child and his/ her caregiver that are crucial for optimal cognitive development. Carew (1980) demonstrated that experiences involving an infant's interaction with another person, especially experiences in which the adult reacted to the child or prestructured experiences for him/her, correlated with measures of development earlier, more highly, and more consistently as compared to intellectual experiences that were created and experienced by the child him/herself. More specifically, mothers of those children defined as competent infants were found to spend more time teaching the infants, facilitating their activities, and stimulating them intellectually.

What does teaching an infant mean? Are all adult–child interactions equally contributive to differential cognitive development? White, Kaban, and Attanucci (1979) suggested that environments that teach children to gain adults' attention, to please adults, to learn from looking and listening, are environments that promote cognitive development. Yet, the basic question of identifying the potent factors or processes within an interaction between a child and his/her caretaker that promote the development of the previously identified variables, remains largely unanswered.

Numerous studies have repeatedly demonstrated significant relations between various criteria of development and maternal behavior such as attentiveness, warmth, responsiveness, and nonrestrictiveness.

Most of this research, although indirectly supporting the role of an adult mediator between an infant or child and his/her environment, has not yet presented a universal rather than specific content-related theoretical conceptualization of the characteristics of mediation, interaction, or teaching that precede differential cognitive development. An attempt to answer this question will be suggested through the presentation of the theoretical framework of the mediated learning experience.

What Is a Mediated Learning Experience?

The theory of MLE is part of the theoretical framework of *cognitive modifiability* (Feuerstein, 1979), based on the conceptualization of intelligence as the capacity of an organism to use previous experiences for future learning.

What processes must take place in a child's life, what type of learning is required to assure his/her learning how to learn, to assure flexibility or plasticity of mind? There are two basic ways in which an individual is modified (changed) through interaction with his/her environment. The first is modification that occurs as a result of direct exposure to stimuli, that is, direct contact or exposure to stimuli perceived or experienced through the sensory channels. The second process of learning, mediated learning experience, is the process of learning that occurs when another person serves as a mediator between the child or learner and the environment, preparing and reinterpreting the stimuli from the environment so that they become meaningful and relevant for the child.

Mediation is an active process. The mediator acts upon the stimulus by selecting, accentuating, focusing, framing, providing meaning, and locating the stimulus in time and space. The mediation enables individuals to benefit from experience; it actually prepares them to learn, to become modified.

Based on the theory of MLE, the following criteria were identified as universal characteristics of an interaction between an adult and a child, turning that interaction into a mediated learning experience for the child. The identification of these criteria bears far-reaching implications for the construction and evaluation of environments that promote cognitive development of young children and identify risk factors within such environments.

Basic Criteria of an MLE-Type Interaction

FOCUSING—INTENTIONALITY AND RECIPROCITY

In simple terms, this criterion can be described as an attempt on the part of the mediator or caregiver to focus the child's attention on something in the child's surroundings. There must be a clear indication of the adult's intentionality to mediate, and of the child's reciprocity. Reciprocity is achieved when the caregiver has succeeded in catching the child's attention so that the child responds vocally, verbally, or nonverbally to the adult's behavior. Intentionality of the mediator is communicated to the child at a very early stage and creates a joint intention, an openness, a readiness to perceive changes and respond on the part of both parent and child.

A behavior that is intentional is considered reciprocal when the infant or child in the interaction responds vocally, verbally, or nonverbally, even by visual focusing only, to an adult's directive behavior. Taking or handing a toy to a child, for example, is considered focusing only when it is clear that the parent's behavior is intentional and not accidental, and when there is an observable response from the child that he/she saw or heard the intentional behavior of the adult.

The intention to mediate between the environment and the child has several basic components, such as regulating the state of arousal of a child, calling his/her attention to stimuli, and affecting his/her response.

MLE is not accidental; it is a conscious, intentional act. It is a dynamic process in which the mediator (most frequently the mother) attempts a series of actions to reach the objective of her mediation. She moves her head toward the infant or away from the infant's face until he/she focuses on her eyes, or she moves an object until the infant focuses on it. She may vary her tone of voice or rhythm of speech until the infant responds in line with her intentions. Intentionality affects the manner in which a stimulus is presented and attended to by the child. The mother, through adjustments of her behavior, selects that part of the environment on which she wishes to focus the child's attention and chooses and regulates the modes of his/her response.

Intentionality affects the basic processes of arousal. The mother may calm the baby before starting to mediate. She will not engage in MLE if the infant is too sleepy. She does it, for example, through introducing body movement or vocalization in accordance with the child's momentary rhythmic behavior and gradually reduces or increases the pace in the direction intended. Stern (1977a) gives a detailed account of the "atoms" of such interactions. He speaks of the differences in adults' behavior toward infants as compared to their behavior toward other people. Components such as exaggeration in facial expressions, variation in rate of speech and vocal tone, may be considered as parts of the MLE, as tools of intentionality, although these various components may not necessarily be consciously directed. The need to mediate, in itself, is intentional. The component expressions of intentionality are not necessarily consciously controlled. There are intentions that stem from the fact that mothers belong to or are part of a cultural, social, or ethnic group.

What mothers think about their infants, their "naive theories" of childrearing, their image of what a child should grow up to be, shape their behavior toward the infants and are included and expressed in their intentionality, affecting both the manner in which stimuli are presented and attended to.

In one of our studies, we found that mothers' behavior toward their premature infant boys differed significantly compared to their behavior toward premature girls, while still in the intensive care unit in the hospital. Mothers explained this difference by expressing their belief that girls are weaker and therefore need more visiting.

The intention to mediate to the child in a way that will make the stimuli compatible for him/her creates experiences of *mediated sharing*. The need to share experiences with someone else is mediated to the child through interaction with an adult. A child needs experiences of sharing objects, thoughts, points of view, and experiences of empathy in order to expand his/her needs system to include the need to share with another person; for example, the parent's repeated focusing of the child's attention, "Look, look here is . . ." can later be reflected in the child's need to share his/her own perception and experiences with others. One of the basic factors enhancing a breakaway from egocentric perception, processing, and communicating is related to the need to affect the other person, to make him/her understand, to create experiences in which a child has to explain to someone, to show him/her something or ask for something. In order to perform this sharing in a manner that will produce the expected or desired results, egocentric thinking or communicating will not suffice. Sharing is mediated through modeling, scheduling of experiences in which sharing must occur, identification, and reinforcement of sharing experiences or their components in the child's behavior. Mediated sharing serves as the basis for the need to mediate to others, and this affects both a child's cognitive performance as well as his/her social–emotional behavior.

It should be added that children need mediated learning experiences in order to enhance their capacity and need to share with others and interact with them. Without this basic need, toddlers would probably not be able to benefit from being together.

EXPANDING AND GOING BEYOND THE IMMEDIATE (TRANSCENDENCE)
In simple terms, expanding is present when the caregiver tries to extend the child's understanding of what is in front of him/her by explaining, comparing, or adding new experiences that may not be necessary for the ongoing interaction. For example, talking to a child about food during feeding is

beyond what is strictly necessary for the feeding itself, or exploring body parts during bathing is not necessary for bathing. At a higher level, one explains to a child why certain things happen, telling a story about it or showing a child something and comparing it with something he/she has experienced before.

This criterion relates to the fact that through an MLE-type interaction the goal of the interaction is expanding and going beyond the immediate experience, from its immediate precedent and consequences to others that are remote in time and space. A mediated experience is not restricted to the satisfaction of immediate needs. It is by going beyond the immediate that structural changes occur in the child, structural changes in the sense of anticipation of, search for, and need for information beyond the immediate. White et al. (1979), in their description of competent and less competent infants, indicate that competent children ask for adults' assistance; they know how to ask for assistance or information. But how do children know that they can expect more information, that every experience can be viewed as part of other experiences that may expand it? How do children know that there is more to an experience than what meets their eyes or other senses? If one asks a child to carry out a chore, such as bringing an object, the command is sufficient to bring about the desired behavior, but not a mediated learning experience. In essence, the mere fact that the child has carried out the chore indicates that he/she has achieved the immediate goal of the command. However, it has not served as expansion until placed by a mediator in relation to a more distant cause, effect, or any other expansion beyond the immediate. The conceptualization of expansion is thus different from reinforcement; it is also different from explaining an act or merely labeling it verbally. Saying "Thank you" to children or smiling at them would reinforce their acts and perhaps their tendency to do what we ask, but telling them, for example, what the tool is needed for and what may happen if the tool is not used properly, is expanding beyond the immediate and constitutes an MLE. Expanding as described previously is perceived by mothers in non-Western traditional cultures as "teacher's" way of speaking.

MEDIATION OF MEANING AND EXCITEMENT
An adult's behavior that expresses verbal or nonverbal appreciation or affect in relation to objects, animals, people, concepts, and values endows these stimuli with feeling and meaning so that they "stand out" in the child's experience.

These behaviors include facial gestures (e.g., exaggerated opening of the eyes and mouth), sounds (e.g., a sigh or scream of surprise), and verbal expression of affect or labeling (e.g., giving an object a name). All these re-actions make the objects stand out for the child; they become distinctive and meaningful.

The objects that surround us (with the exception of a few that sat-isfy basic needs) have no meaning to the child unless they bear meaning to the mediator: an affective, value-oriented connotation that can be transmitted to the child through the MLE and cannot be obtained through direct expo-sure to stimuli. As strange as it may sound to some people, one has to learn how to pause and wonder.

A child has to learn to expect relations between what is perceived or experienced, and emotional connotations and undertones that may derive from cultural values or other parental experiences. Through mediation the child learns that things and events have a significance beyond what he/she has directly experienced.

Through direct exposure, the child perceives the world, but seeing it without the mediation of its value or the affect it arouses in the adult might not bring about the effect of wonder or attachment and thus will not en-able the child to form this type of relation with future experiences that would present other meaningful objects or relations. I would like to stress that mediation of meaning includes mediation of the meaning of emotions. Chil-dren may experience emotions; they may feel content, angry, or fearful, but if not mediated, the experience may remain isolated, unrelated to its prece-dents and consequences, or to other similar experiences of the children them-selves or of others.

REWARDING—MEDIATING FEELINGS OF COMPETENCE

When adults express satisfaction with children's behavior and explain why they are satisfied, this is an example of mediation of feelings of competence: "Very good, you remembered to take the large blocks first and the small ones afterward."

Through mediation of feelings of competence, children acquire a sense of mastery, a feeling that they are capable and successful, which contributes, no doubt, to their willingness to explore the new and attempt to apply them-selves to new and challenging endeavors. If we want to encourage curiosity and active exploration, we must encourage mediated feelings of competence.

The existing theories of child or personality development relate to the accumulation of success experiences, to the end product, to the sum. The MLE focuses not only on the direct exposure to the success or failure, but also to its interpretation by a human agent as to the place of these experi-ences in relation to other actions of the child, to other parts of the same activity, to possible events that could have led to the outcome and to possible consequences. Merely saying to children, "This is very good," is reinforcing their feelings of competence, but it is limited and its effect may be an increase of similar types of activities. The mediation in this case, as in other MLE, is helping children, not just by reinforcing their efforts, but by focusing on the processes that led to success and on the mental process that preceded it. This form of mediation enables children to use their experiences to construct a realistic picture of their success and of specific components of behavior that led to it. The fact that children experience success is in itself not sufficient to produce feelings of success. In addition, young children may not realize that they have succeeded in performing part of what they attempted to achieve. They need an adult to "scale" their success relative to their abilities and not, as often seen by children, relative to the seemingly perfect performance of another adult. In areas of performance in which we have had fewer mediated learning experiences, we are less capable of learning from direct exposure to our successes, and we are more vulnerable to criticism and more unsure of ourselves. (In most non-Western, traditional cultures, praise is rarely noticeable. It is infrequent, and when given, it is very subtle.)

REGULATION OF BEHAVIOR—HELPING THE CHILD TO PLAN BEFORE ACTING

The parent (or another adult) brings to children's awareness the possibility of "thinking" before doing, of planning steps of behavior toward attaining a goal. Repeated experiences in which mediated regulation of behavior occurs create in children a need for such regulation in their future experiences. The adult, by modeling, demonstrating, or scheduling objects or events in time and space, introduces a pattern (plan) of activities for children, thus regulating the pace and reducing children's impulsiveness in perception, elaboration, and expression. Regulation of behavior entails matching the characteristics of the task to be performed with children's capacities and interests, as well as organizing and sequencing steps toward success. For example, "It is hot. Cool it first before you put it into your mouth," "Let's wash your face slowly, so no soap will get into your eyes," "Slowly, not so hard. It is delicate. Do it softly," or "First, turn all the pieces over, then search for the right piece."

Through this process children learn to match their behavior to the nature of the task, which is required for goal-directed action and problem solving.

In general, MLE prepares the individual to seek experiences of new learning. It instills new needs in the child, that is, the need to go beyond the satisfaction of the body's physical needs; the need to have one's experiences interpreted, related to past and future sequences, and embedded in a meaningful frame of reference that is relevant to the individual.

2 ENHANCING LEARNING POTENTIAL AND LITERACY IN YOUNG CHILDREN

The acronym MISC stands for both the process and the objective of the approach discussed in this book. Through the process of a mediational intervention for sensitizing caregivers of infants and young children, these children stand a better chance of becoming more intelligent and sensitive children, ready to benefit from cultural transmission and new experiences.

How Does the MISC Differ from Other Programs?

The overall objective of the MISC program is to help and sensitize parents (and educators or other caregivers) so that they can relate to their children in a way that will enhance their children's cognitive, socioemotional, and moral development, and prepare the children to benefit from future learning.

The MISC program was designed to overcome some of the difficulties that were inherent in ongoing intervention projects in various countries in Africa, Asia, the United States, and Europe. Although different programs were ongoing in different communities, the same problems were reported repeatedly in most of them:

1.   Parents from various ethnic backgrounds, especially those of low socioeconomic status, were led by professionals to believe that there is one ideal model, a "better way" of raising young children, better than the traditional way they brought with them from their old homes. The transition from the old to the new most frequently led to a feeling of alienation. Parents felt that what they had to give or transmit to their children was not sufficient to promote later development, and therefore, they could only contribute to the development of the infants the little they had been taught by the visiting specialist in the ongoing programs.

2.   Structured, content-oriented programs using specific materials tended to create a dependency on these materials (toys, booklets, etc.). In several communities where mothers were engaged in intervention programs in which structured materials such as toys or exercise booklets were presented, mothers requested these same materials for their younger children and were completely unable to transfer from a previous intervention to another child any general understanding about underlying processes or functions necessary for their child's development. In fact not only did they not gain from the project, they frequently lost their own initiative and trust in themselves as, first and foremost, teachers of their children. These programs led parents to believe that children learn only when one sits with them to do the exercises incorporated in a structured program or game.

3.   Structured programs typically include materials that are suitable for a specific age group or a defined situation. Once these characteristics were no longer relevant (i.e., children grew older), programs were terminated and parents did not know what to do.

4.   One of the basic differences between the MISC program and other early intervention programs is the fact that, whereas other programs aim to affect cognitive skills or processes, *the prime objective of the MISC program is to affect a child's need system, to create new, more differentiated needs that will promote his/her future appetite and capacity for learning.* It is a mistake to think that merely bringing people into contact with new experiences will help them develop a differentiated taste or need for them. We can take children to the theater, to the library, or to a concert, but will merely taking them create in them the need to seek cultural experiences of this kind in the future? An infant or young child experiencing pleasant feelings in the presence of an adult will learn to want to be with him/her even after basic needs have been fulfilled. Hearing the adult, pointing to things, explaining them, associating, comparing, contrasting, and so on, becomes desirable as well, and thus more needs for specific types of "educational" interactions are created. It is through human mediation that an infant or young child learns to need and seek more information, beyond what is directly perceived by his/her senses.

What makes the adult–child interaction a pleasant experience is to a large extent related to how successful the two partners are in matching and synchronizing their behaviors, as described earlier. Both the child and the adult play a major role in this interaction; there is no doubt today that we are dealing here with a two-way process, parent affecting child, and child affecting parent in return.

As the MISC is focused on the quality of interaction between caregiver and child and not on the content or the material used in this interaction, it is not a "program" in the traditional sense. It is more a method for sensitizing mothers (or other caregivers) to the positive aspects of their existing interaction and childrearing practices. As such, it can never be in conflict with their own traditional way of childrearing. As stated earlier, imposing structured programs based on other people's cultural standards tends to produce three negative effects:

1. Dependency
2. Alienation
3. Feelings of inferiority in parents

In the MISC these effects are counteracted by helping caregivers to see the positive aspects of their own interaction with their children, thus strengthening their self-confidence and trust in their capacity and in their traditional knowledge of childrearing.

Typical Features of the MISC Program

The essence of this program is sensitization and consciousness-raising of the trainees regarding key issues in the relationship between caregiver and child. In practice this means trying to convey a practical understanding of the criteria of mediation to the caregiver through a participatory educational approach.

The objective of the MISC Program is to promote a sound, facilitative adult–child relationship. The program *can be implemented with any group of children, in any context where interaction is taking place,* from nursery and preschool to large-scale community-based projects involving local resource persons who are trained to do "home training" with parents.

The training in sensitization and consciousness-raising is usually done in the homes (in parent groups, in day-care settings, or kindergartens) through *a participatory approach* in which a series of interactive techniques are used, for example, role playing and modeling; emphasizing empathy by focusing on "How would you feel if . . ."; analyzing concrete examples from parents' daily experience with their children; and if a video is available, parents (or other caregivers) may view themselves interacting with their own children and afterward analyze this interaction according to some basic criteria of mediation.

In this program only positive aspects of the parents' interaction with their children are pointed out. This leads parents to become more motivated and interested as they gain feelings of competence as caregivers. The latter is most important for the long-term effects of the program.

RATIONALE: THEORY AND RESEARCH

Countless efforts have been made to develop early-intervention programs designed to enhance cognitive development of young children. Inconsistent and disappointing findings have been reported in several major studies concerning the efficacy of early intervention (Clarke-Stewart & Fein, 1983; Collins, 1984; Lazar, Darlington, Murray, Royce, & Snipper, 1982; Ramey, Bryant, & Suarez, 1985; Scarr & Weinberg, 1986). These major syntheses of early intervention studies report an increase of about 0.5 *SD* IQ following various compensatory interventions with disadvantaged preschool children. Even this effect was found to fade with the passage of time. In the existing literature the reasons for these discouraging findings are as yet unclear. Some of the programs, for example, the Family Development Research Program (FDRP; Lally, Mangione, & Honig, 1988) presented a full complement of educational, nutritional, health and safety, and human service resources. This intervention continued for five years, starting at birth. The omnibus conceptualization behind this type of program seems desirable; however, its applicability for use with large populations cross-culturally may be limited. It is also quite difficult to assess the differential effects of variables within the intervention on various outcome measures.

Dunst and Trivette (1988) summarized the results of eight studies on the effects of different forms of social support on child, parent, and family functioning. They suggested that social support affects well-being of parents, which in turn affects parents' interactional styles, which in turn influence child behavior. I believe this sequence is not exclusively unidirectional and that it is possible to affect the quality of parent–child interaction and the child's behavior, and consequently to empower parents to give them a sense of hope and a feeling of active participation in the future of their children and in their own well-being.

Three major themes that I believe are prerequisite for any successful intervention with infants and young children have not been seriously taken into consideration in earlier intervention attempts. These themes include (a) cultural variability in relation to educational goals, philosophies of childrearing, parental roles, and perceptions of the child; (b) the role of parental mediation in children's emotional development; and (c) parental mediational behaviors that constitute a quality mediated learning experience.

Cultural Variability: Parental Perceptions and Goals

Parents' values, assumptions, and educational philosophy, as well as their perceptions of their children, were found, in numerous studies, to guide parental behavior (e.g., Bell, 1979; Freeberg & Payne, 1967; Klein, 1984).

A careful assessment of cultural–psychological variables should constitute a major prerequisite of any early intervention because of the dramatic effects of these variables on the quality and style of parental interaction with their children.

Objectives "imported" by psychologists or educators from one culture may be unsuitable, and therefore stand little chance to be effective with parents of another culture. In my own work with parents and caregivers in Sri Lanka and Ethiopia, it became apparent that they did not want what they called a "Western-type" of "pushy," self-centered, competitive, "intelligent" child. Their educational objective was a noncompetitive, caring, sharing individual. Similar reports were made for Indonesian parents (Hundeide, 1988). For these parents, an objective such as enhancing flexibility of mind was not desirable unless it was clearly related to their own educational objectives for the child.

Mothers' ideas about the timetable of development in infancy and childhood are influenced by cultural factors significantly more than by information gained in the course of parenting. It appears that more westernized cultures believe in an earlier timetable of infant development than the more traditional cultures (Goodnow, Cashmore, Cotton, & Knight, 1984; Hess, Kashigawa, Azuma, Price, & Dickson, 1980; Rosenthal, 1985).

Differences in parental philosophy of childrearing or perception of children's development go far beyond timetables of developmental landmarks. Their view of the ideal child, and consequently their objectives for the child, may differ dramatically.

In addition to the sociocultural effects on parents' view of their children, mothers' perceptions of themselves as effective agents in child development, their styles of coping with their life stresses, their support systems, and so on, must be taken into serious consideration in an attempt to understand and affect parental mediation to the child. Understanding the parent–child relationship within its cultural context must include an attempt to understand the unique meaning ascribed to the basic concepts used by parents in expressing their wishes, philosophies, and perceptions of themselves and their children. When parents say they want a wise or a clever child, it may have a different meaning in Western cultures as compared to some other cultures. For example, for the Clee aboriginal people of Northern Canada, *wise* means something close to "respect and respectful, thinks hard, presistent," whereas the Western *intelligence* may be perceived as more in line with what they call "backward knowledge, cunning knowledge used to manipulate others" (Berry & Bennett, 1992).

The factor of cultural impact on parental behavior is especially dramatic in relation to populations of children with special needs. In some traditional rural communities (e.g., in Portugal, Indonesia, and Ethiopia), the disabled or mentally retarded child is viewed as a punishment from God and thus parents have to accept it and not make any attempts to change the situation or help the child reach normal functioning.

A mother's knowledge about the environment (i.e., her level of differentiation between trees, flowers, birds, objects, etc.; her acquaintance with her own culture; and her appreciation of its songs, customs, foods) may limit or enhance her capacity for cultural transmission and help her develop her child's differentiated awareness of the world in which he/she lives. If one does not focus on detail in the environment, how is he/she going to point it out or mediate to a child?

Knowledge and feelings affect parental behavior, both consciously and subconsciously, for example, differential treatment of boys versus girls with a similarly perceived temperament (Klein, 1984). Boys and girls who were perceived as more active received a higher frequency of "stimulation," but whereas boys received predominantly motor and physical stimulation, girls received more visual and verbal stimulation.

A mother's style of interaction with her baby is strongly affected by her basic perception or model of the interaction she holds in her mind of what "good mothering" should be. Parents' childhood experiences, and memories of their own relationship with their parents, were found to provide a filter through which parents view and respond to children's characteristics and behaviors (i.e., Belsky, 1984; Crowell & Feldman, 1988; Ricks, 1985). It has been postulated that children create an internal mental representation or working model of self and others based on their experiences with their parents (Bowlby, 1980). It has been further postulated that internal models have a propensity for stability and, once established, tend to be perpetuated (Bowlby, 1980). We have recently found that *quality of mediation*, as empirically defined in our study (Klein, 1987b, 1989, 1991), is related to the quality of mother–infant attachment and can be modified through direct intervention designed to raise the frequency of the basic criteria of mediation (Tal & Klein, 1994).

Mediation implies a communication between two individuals in which each is adjusting the form and content of a message to the communicator's definition of the nature of the receiver and the situation (Rommetveit, 1974; Labov, 1979). In line with this general principle of communication, an adult may be a "good mediator" to one child but not to another, based on the adult's perception of the child and the child's perception of the adult. Hundeide (1988) speaks of a tacit "contract" that may exist between the adult and the child: that is, we adjust our communications to the way we interpret the nature of the receiver and the situation, and after some time, this may become stabilized into a relationship, a contract, in relation to which the two participants invite particular styles of interaction with each other. Consequently, for example, mothers categorized as low mediators, may be able to interact with their child in a high mediational style, provided the context, situation, and definition of their child are such that they invite such a style. *The culture may define the "right" and "wrong" styles of communication with children at different age levels.* For example, mothers observed sitting behind their children, quietly watching them play, were found to believe that children should be given the freedom to choose what they want to do with no interference from the adult. These mothers followed a model of mothering dictating that uninvolvement equals good mothering.

The dynamic nature of the style or code of interaction has been demonstrated, for example, in studies by Ginsburg (1972), who found that what Berenstein (1970) defined as an *elaborated code of communication* depended on the way the speaker defined the receiver and the situation. This orientation has significant implications for intervention strategies. If we become aware of mediational skills, we may be able to find the characteristics of the specific situations and perceptions yielding the highest forms of mediational styles within an individual and attempt to approximate those in other situations (provided they are culturally plausible).

Prior to the planning of any intervention with very young children, it is necessary to answer the basic questions related to the issues discussed earlier: What are the parents' goals for the child? How do they view the child as compared to others? What do they see as their role? What do they consider good parenting and how much effect do they think they may have on their child's development? In addition, the MISC approach advocates a special focus on the specific themes and areas of interest of the parents within their own life space and culture and encourages them to use these in their interaction with their children.

Despite the universality of the criteria determining the occurrence of mediation, the quality of mediation may vary depending on the personal involvement of the mediator in the subject he/she is attempting to mediate. Mediators may show their best mediational skills when attempting to mediate to a child something they are excited about and are well familiar with. *Cultural themes that are highly valued by parents and with which they are well familiar may thus be considered as excellent mediational contents.* In terms of implications for intervention, it may be a good starting point to identify the particular preferences, hobbies, and interests within a family and suggest those as a content area for mediation to the child.

Cultural variability is assessed prior to the onset of the MISC intervention through observations, collection of basic data regarding the participating population, and an in-depth structured interview of the adult members of each participating family or center.

Based on the parents' responses to these questions, decisions are made as to the starting point and the direction of the intervention. It starts with a parental need that could be met through the intervention. For example, rural parents in Indonesia, Sri Lanka, or Ethiopia want their children to help out on the farm. The parents may not be interested in a program unless it is clear to them that it may help them raise a child who will be better able to understand and find solutions to problems related to life on the farm. A literacy program introduced in this context has a better chance of meeting parental needs and motivation to continue with it. Parental interests, special likes, and skills are focused on throughout the intervention process.

RESEARCH ON EARLY MEDIATION AND ITS EFFECTS

The relationship between various parental behaviors and infants' development has been studied widely and intensively. However, available research pertaining to cognitive development does not clarify the specific elements of adult–infant interaction that constitute a learning experience for the child.

Bryant and Ramey (1987) conclude their review of early interventions by saying,

> We are still unclear about which specific aspects of early experience are causally linked to specific aspects of intellectual development. Did children learn more from their many experiences with educational materials and toys, or from the expressive descriptive language used by their caregivers as they played with the toys, or from the emotional support they felt, allowing a more confident exploration of the environment? The theoretically important point seems to be that intellectual development can potentially be influenced by systematic efforts aimed at a variety of modes in the social–interactional system of infants and their caregivers. (pp. 74–75)

There is a theoretical base (Feuerstein, 1979, 1980) and empirical data (Klein, Weider, & Greenspan, 1987b; Klein, 1988, 1991) suggesting that specific characteristics of adult interaction with children constitute mediational behavior and may affect children's predisposition to learn from new experiences. Mediated learning, as distinct from direct learning through the senses, occurs when the environment is interpreted for the child by another person who understands the child's needs, interests, and capacities, and who takes an active role in making components of that environment, as well as past and future experiences, compatible with the child. Mediation affects the individual's present learning and may improve his/her opportunity to learn from future experiences.

BASIC ELEMENTS OF MEDIATION
Empirical Definitions

Basic elements of what constitutes a teaching mediational interaction between a caregiver and a child at any age were identified, based on Feuerstein's (1979, 1980) theory of cognitive modifiability, a summary of available research, and a series of studies carried out by the author. The most salient of these factors, mentioned earlier in this book, were empirically defined (Klein et al., 1987a, 1987b; Klein, 1988, 1991).

- *Focusing* (Intentionality and Reciprocity): Any adult act or sequence of acts that appears to be directed toward achieving a change in the child's perception, or response (e.g., selecting, exaggerating, accentuating, scheduling, grouping, sequencing, or pacing stimuli).
- *Affecting* (Mediation of Meaning): An adult's behavior that expresses verbal or nonverbal appreciation or affect in relation to objects, animals, or concepts and values.
- *Expanding* (Transcendence): An adult's behavior directed toward the broadening of a child's cognitive awareness, beyond that which is necessary to satisfy the immediate need that triggered the interaction.
- *Rewarding* (Mediated Feelings of Competence): Any verbal or nonverbal behavior of an adult that expresses satisfaction with a child's behavior or identifies specific components of the child's behavior that the adult considers successful.

It was found that the factors of quality mediation, as empirically defined before, predicted cognitive outcome measures up to four years of age better than did the children's own cognitive test scores in infancy, or other presage variables related to pregnancy and birth histories and to mothers' education (Klein, Weider, & Greenspan, 1987). Similar findings were reported for a sample of very low birth weight infants (Klein, Raziel, Brish,

TABLE 1.1 DEFINITION AND EXAMPLES OF BASIC CRITERIA OF MEDIATION

Definition of Criteria	Examples
Intentionality and reciprocity (focusing behavior): Any act or sequence of acts of an adult that appears to be directed toward affecting a child's perception or behavior. These behaviors are considered reciprocal when the infant or child in the intervention responds, vocally, verbally, or nonverbally.	Selecting, exaggerating, accentuating, scheduling, grouping, sequencing, or pacing stimuli. Talking or handing a toy to a child is seen as intentionality and reciprocity only when it is apparent that the adult's behavior is intentional and not accidental, and when there is an observable response from the child that he/she saw or heard the intentional behavior. Examples of intentionality might include a parent making a visible effort to change his/her behavior and the environment by (a) bringing an object to the child, moving it back and forth, observing the child and continuing to adjust the stimulus until the child focuses on it; (b) moving a bottle or a particular food item in front of the infant's eyes until he/she focuses on it; (c) placing toys in the bath water; (d) placing oneself in front of the child to obtain eye-to-eye contact; (e) placing objects in front of the child at a distance requiring that he/she will attempt to reach them.
Mediation of meaning (exciting): An adult's behavior that expresses verbal or nonverbal excitement, appreciation, or affect in relation to objects, animals, concepts, or values.	These behaviors may include facial gestures or paralinguistic expressions (e.g., a sigh or scream of surprise), verbal expressions of affect, classification or labeling, and expressions of valuation of the child or adult's experience (e.g., "Look, I am washing your foot now," "See how long this macaroni is," "Look at this beautiful flower," or "This cup is special, it belonged to Grandfather").
Transcendence: An adult's behavior directed toward the expansion of a child's cognitive awareness, beyond what is necessary	Talking to a child about the qualities of the food during feeding is beyond what is necessary to assure provision of nutrition; exploring body parts or the characteristics of water during bathing is not necessary for bathing. Transcendence maybe provided through expressions implying inductive and deductive reasoning, spontaneous comparisons, clarification of

Definition of Criteria	Examples
to satisfy the immediate need that triggered the interaction.	spatial and temporal orientation, noting strategies for short- and long-term memory or search and recall memory activities.
Mediated feelings of competence: Any verbal or nonverbal behavior of an adult that expresses satisfaction with a child's behavior and that identifies a specific component or components of the child's behavior that the adult considers contributive to the experience of success.	Such identification can be achieved, for example, by careful timing of a verbal or gestural expression of satisfaction, through repetition of a desired behavior, or through verbal and nonverbal expression (i.e., saying "Good," "Wonderful," "Great," "Yes," or clapping hands and smiling when the child successfully completes a task or part of it).
Mediated regulation of behavior: Adult behaviors that model, demonstrate, and/or verbally suggest to the child regulation of behavior in relation to the specific requirements of a task, or to any other cognitive process required prior to overt action.	Behavior is regulated on a mediational basis by the process of matching the task requirements with the child's capacities and interests, as well as through organizing and sequencing steps leading toward success. For example, "It is hot; cool it first before putting it in your mouth," "Let's wash your face carefully, so that no soap will get into your eyes," "Slowly! Not so hard! It is delicate, do it gently," or "First, turn all the pieces over, then search for the right piece." Mediated regulation of behavior may be related to the processes of perception (e.g., systematic exploration), to the process of elaboration (e.g., planning behavior), or to the processes of expressive behavior (e.g., reducing egocentric expressions and regulating intensity and speed of behavior).

& Birenbaum, 1987). Intercorrelations between mothers' mediational behaviors over time, when their children were 6, 12, 24, and 36 months, averaged .53 and the average interjudge reliability for assessing these behaviors ranged between .74 and .81 in studies of low socioeconomic status (SES) American (Klein, Weider, & Greenspan, 1987b) and Israeli mother–infant samples (Klein, 1988).

Because these studies were correlational and could not lead to cause-and-effect conclusions, another study was designed to examine the sustained effects of modifying the mother–infant mediational interaction on infants' cognitive test performance and behavior. This study will be referred to as the follow-up study.

The research design of the follow-up study included a randomized assignment to the experimental and control groups; an observational assessment of maternal mediation; a "baseline" assessment of the infants' developmental status, using Bayley's Mental Development Scales, prior to training mothers in mediational strategies; and a follow-up evaluation of experimental versus control mothers and children one year and three years after the termination of training.

The total study sample consisted of 68 families in a small, low-SES urban community in Israel, who were randomly assigned at a ratio of approximately 2.5 to 1 to an experimental and control group ($n = 48$ and 20, respectively). This community was singled out for intervention by the Ministry of Education and the Office of Welfare in Israel. Large proportions of children in this community had poor school-readiness records, experienced school failure, and dropped out of school.

Activities developed for the experimental group were based on the MISC Program. These activities were designed to improve mother/child mediation to her child. The level of mediation was defined by the frequency of appearance of empirically defined maternal mediating behaviors and the children's responsiveness. The training of mothers was carried out in the homes by paraprofessional "mediators" and supervised by paraprofessional developmental psychologists.

Intervention in both groups was terminated when mothers could verbally define the basic components of the parental behaviors targeted by the intervention. In the experimental group, these behaviors were represented by the criteria of mediation, and in the control group, by basic aspects of a responsive, nonpunitive yet demanding environment.

Mediation processes affect children's cognitive input, elaboration, and output processes. It was expected that maternal behaviors of focusing, affecting, and expanding would affect children's vocabulary and abstract reasoning and, in general, prepare children to perform better in situations requiring "new learning," such as tasks requiring immediate sequential memory. Thus, children's cognitive performance was assessed using the following measures: Peabody Picture Vocabulary Test (PPVT), the auditory reception, visual reception, visual association, auditory association, and auditory sequential memory of the Illinois Tests of Psycholinguistic Abilities (ITPA), as well as the Beery and Bucktanika test of visual motor integration.

Comparison of the two groups on the separate components of each mediation factor three years following the intervention revealed that the experimental-group mothers showed significantly more mediation behaviors across all components of mediation (Klein & Alony, 1993).

Significant differences in favor of the experimental group were found on the PPVT, auditory reception, and auditory association measures. The average PPVT IQ for the experimental group was 101 (SD = 15.5), and for the control group, 84 (SD = 14.1).

Of all factors of maternal mediation, *mothers' expanding and rewarding behaviors were most frequently related to children's cognitive performance*. Children's expressions of affect were related more to factors of maternal mediation than to any of the other variables of children's behavior, and were mostly related to maternal encouraging behaviors, maternal expansion of ideas, maternal request for affect, and expression of feelings. Focusing behavior was positively and significantly related to all variables of children's expression of affect.

One of the most interesting findings in the follow-up study was the relationship found between maternal mediation behaviors and children's test performance. Mothers' expanding and rewarding behaviors were found to be most frequently correlated with children's cognitive measures. Within these two criteria, *maternal request for expansion of ideas* (rather than provision of information) *and rewarding with explanation* (rather than simply saying "Good," "Fine," etc.) *were singled out as most significantly related to the children's cognitive performance at age four*. These findings coincide with those reported by Collins (1984), identifying the variable of "demandingness" as one of the most essential determinants of the quality of "good" family environments. The current study provided the possibility of exploring the effects of various types of "demandingness."

Children's expressions of affect (including naming, nonverbal expression of feeling, and associating between things) were most significantly related to all criteria of maternal mediation, but mostly to maternal rewarding behaviors, maternal expansion of ideas, and maternal request for "affect," that is, for signs of excitement in relation to some meaningful objects or events.

Focusing behavior, which was not significantly related to any of the cognitive outcome measures, was most significantly related to the children's expression of excitement (i.e., $r = .73$ between maternal focusing of children's attention and the child's spontaneous naming of objects or things, and $r = .58$ between maternal focusing and children's spontaneous provisions of association).

A noteworthy relationship was found between the children and the mothers' nonverbal expressions of feelings. Mothers' expressions of feelings were also found to relate to children's spontaneous provision of rewards to others ($r = .44$). The positive relationship of the criteria of mediation to both cognitive outcome measures and to behavioral assessments is an important finding in itself. It supports those (i.e., Lazar et al., 1982) who claim that a focus on cognition is not an adequate criterion for determining the impact of parent–child interaction.

The MISC program applied in the follow-up study was not designed directly to improve children's performance on specific cognitive tasks. Yet, three years following the termination of the intervention, children in the experimental group outscored the children in the control group with regard to language performance as measured by the PPVT, and two measures of verbal reasoning. These findings suggest that those low-SES children who participated in the experimental group were brought well within the normal range of verbal performance.

Mothers in the experimental group expressed higher aspirations for their children's intellectual growth, but they also expressed a more flexible and balanced view of what factors were important for their children's future development.

Provision of external rewards is frequently criticized (LeVine, 1980; Lepper, 1981). In the Klein and Alony (1993) follow-up study, a verbal or gestural praise contributed favorably to children's cognitive and social–emotional development if it was accompanied by explanations that related the "success" to its causes or associated (compared or contrasted) it with other experiences. With regard to rewarding or encouraging young children, we have to be aware of the pendulum of psychological "style" and its dangers. Young children depend on adults for mediation of competence. Quality mediation requires a recognition of children's individual needs, including those related to the amount and type of reward they may require.

It has been well established in psychoeducational literature that children from poor families generally score lower on a variety of cognitive measures related to intelligence and academic performance as compared to middle-class children. Mothers' intelligence or years of schooling were repeatedly pointed out as a powerful predictor of children's future cognitive performance. The following finding from the MISC intervention and follow-up study is of special interest in view of the above facts. The correlation between mothers' years of schooling and their mediation to their infants and young children prior to the intervention was almost identical in the intervention and the comparison (control) group (for the intervention group, $r = .43$, and for the control group, $r = .45$). Three years following the intervention, the correlation between mothers' years of schooling and their mediation went down (to $.21$; $df = 41$; $p > .05$) in the intervention group, while remaining almost constant ($r = .42$; $df = 16$; $p < .05$) for the control group. Furthermore, the correlation between mothers' years of schooling and children's Bayley Mental Development Scales for both groups prior to the intervention was $.36$ ($df = 57$; $p < .01$). Following the intervention, the correlation between mothers' years of schooling and children's PPVT scores was $.23$ ($df = 41$; $p > .05$) for the intervention group and $.41$ ($df = 16$; $p > .05$) for the control group. These findings suggest that the quality of maternal mediation can be modified and once modified, the link between maternal schooling and mothers' behavior toward their children can be modified as well, resulting in a breakup of the commonly found linkage between mothers' education and children's cognitive achievements. Poor mothers can improve their mediation and contribute to their children's cognitive development as well as middle-class mothers.

Long-Term Intervention Effects on the Mothers

In a follow-up study carried out six years following the MISC intervention in Israel, it was found that 75% of the mothers in the intervention group (though none of the mothers in the control group) found jobs and were working out of home. Working out of home was coupled with higher satisfaction with one's self. This could be viewed, at least partially, as related to the empowerment effect of the intervention. Those mothers who initially viewed themselves as helpless and as having little potential to affect their children's development, as well as their own lives, gained an awareness of some basic elements of effective interaction with others (babies and children were the direct target, but the objective was to improve the process of adult–child interaction). Mothers clearly expressed in interviews or written reports that they had begun to use the criteria of mediation in their everyday lives in relation to other members of the family, as well as friends and authority figures.

Hana, a thirty-five-year-old mother of three children, reported the following:

With my teenage daughter nothing works except for lots and lots of mediated competence. If I want to get anywhere with her I must first find a few good things she did or comment on something she is wearing that looks nice. I used to have terrible fights with her trying to start the simplest conversation. Now I am trying to match my objective with her mood or what I know she wants and compliment her a lot and we are all happier.

Sara, a thirty-two-year-old mother of four children, told the following at a group meeting:

I have learned to express positive emotions and mediate competence to others. My husband lost his job. It was very hard on him sitting in the house and doing nothing. He was finally given a small job by the local community center. He was asked to paint tree trunks and hated it. He was ashamed to be seen by his friends. On Saturday when we were walking down the street with our kids, I wanted to make him feel better so I mediated competence to him. I said: "Look how festive the street looks with all those tree trunks white and clean."

Jasmin, a twenty-three-year-old mother of two babies, told about her own experience.

I used to get up in the morning and start with some chores. By the time it was noon and I had to feed the children, I realized I have not done anything. I would do part of one thing, then go to another, then remember that I have to finish the first. I was disorganized. When I tried to improve my own mediated regulation of behavior to my son, I realized that I need it myself. I need to plan before doing to decide what to do first and what to do later. If I had to buy milk, I checked if there is anything else I need at the grocery or the bank, which is right next to it. This way I saved myself a lot of time and effort. I used to have problems with my neighbor, so I decided to use some mediation of competence. It worked wonders. Now I really see the good in her and she sees the good in me.

Mothers expressed the changes that took place in their own attitudes toward school authorities and their feelings toward school.

Tamara, a twenty-eight-year-old mother of two children, told of her experience with school:

I used to hate coming to school with David [her older child, six years old]. The teacher attacked me first thing in the morning: "David was a bad boy yesterday." I used to get angry and shout at him in front of the other children. I thought that a good mother should discipline like that. Now with my younger son Rafael, three years old, I can tell the caregivers to look at what he does well and encourage him. I could tell who mediates well and who is just talking a lot. I wish I could choose the teacher who would teach my children. . . . I am sometimes disturbed by things I see in kindergarten and I see it as my duty to talk to the teacher about it.

The distribution of parents' perception of what they wanted their children to become showed that more parents in the intervention group following the MISC program wanted wiser children, children who could learn better, whereas parents in the comparison group expressed wanting more disciplined children.

Parents who participated in the program expressed feeling more capable of affecting their children's development as compared to parents in the comparison group (Klein & Alony, 1993). Differences in attitudes and aspirations of parents in relation to boys as compared with girls were less marked in the group that participated in the program as compared to the comparison group. It seems that sex differences become a part of other characteristics of the children that need to be considered and responded to in the process of mediating to them.

It appears that mothers use concepts of mediation criteria and apply those to their benefit in understanding, criticizing, or constructing interactions with others. In the three-year follow-up study described earlier, it was clearly demonstrated that significant differences in the quality of mediation occurred following the intervention and that those lasted at least three years following the intervention. Based on mothers' interviews six years following the MISC intervention, it appears that mothers felt more competent about their parenting, as well as their interaction with school authorities and other adults in general.

Parental Mediation and Emotional Development

A positive emotional climate is a prerequisite for a quality interaction with a young child. Love is difficult to define and many researchers have rejected this aspect of mothering as introducing mystical and immeasurable elements. However, the quality of family relationship has been found to be strongly associated with the nature of the child's psychological development. Where warmth in the family is lacking, there is a higher risk of the child developing deviant behavior (Rutter, 1981). The growing interest in the scientific study of "attachment" is in my opinion the back door through which the concept of love is returning to the scientific arena.

It is accepted that in order for attachment to occur, the same person must have contact with the child over a prolonged period of time. However, the absolute amount of time spent with the child is not the major determinant of attachment. It was suggested in early studies (Schaffer & Emerson, 1964) that the intensity of parental interaction with the child is an important factor. In studies of kibbutz children (Bowlby, 1969), children were found to be more often attached to their mothers, whom they saw for a short period of intensive interaction, than to the *metapelet* (the caregiver) who cared for them all day.

From a cognitive-development perspective, there is a special impact of early infant–parent interaction on later emotional development. In infancy there is an absolute predominance of imaginable schemata. Because internal language does not exist yet, it is impossible to decentralize these images; for the infant they correspond to reality. These basic images have a strong impact on the developing child; they cannot be modified, placed in a temporal dimension, or thought of, because they are not coded in words; they resist change. Infants internalize their experiences with their parents as the only existing reality and therefore the image of that reality and of themselves in it is so central to future development (Guidano & Liotti, 1983).

EFFECTS OF THE MISC ON MOTHER–INFANT ATTACHMENT

The link between mediational experiences as defined within the framework of the MISC approach and type of attachment as defined by Bowlby (1980) recently has been reported in research (Tal & Klein, 1994). The type of attachment between infants and their mothers at twelve or eighteen months was found to be related to children's subsequent cognitive and social emotional development. Children who were rated as securely attached to their mothers at one year of age were found to score higher on school achievement measures and displayed less adjustment problems in later life as compared to children who were not securely attached (displaying anxious and avoidant attachment). In recent years several intervention programs have been designed in an attempt to prevent attachment problems or reduce their effects (Lyons-Ruth, Connell, Grunebaum, & Botein, 1990; Lieberman, Weston, & Pawl, 1991). These programs are based on a psychotherapeutic approach with some developmental guidance. The MISC approach, designed to enhance the quality of mediation provided to the child, with its special focus on the affective as well as the cognitive components of a mediational interaction, was hypothesized to affect the quality of attachment as well as cognitive development of infants and young children.

The study was conducted in Givat Olga, a small urban community in Israel, located near the city of Hedera. All families who had babies born between February 15, 1990 and February 28, 1991 were contacted and asked if they would be willing to participate in a study of child development that would involve videotaping their babies and discussing their development. Of all mothers contacted, 115 mothers, comprising 75% of the mothers contacted, agreed to participate. Throughout the study, 14 of them left for various reasons (moving to another location, illness in the family, mothers going out to work, etc.). The mothers and infants were randomly divided into two groups: 50 mother–infant pairs in the intervention group, and 51 in the control group. The final sample included 45 boys and 54 girls, equally distributed between the two groups. Of the infants in the study, 36% were firstborn children. The average number of children per family was three. All the participating infants had normal Bayley Mental Development Scale age scores.

The research design included a preassessment, intervention, and a postassessment. The pre- and postintervention assessments included a ten-minute videotaped session of mother–infant free play, (analyzed using the Observing Mediational Interaction [OMI]; Klein & Alony, 1993), and an interview designed to obtain basic information about mothers' perceptions of their children, themselves, their potential to affect their children's development, the children's day, and so on. The intervention program for the experimental group was based on the MISC and included eleven individual guidance meetings with the mothers and four videotaping sessions at the mother–infant local health centers.

The intervention proceeded as follows: One videotaping session was followed by three guidance meetings in which the videotape was analyzed in line with the mediation criteria observed. A similar procedure was carried out following the second and third videotaping sessions. Two meetings were scheduled after the fourth and last taping. The taping occurred once every two months and the meetings approximately once every two weeks. The control group had the same number of videotaping sessions as well as meetings, but the discussions about the videotaped sessions focused on general issues related to feeding, motor development, or other questions raised by the mothers. No information was given to the control group mothers regarding the criteria of mediation that are basic components of the MISC.

Following the intervention, when the infants were about twelve to

TABLE 1.2 MISC PROGRAM: INTELLECTUAL AND SOCIAL–EMOTIONAL NEEDS IN RELATION TO MEDIATION

Mediation Processes	Examples of the Process	Intellectual Needs	Social–Emotional Needs
1. Focusing (intentionality and reciprocity)	Making the environmental stimuli compatible to the child's needs, e.g., bringing closer, covering distractions, repeating, sequencing, grouping, helping the child focus, see, hear, and feel clearly.	Need for precision in perception (vs. scanning exploration). Need for precision in expression.	Need to focus on and decode facial and bodily expressions of emotion. Need to modify one's own behavior or the environment in order to mediate to others (to make the other person see or understand).
2. Exciting (meaning)	Expressing excitement vocally, verbally, or nonverbally over experiences, objects, people, etc. Naming, identifying.	Need to search for meaningful new experiences (i.e., listen, look, taste things that remind one of past experiences). Need to respond in a way that conveys meaning and excitement (sound, look, and feel excited). Need to invest energy in meaningful activities (along the lines of intrinsic motivation).	Need to think about one's own feelings and the feelings of others. Need cause and cause-and-effect sequences in social interaction. Need to associate between experiences, recall past information, and anticipate future experiences.
3. Expanding (transcendence)	Explaining, elaborating, associating, and raising awareness to metacognitive aspects of thinking. Relating past, present, and future experiences. Relating to physical, logical or social rules and framework.	Need to go beyond what meets the senses. Seek out further information through exploration. Request information from other people and from other sources. Need to seek generalizations. Need to link, associate, recall past information, and anticipate future experiences.	Need to think about one's own feelings and the feelings of others. Need cause and cause-and-effect sequences in social interaction. Need to associate between experiences, recall past information, and anticipate future experiences.

Mediation Processes	Examples of the Process	Intellectual Needs	Social–Emotional Needs
4. Encouraging (feelings of competence)	Praise in a way that is meaningful to the child. Clear isolation and identification of the reasons for success. Well timed in relation to the experience.	Need to seek more success experiences. Need to summarize one's own activities and determine what led to success.	Need to please others and gain more mediated feelings of competence. Need to identify what pleases different people. Need to provide others with mediated feelings of competence.
5. Organizing and planning (regulation of behavior)	Regulation with regard to speed, precision, force, and preferred sequence of activities.	Need to plan before acting, e.g., consider possible solutions prior to responding. Clarifying goals, meeting subgoals. Need to pace one's activities. Need to regulate the level of energy invested in any given task.	Need to control one's impulses in social situations. Learn acceptable ways of expressing one's emotions (i.e., regulate the pace and intensity of one's social responses to anger and joy).

thirteen months old, they were videotaped during another ten-minute free-play session and in the sequence of short experiences comprising Ainsworth's "Strange Situation" paradigm. Children were assessed again using the Bayley Mental Development Scales. The assessments and ratings of attachment were carried out "blindly" (by people unaware of whether children were in control or experimental groups). The findings confirmed the basic hypothesis that improving the quality of mother–infant mediational interaction in the experimental group will reduce the number of anxious attachments in this group. Nine out of 49 children in the experimental group, as compared with 19 out of 50 children in the control group, were found to be anxiously attached. In addition (as was found in the other studies on the effects of the MISC), the experimental-group children scored an average of 132 (SD = 9.41) on the Bayley Mental Development Scales as compared to 122 (SD = 9.45) for the control subjects.

The most important factor in mothers' interaction with their infants in relation to attachment was the frequency of their responding to the infants' initiatives, especially when the responses appeared together with behaviors that conveyed acceptance and mediated competence to the young children. This study confirmed the possibility of enhancing the learning potential of young children and ensuring a positive, healthy social–emotional adjustment through the application of an intervention designed to enhance the quality of mediation provided to infants during their first year of life.

DIRECT PARENTAL MEDIATION OF AFFECT

Based on analysis of videotaped observations of parent–infant interactions carried out by the author in Israel, the United States, Norway, and Sri Lanka, three basic types of situations in which feelings are mediated to infants and young children were identified. These situations may be described as (a) face-to-face (Type I) interchange of affect, (b) affect directed toward anything (or anybody) in the environment, (c) face-to-face (Type II) mediation of affect interpretation and empathy. These three types of situations differ also in the tacit message mediated through each.

"I love you"; Face-to-Face (Type I) Mediation of Affect. During the initial stage of face-to-face mediation of affect, the objective of mediation is to convey to the infant the message: "I love you." This message is expressed through physical closeness, warm contact, and satisfaction of basic physical needs. The more abstract general message mediated is the association between the presence of a particular person (most frequently a parent) and a sensation of pleasant comfort and positive, satisfying sensations with an-

sations with another person.

The ongoing processes of mediation during early infancy include an array of behaviors ranging from holding the baby, touching, and caressing, to eye contact, smiles, and imitation of signs of joy or discomfort. Parental imitation of the baby's initiated signs of emotional expression begins during the first few months of life; later, processes of attunement appear alongside of imitation. Attunement (Stern, 1989) represents the attempts on the part of an adult to mediate to the child the feeling of "I feel with you," "I share your excitement," or, in other words, conveying the message of emotional togetherness and emotional understanding. It occurs through a process resembling a form of imitation that is cross-sensory; that is, the mother "translates" signs of emotion expressed by her infant into other forms of behavior that bear some basic characteristics (i.e., rhythm, intensity) in common with the infant's attempt.

In terms of affecting the child's needs system, face-to-face mediation of affect enhances the need to seek human, face-to-face interaction as a source of pleasure and satisfaction.

"Look how exciting it is"; Affect Directed Toward the Environment. During this phase, the objective of mediation is to focus the child's attention on exciting objects or people in his/her environment. Mediating to the child the beauty, the meaning, the significance of things, is to share one's own appreciation and joy with the child. This type of emotional interchange can occur if children experience Type I situations in which their own initiated signs of excitement are recognized and shared by the adult mediator. This category includes those experiences that affect children's predisposition to seek meaning and excitement in their experiences, and clearly represents the close interplay between cognitive and emotional mediation. This type of mediated affect enhances a double set of needs in the child, one in relation to seeking excitement and meaning in things around him/her, the other pertaining to the ways in which these are expressed in mediation. In other words, the message conveyed through mediation at this stage is "Look how exciting it is" and "Look how I express excitement."

"Look how I feel"; Developing Empathy and Understanding of Emotions. This phase involves expanding children's understanding and empathy toward other people's emotions, as well as toward their own emotional experiences. This type of mediational experience requires the prerequisites of both Type I and II experiences, helping children "read" and label feelings, and reach a finer differentiation of feelings within themselves and others, while identifying cause-

and-effect relationships, namely, conditions leading to various feelings.

One possible initial link between infants' expressions of emotion and their cognitive functioning has been proposed by H. Papousek, M. Papousek, and Koester (1989). They suggest that the infant activates his/her capacities to collect, process, and integrate information. When this effort strains the cognitive mechanisms but does not lead to an effective solution to a problem, the infant shows signs of displeasure. Successful adaptation elicits vocal and facial expressions of pleasure. The same process is also evident in social situations. Signs of pleasure on the infant's part call forth intuitive empathic matching by the parents. The infant's smile (perhaps the result of a cognitive event) is followed by the parents' smiles, and mutual matching provides continuous pleasure in the evolving social interaction. Thus in many ways the interconnection between cognitive and emotional processes becomes particularly meaningful in the context of the infant's interaction with his/her social environment.

A good example of this interconnectedness may be found in relation to parent–infant vocal interaction. Infants' vocalizing is considered to be an especially sensitive indicator of emotional states, because it is closely related to breathing and vegetative functions. In an interactional context, mothers and fathers use simple, enhanced, melodic vocal contours at a relatively higher and extended pitch range when interacting with three-month-old infants as compared with younger infants. These contours occur in response to the infants' vocalization and gestures; that is, infants' expressions of excitement elicit primarily rising contours in parental vocalization, and the opposite occurs in response to infants' signs of fussiness (M. Papousek, H. Papousek, & Bornstein, 1985). Parents' behavior in this case should not be understood as a mere sharing of emotionality; there is a didactically meaningful intention on the part of the parents to affect the child's behavioral–emotional states. Rising contours may be perceived as encouragement, and falling contours as calming and soothing.

Indirect Effects of Parental Mediation on Emotional Development

Emotions may be regarded as "seeing-as." One's emotional reaction reflects how one sees a situation. Shades of emotion change with each way one views the situation. The description of a situation to oneself is crucial in terms of the emotional effect it triggers.

Thus, by helping children "know" or understand, one also helps them differentiate and develop feelings. In this context, parents as mediators have an effect on children's early development through implicitly constructing the experimental pool into which all future experiences will fall and be coded.

With the emergence of children's language skills, parents can rely more on words to affect emotional development through mediational behaviors of affecting and expanding (i.e., labeling, explaining, and relating experiences to events in the past and in the future). Another avenue for indirect parental influence on emotional development is imitation. Imitation may be designed by parents, facilitated by their intention to mediate. Inviting children's imitative behaviors may include contrasts, repetitions, and exaggerations. Few people are aware that emotions, as well as actions, are copied. A mother's complaint about her work may convey a message of negative feelings around work in general.

Ethics are also mediated to as large an extent as emotions. Mediation is extremely important in development of both emotions and ethics because both are open ended. There are subtle relations between the two. For example, a member of the family tends to express emotions about something. Even if he/she does not clearly say "x is good" or "x is bad," his/her intonation and expression present a value judgment that is adopted by young children at a stage when they cannot yet judge for themselves.

It has been suggested (Perkins, 1966, cited in Shibles, 1971) that statements about emotions do not describe behavior but rather interpretations of it. Words conveying emotions form part of the vocabulary of appraisal and criticism, which again brings into focus the importance of mediation. We have an innate need to "feel good." This need is cultivated by early experiences. What is defined as "feeling good" is mediated, and most of the strongest mediations of this nature occur early in life.

People usually think that emotions happen to them and that they cannot influence their course, whereas, in effect, a large component of our emotional experience is actively determined and created by us. "Actively" implies consciousness or "knowing."

From this point of view it becomes clear that parental effects on the emotional development of their children do not occur independently of their effects on their motor and cognitive development.

> Emotion is not the opposite of thinking, rather it is partially comprised of thinking or reason. . . . Emotion does not exist in its own right, as a special and almost mystical sort of entity; it is rather an essential part of an entire sensing-moving-thinking-emotion complex. (Ellis, 1962, p. 47)

Positive human emotions, such as feelings of love or elation, are often associated with or result from thoughts that are related in some form with variations of phrases such as "This is good" or "This is bad."

Parents as well as professionals are more aware of educational goals related to teaching children new skills or ideas, and are less conscious of mediated feelings, directly through the processes discussed earlier, as well as indirectly through mediation commonly associated with cognitive enhancement.

An optimal organization of affect exists when a person experiences a rich variety of developmentally advanced affects that are selectively used in response to internal and external stimuli (Greenspan, 1989). A less optimal capacity in displaying advanced and selective use of affects occurs when the person is under stress. In more severe disturbances, usually a few affects predominate and are representative of pregenital concerns (e.g., emptiness, rage, envy, pseudowarmth). In the most severe disturbances, the affect system is not fully developed, resulting either in a lack of affect or in inappropriate affect.

The most advanced, or developmentally mature, state is dependent on formal operations in which combinatorial thinking is possible. The structure can process a wide variety of affects, some of them discordant, and can find a way to integrate and synthesize them. The type of affect selected can reflect both the current situation and earlier developmental levels, as well as future anticipations.

In order to have the opportunity for emotional development, a young child needs guided experience and adult mediation that is stable, consistent, and positive. These experiences include both direct and indirect mediation of emotions. Through the use of videotaping and video feedback, parents participating in the MISC are helped to form a positive cycle of communicative interaction with their infants. Mothers and infants are videotaped during various caregiving and play activities at home. Infant behavior (eye contact, smiles, vocal responses, expressions of joy or stress, level of body tension, etc.) is identified. The relationship of those infants' behavior to their general state and to the parents' behavior is identified in cooperation with the parents. Parents are encouraged for initiating and maintaining a positive cycle of interaction as a goal in itself and as grounds for continued mediation. Parents are encouraged to identify on video the behaviors that represent the three levels of mediation of emotion discussed earlier. Different parent–infant dyads may differ with regard to the number of sessions required to achieve the criteria of a positive, expressive communication cycle. However, it is not recommended to introduce all of the information mentioned previously in less than three sessions. It is necessary to follow the process of change, allowing the parents to identify the target behaviors on tape (rather than doing it for them) and providing them with mediated competence regarding their parenting skills.

In conclusion, the importance of early experiences is in the primacy of their occurrence, in the fact that they set the basis, the frame of reference, or the disposition, for later experiences. Parents play a major role in affecting their child's cognitive and emotional development directly and indirectly. The MISC represents an attempt to improve the quality of the human environment for young children. It includes three major components:

1.   a focus on parents' cultural and personal background, their perception of their role as parents, their view of their child, and their educational objectives for him/her;
2.   a focus on the emotional climate of the parent–child interaction to ensure the availability of the types of interaction that are essential for mediation of emotion;
3.   a focus on basic characteristics of a quality mediation for young children, namely, the kind of human mediation young children need in order to adjust to our changing world, benefit from new experiences, and become caring and intelligent human beings.

How Can Mediation Be Enhanced?
An Outline of the Intervention Procedure

The MISC project includes a structured and an unstructured component. The structured component relates to the training of mediators who are expected to carry out the intervention. The unstructured component is related to the cultural interpretations of the objectives and the content through which the criteria of mediation are introduced and demonstrated in the homes.

Mediators (persons who carry out the intervention) must have a basic knowledge of general principles and landmarks of child development, an appreciation of individual differences in development, and a deep understanding of the cultural and socioeconomic reality of the population in which they work. They should be capable of forming an empathic relationship with the mother or caregivers and function in an accepting, nonauthoritative manner. They are expected to encourage rather than criticize or evaluate, and to convey enthusiasm and hope regarding the role of the parent (or caregiver) in promoting the chances of child development.

Because the criteria of mediation are not relatively culture or content specific (i.e., it does not matter whether the child learns to associate meaning with one object or another as long as he/she experiences the association of any experience with meaning), each criterion may be demonstrated in relation to different cultural experiences, objects, or people in every one of the families. More about the procedure adopted for use in different countries will be presented in the following chapters.

The Basic Process of MISC Intervention at Home

The MISC can be implemented in various settings, including homes, day-care centers, kindergartens, or health centers. The following section presents the basic characteristics of the MISC as a home-based program. The following basic procedure has been used to implement it:

1.　　Every participating family is visited at home prior to the onset of the program. During these visits, mother–child interactions during feeding, bathing, and play are observed. Based on these observations and on an interview with the mother (assessing attitudes toward the child, educational philosophy, objectives of childrearing, and an overview of what happens to the child throughout the day), a typical profile of the mediation provided to a child in each of the families is constructed (if possible, focusing on the type of mediation provided by each of the family members) and a general outline of the plan of intervention is then drawn up.

2.　　In some families the primary emphasis of the intervention may be to establish a positive cycle of expressive adult–child interaction. Such a relationship is necessary for the formation of a sound basis for mutual acceptance and an affective bond between the adult caregiver and the child he/she cares for. This form of intervention is required for the establishment of intentionality and reciprocity in the adult–child relations.

3.　　In every family the mediator begins by mediating feelings of competence to the mother regarding those behaviors in which she mediated most successfully and demonstrated the highest frequency of mediation criteria (as found during the initial observation). A specific criterion is brought to her attention and is clarified for her using the technique described in the following pages. Once a criterion is identified and clarified, the mother is helped to find more ways to demonstrate it in her everyday life with her own child at home or in the street. The sequence in which the criteria are presented depends upon the mother's strengths and weaknesses in mediation, starting always with relative strengths in order to ensure mediating competence to her.

4.　　Every session begins with a review of the criteria of mediation and examples presented at the previous meeting, and ends with a summary of mediational behaviors presented in the current session. Every family participating in the program is visited periodically, once a week or less frequently, as needed, by a mediator assigned to it. Each mediator reviews the session with an instructor (supervisor) and prepares a summary of the session, as well as objectives and plans for the next session.

5.   General meetings are held monthly or bimonthly for all participating parents. During these meetings parents are asked to analyze videotaped mother–child interactions and suggest alternative ways of mediating.

A Sample of Intervention Strategies Used

1.   Parental guidance is most efficient when mother–child interactions are *videotaped* and mothers view the tapes with the mediators. Every one of the basic criteria of mediation is used in the mother–mediator interaction and mothers are helped to identify those criteria.

2.   Mediation of the MLE criteria to the adult caregivers, in most cases to the mother, is focused on situations from adult daily life. Following the initial stage, the criteria are identified as they appear in daily activities in the home, and expanded to demonstrate other possible ways of expressing the same criteria in different interactions with the child. For example, your mother-in-law comes to visit, and you make an effort to clean the house, cook a good meal, wash and dress the children. Your mother-in-law does not say anything. In other words, after all the work you have done, you do not get any mediated feelings of competence. How do you feel? There are other possibilities: Your mother-in-law says, "Thank you I enjoyed my visit" or another possibility, "Thank you, I love to see you and the children look so nice." Both possibilities provide you with feelings of competence. It does feel good to hear good things said about yourself; however, only the second possibility is specific enough and provides you with an idea that may help you do things better next time. In other words, if your mother-in-law enjoyed seeing you and the children look nice, why put much effort into cleaning the house or cooking? Following examples such as the one presented here pertaining to the criteria of mediation in adult life, the same criteria are discussed as they appear in the interaction between the adult and the child. For example, your child scribbles on a piece of paper and brings it up to you. Don't ignore it, provide mediation of competence. Tell him/her it is beautiful and why you consider it to be beautiful (provided you want him/her to do it even better next time). "It is very nice. I see you have used many colors" or "You have filled the entire page." (Your comments depend on what you consider a desirable goal in your child's development and future behavior.) We have found that it is easier for mothers to identify with and remember better the criteria of mediation as they are represented in their own lives, and only later to view these in rela-

tion to their own interactions with their children.

Mothers have been found to develop the ability to use the criteria of mediation in order to evaluate the ongoing mediation between different members of their family and their young child, as well as between day-care workers or kindergarten teachers and their child.

3.   Role playing is mediating to the mother the possibility of understanding the child's behavior if placed in his/her position. For example, let's suppose that you are the child. The entire family is in the living room, and you are taken away to a dark room and asked to go to sleep. How do you feel?

In order to help the mother realize how the child feels, it is sometimes necessary to start role playing with her in her regular role as mother and with the mediator as the child. In the role of the child the mediator can verbalize how the child feels or what he/she thinks, helping the mother to gain insight regarding her child's behavior. This procedure is primarily helpful when mothers view their child's behavior as caused by negative intentions.

4.   Sharing is verbal or nonverbal demonstrations of the thinking processes, overt behavior sequences, or methods one uses in different situations (e.g., "When I look at this kind of question, I feel confused and so I ask myself first . . . and then . . .").

Sharing is primarily important in focusing a mother's attention on her own feelings and on their causes and consequences. Through the process of sharing, one can convey "cultural wisdom" in the form of folk sayings, or stories, or efficient strategies for communication, of affect, or for cognitive processes such as memory, planning, evaluation, and so on. For example, "When I want to remember something, I try to see it very clearly and vividly in my mind, in full detail and color, and in the funniest way . . . that helps me remember it later."

5.   Use of stories, nursery rhymes, songs, dance, and music that are typical to a culture may be reactivated and used to improve mediation to young children. Mothers are encouraged to tell stories or sing and dance with their children and are helped to identify elements of quality mediation within this type of interaction.

Affecting Caregivers' Perceptions of, and Attitudes toward, the Child

Parents' normative conceptualizations of their children are normally part of a cultural tradition and practice that need to be respected. In fact, it is impossible to expect long-term, sustainable effects of any intervention if we do not cooperate and work within these cultural norms. Still, we assume there are certain universal basic conceptions, feelings, and attitudes in the relationship between caregiver and child that are crucial for optimal development of a child in any culture. Examples of these basic attitudes and feelings are as follows:

1. I gave birth to a wonderful human being.
2. I am very important to my child; he/she loves and needs me.
3. I can help my child develop physically and mentally.

WHAT CAN BE DONE TO ACHIEVE THESE ATTITUDES AND FEELINGS? (SAMPLE ACTIVITIES)

• Compliment the parent for having a nice baby. Point out special features, such as beautiful, lively eyes, shiny hair, soft skin, delicate hands and fingers, and so on. (In some cultures compliments should be stated carefully. In Ethiopia, for example, compliments are considered dangerous because they may elicit jealousy and the "evil eye." In addition, praise is viewed as unnatural in an authority-based adult–child interaction. Thus, in working with the Ethiopian population in Israel, special care was taken to avoid mediating competence in the presence of strangers.)

• Indicate positively the similarities between the baby and the parents in the way they look and smile.

• If the parents have photos of the baby, these may be used to enhance positive feelings for the child and to demonstrate how much the child has grown since the picture was taken (stressing that "You are a good mother, see how well he/she develops").

• Provide parents with a simple, basic view of sequential development of babies in various areas, so they can become aware and enjoy even small steps in their child's development. (In order not to overwhelm parents with information, be aware of what they consider important areas in child development and relate primarily to these areas.)

• Demonstrate to the parents that their baby responds to them more than to anybody else. For example, let the mother call the baby and point out the response. Ask the mother if the baby would go to anyone else when she holds him/her. Again, stress the special relationship between the two.

• Point out the positive qualities that may be found in the parents' existing childrearing practices and interactions with their child.

Establishing a Positive Cycle of Early Caregiver–Child Interaction

The following is a simplified, practical approach to identify and encourage behaviors that promote the formation of a positive cycle of interaction between an infant/young child and the adult caring for him/her. Establishing a cycle of positive, expressive interaction is a necessary condition for mediation.

The infant should learn that the world around him/her is predictable and responsive to his/her signals of distress, as well as to behaviors expressing positive excitement (i.e., vocalization, facial expressions, and other bodily signals).

The infant needs to learn that it is worthwhile "to do something," to be active rather than passive, frightened, uninterested, or apathetic (conditions that are found in children who have suffered from a lack of responsive human contact in infancy). The infant seems to have been born equipped to learn the signs that are basic for human interaction, but he/she needs mediated learning experience to further develop these communicative skills and the needs for such communication.

SAMPLE ACTIVITIES FOR ESTABLISHING A POSITIVE CYCLE OF INTERACTION
In order to establish a communicative cycle with an infant or an adult, it is necessary to interpret a partner's behavior as if it is intentional, namely, expressing the wishes, needs, and ideas of the communicative partner (and not just an accidental or a mechanical movement). An awareness of the child's intentions is a very important factor in determining the quality of interaction with that child. It is quite usual to hear caregivers say that there is no point in talking/communicating with a young child because he/she does not yet understand. This may be true in a sense, but the point is that the child needs, from birth onward, sensitively adjusted, expressive communication in order to form an attachment to other people so that he/she can develop socially and cognitively.

The best way for a caregiver to start such a cycle of expressive communication with a baby is to have the attitude that the baby is intentionally expressing a "message" through his/her gestures, and that he/she "understands" in a way, sensitively adjusted "replies" from the caregiver. Such an interpretive attitude, which most mothers intuitively take, makes communication with a baby natural and easy.

Parents are encouraged to ask the following questions: What is the baby doing now? What is he/she trying to tell you? What are his/her initiatives? Beyond the need to satisfy their basic physiological needs, most babies want to touch and feel, see, hear, and experience the world around them, but most of all, to experience human warmth and closeness to one loving person and to receive confirmation of this contact through the adult's expressive behavior. The parents are helped to identify the specific message their baby may be trying to convey at any particular moment.

Parents are encouraged to respond to the baby's initiative with the following behaviors:

- Maintain eye contact with the baby, smile at him/her, respond to his/her behavior, including movement and vocalizations, for example, by patting or by making similar sounds to his/her own. Reflect his/her behavior in a positive, confirming, and reassuring way.
- While interacting vocally or otherwise, make sure to tune in and "dance in rhythm," "taking turns," waiting and respecting each other's turns. Once he/she has a go, then you go; follow his/her initiative.
- Express happiness and excitement in being with the baby; respond to him/her by making happy faces or happy sounds.

It should be noted here that these examples relate to the establishment of a positive communication cycle and are not sufficient for quality mediation. The latter includes the additional elements of exciting, conveying meaning, expanding, associating, encouraging, and regulating behavior.

Termination of the Intervention

The intervention was terminated when mothers (caregivers or educators) could verbally explain in their own words the criteria of mediation, as well as demonstrate this understanding in their actual daily interactions with their children. In most of the participating families in Israel, mothers demonstrated a change in behavior toward their children before they were capable of verbally explaining what they were doing. This was confirmed in other countries as well. One may claim that if the natural sequence is action before conceptualization, then perhaps one should use more modeling techniques first rather than try to explain and help conceptualize. The basic idea behind the MISC intervention is not to teach mothers and educators specific behaviors, but rather to help them identify behaviors that exist within their own repertoire and explain why behaviors of this nature may help their child develop. The objective is to overcome the difficulties of generalization and transfer that plague many educational programs. It seems that clarifying for the parents the behaviors that are essential for a quality mediational interaction and mediating competence to them, helps them learn to use these behaviors more frequently and internalize them as decontextualized knowledge that can be applied in many situations.

The parents not only use these behaviors more frequently, but they also learn to match their own behaviors with signs of initiation or reciprocity from their child. Explaining, demonstrating, and focusing the child's attention may be a "wasted" educational experience, or worse, a disturbing experience, if the child is interested in something else, tired, or overexcited. Parents learn to do or not to do in synchrony with the child's behavior. This synchrony cannot be readily learned by repeating modeled behavior. It is learned through a process of developing insight about one's own behavior in relation to the child's. It seems that this insight was expressed in actual improvements in the quality of mediation and only later was crystallized into words. The objective of the intervention should be to reach the stage of verbal representation of the criteria of quality mediation and not to be satisfied with a change in behavior only. Mothers who can verbalize clearly what constitutes quality mediation (independent of specific contexts) could be expected to use it in different situations as their children grow and encounter new experiences.

3 INTERVENTION WITH SPECIAL POPULATIONS

THE MISC WITH VERY LOW BIRTH WEIGHT INFANTS AND YOUNG CHILDREN

Very low birth weight (VLBW) infants are considered to be "at risk" for developmental difficulties and have been found to be highly susceptible to variations in the quality of the environment in which they live. The current section summarizes the results of a series of studies involving a population of VLBW Israeli children and their parents, and a follow-up study with the same population three years after the MISC intervention.

Study 1

A study by Klein, Raziel, Brish, and Birenbaum (1987a) was designed to compare the performance of 42 VLBW three year olds with two control groups: one composed of their siblings (15 children), and another composed of 40 normal-birth-weight children, on a series of cognitive measures, including several subtests of the Wechsler Intelligence Scale for Children-Revised (WISC-R), the Illinois Test of Psycholinguistic Abilities (ITPA), and the Developmental Test of Visual Motor Integration. The study was also intended to assess the relationship between the quality of parental interaction and cognitive performance of children born weighing below 1.5 kg, which is considered the cutoff point for infants at special risk of nonsurvival and/or developmental lag.

Parents' quality of interaction with their children was assessed using the Observing Mediational Interaction (OMI) method (Klein & Alony, 1993) that will be described later in this book.

VLBW children were found to perform as well as their siblings and the normal-birth-weight control group on most of the cognitive measures used, with the exception of auditory sequential memory (ASM) on the ITPA and understanding of word meaning, as measured by the Peabody Picture Vocabulary Test (PPVT).

The observational measure of the quality of parent–child interaction based on mediational criteria was found to correlate with cognitive performance of the VLBW subjects (Klein, 1988), whereas no significant correlations were found between birth weight and those same cognitive measures. In other words, the quality of parent–child interaction was a better predictor of these children's mental development than their birth weight. Study 1 was the first in which mediational observation was applied with VLBW subjects. Based on the findings of this study, the OMI was found to be a powerful predictor of cognitive performance of VLBW children.

Study 2

Correlations between the quality of mediation and test performance of the VLBW subjects found in Study 1 were not deemed sufficient for drawing conclusions regarding a cause-and-effect relationship between these variables. In order to examine the latter relationship, VLBW subjects in Study 1 were randomly divided into an experimental and a control group. No significant differences were found between the intervention and control groups on all background variables. The average birth weight of the intervention group was 1,207 g (*SD* = 246) and of the control group, 1,231 g (*SD* = 170).

The MISC intervention was offered to all participating parents of VLBW subjects in the experimental group. The objective of this intervention was to improve the quality of parent–child interaction in the VLBW group and to assess the effects of this intervention on the children.

The intervention began with two observations of parent–child interactions at home. Each observation included a feeding, a bathing, and a play session with the child. Based on the observational data, a profile of results for the five primary mediational criteria was constructed for each mother–child dyad. A trained mediator described and clarified to the mother those criteria on which she had shown evidence of constructive interactions with her child. Only later were these criteria related to those that needed to be encouraged and reinforced. Mediators did not come into the subjects' homes with a set of preplanned exercises or toys. They related to what was available in the home and to the ongoing content of mother–child interaction at that time. Indicators of success of the intervention were (a) change in mothers' behavior toward the children as measured by an increase in the frequency of the occurrence of behaviors exemplifying the basic criteria of mediation, and (b) improvement in mothers' ability to verbalize basic aspects of a quality interaction. The intervention took place over a period of seven months, with most families receiving home visits every month to six weeks, depending upon the extent of mediation shown in the initial home profile. One year after the intervention, the quality of parent–child interaction was found to have improved significantly on all five of the primary criteria of quality interaction. Furthermore, test scores of the VLBW subjects in the experimental group were shown to be consistently higher than those of the control group, although none of these differences reached statistical significance. On two measures (ASM and PPVT), VLBW subjects in the experimental group scored as well as or better than their siblings or normal controls. In contrast, it should be noted that prior to the intervention, members of the VLBW group had scored significantly lower than the other groups on both of these measures. Following the intervention, parents of small for gestational age (SGA) children, who are typically viewed as most at risk, interacted with their children better than did parents of VLBW children who were born appropriate for gestational age (AGA).

Study 3

Three years after the intervention described in Study 2, when the children were six years old, the families were visited again by graduate students trained in observation and testing procedures, and who were unfamiliar with the family visited. Of the original 42 families of VLBW subjects in Study 1, 36 families were contacted, and 29 of them agreed to participate in the follow-up study. It should be noted that all of the parents in the experimental group who could be reached agreed to participate; four families could not be located, and two parents in the control group refused to participate because their children "were in special education classes and were overtested already."

The quality of mediation was assessed using the OMI at the home of each family. Mothers were asked to play with their children using a puzzle task with an eighty-piece puzzle brought by the observer. In addition, the children were individually tested in their homes on the following measures: the Vocabulary and Similarities Subtests of the WISC-R, PPVT, Draw a Person, the Developmental Test of Visual Motor Integration, and the Auditory Sequential Memory Test of the ITPA. Mothers were asked to evaluate their children's performance and to rate them on a five-point scale with regard to language development, gross and fine motor coordination, and sociability.

The effects of the intervention on the quality of mother–child interaction persisted three years after the intervention. Significant differences were found between the mothers in the intervention group and the control group on each of the five criteria of mediation. All differences were in favor of the intervention group.

The VLBW experimental group showed significantly more spontaneous sharing of information with their mothers than did the control group, and spontaneously pointed out more associations between things than the control group.

No significant differences in performance of VLBW children in the intervention group as compared to the control group were found on most of the cognitive measures, with the exception of the PPVT. However, a consistent trend in favor of the experimental group was found on all of the seven measures used in this study. Similarly, no differences were found between the SGA and AGA following the intervention.

Comparing the children's scores on the cognitive measures one and three years after the intervention in the experimental and control groups, and for the SGA and AGA groups, revealed that on the auditory sequential money test the SGA children in the intervention group scored higher than those in the control group, and higher than the AGA subjects in both the experimental and control groups. In other words, the group of children that was expected to do worse achieved the highest scores following the intervention.

Mothers' evaluations of their children's performance with regard to language, gross- and fine-motor coordination, and sociability, revealed that more children in the control group, as compared to the intervention group, had difficulties in these areas. At Follow-Up 1 (one year following the intervention), 5 children in the intervention group were rated by their parents as having language problems, as compared with 5 children in the control group. At Follow-Up 2 (three years following the intervention), 2 children in the intervention group and 5 in the control group were rated as having such problems. One child in the intervention group and 4 in the control group were rated as having gross-motor coordination difficulties on Follow-Up 1, and none was rated as such in either group on Follow-Up 2. As for fine-motor coordination, none of the intervention group children and 4 of the controls were rated as having difficulties one year following the intervention, and none of the intervention children and 2 of the control group children were rated as having fine-motor problems three years following intervention. Regarding sociability ratings, 1 child in the intervention group and 2 in the control group were rated as having sociability difficulties on Follow-Up 1. Three years following the intervention there was still 1 child in the intervention group and 4 in the control group who were rated as having sociability problems. Two of the children in the control group and 1 of the children in the intervention group were attending special education classes three years following the intervention. It should be noted that the children in special education classes were not tested because of parental refusal to participate in the follow-up.

Summary

The MISC intervention was designed (a) to enhance the quality of interaction between parents and their children who were born at VLBW and, consequently, (b) to improve the children's cognitive performance. Despite the fact that the intervention was not intensive (one home visit every four or six weeks), it was found to have a significant and long-lasting effect upon parents' behavior. Three years after the intervention, intervention group mothers showed more focusing, exciting, expanding, rewarding, and regulating behaviors as compared to control group mothers. The differences between parents in the intervention and control groups appeared to grow over the years with regard to the amount of mediated encouragement and expansion of ideas. Learning the criteria of mediation apparently sensitized parents in the intervention group to notice more opportunities for mediation of competence and transcendence as their children approached school age. Parental expanding and rewarding behaviors appeared to be predictive of young children's cognitive performance at a later age more than most of the other criteria of mediation (Klein et al., 1987b). Thus, it may be expected that the intervention group will continue to perform better than the control group on various cognitive tasks. It appears that for the population of parents of VLBW children, even a brief intervention enhancing parental awareness of the determinants of a quality interaction is sufficient to produce long-lasting changes in the quality of their interaction with their children. In other populations, such as low-SES families, the same objective required a more intensive intervention (Klein & Alony, 1993).

The effectiveness of the intervention described in the current study could also be related to the *how* of the intervention in addition to the *what*. In every home visit, the mediators used all the basic criteria of mediation in their own interactions with the parent. The meetings between the parent and the mediator consisted of quality interactions (i.e., focusing, exciting, expanding, rewarding, and regulating behaviors). Parents were guided to do what they did naturally with their children, but with greater awareness of the potent factors within each interaction. Several of the mothers in the intervention group remarked that following the intervention they had gained more confidence in what they were doing with their children, had more patience, and enjoyed the children more than before. One of the mothers said:

"I always wanted to do more for my child. I was told to stimulate, so I showed her things and spoke to her, but once I caught her attention I did not know what to do. . . . I took another object and again tried to catch her attention. Now I know how to make things excite her. I show her what they mean, how to find other things like them, or how to connect one experience with others she has had in the past."

No differences were found between the groups following intervention with regard to the number of items listed in response to the question "What can be done to enhance a child's cognitive development?" It is interesting to note, however, that whereas control group parents listed what could be done *to the child*, parents who participated in the intervention repeatedly referred to the need to *match* what they want to do with the *child's needs, capacities, and preferences.*

In the current study, parents in the SGA group were found to provide their children with significantly more intentionality and reciprocity, more mediated feelings of competence, and more regulation of behavior than the parents of the AGA group. A possible explanation of these findings could be related to the fact that the VLBW children born SGA have been found to be more at risk than VLBW AGA infants. Parents of at-risk infants were reported to increase their mediational efforts in line with their perceptions of the urgency of their infants' position. Extra parental efforts to enhance the development of the smaller, apparently weaker babies were discussed previously by Field, Walden, Widmayer, and Greenberg (1982) in their report on the early development of preterm discordant twins. The finding regarding higher levels of parental mediation provided to SGA as compared to AGA children could at least be partially related to the fact that the SGA babies in the current study stayed in the hospital an average of 8.5 days longer than did the AGA babies. During this period and the follow-up visits, the parents were instructed to interact with the babies and to stimulate them, particularly in face-to-face interactions. The parents' sharpened awareness of the infants' need for interaction and the greater urgency of their condition could have increased the SGA mothers' behaviors directed toward focusing, rewarding, and regulating the children's attention. It is interesting to note that the SGA parents did not provide their children with more mediation of meaning, nor did they expand and explain more than the AGA parents. Parental concern to be active and enhance their children's development was not sufficient to produce differences with regard to expanding and exciting behaviors (transcendence and mediation of meaning). Apparently, a change in mediation regarding the latter criteria requires more than a natural concern or general instructions to stimulate the child (i.e., to do more for or with the child).

The population of VLBW children in the current study was originally found to perform as well as their siblings and normal controls on all measures of cognitive performance, with the exception of ASM and vocabulary. Following the intervention, no differences were found between the experimental group and the control group with regard to most of the measures, including ASM. All VLBW subjects appeared to function on norm on the ASM measure. The intervention group did, however, score higher than the control group on the vocabulary measure (PPVT). Considering the central role of language and verbal intelligence in cognitive performance of children, this finding is extremely important.

In a recent follow-up study (Klein & Alony, 1993) of normal birth weight, low-SES infants and their families who had received the same intervention as described in this study, it was found that an improvement in the quality of maternal mediating behavior not only affected children's performance on language and reasoning measures, but also increased children's spontaneous naming of things and the expressions of relationships or associations between various objects and behaviors. These children requested more information, showed more excitement, and spontaneously used more verbal rewards for other people's performance. In short, all these behaviors actually mirror the type of mediating behaviors used by their parents. It is possible that these behaviors of spontaneously sharing or mediating to others found in the experimental group children may affect the ease and quality of their social interactions with their parents, as well as with teachers and peers throughout their development. This possibility is especially important in light of the finding that VLBW subjects are rated as passive, withdrawn, or shy (Bjerre & Hansen, 1976; Wallace, 1984). If the current intervention affected the children in the direction of more spontaneous, meaningful verbal interchange, the outcome of the intervention may be more significant when the child is found in more and more situations in which learning and social adjustment require enhanced active participation in social interaction.

Although the criteria of mediation may be regarded as criteria of maternal teaching behaviors and, as such, focus on cognitive aspects of development, achieving quality mediation implies creating a good match between the adult's intention to interact with the child and the child's needs and interests. This basic requirement, combined with the criteria of sharing excitement (mediating meaning) and encouraging the child (mediating competence), could be considered as important contributors to a supportive parent–child relationship with the potential to affect emotional as well as cognitive development.

The MISC program for children with Down's syndrome (MISC-DS) is one of a series of MISC programs implemented with infants and young children with special needs.

The MISC-DS program has been ongoing at Bar-Ilan University under the auspices of the Baker Center. The center provided direct services to over 200 children, ranging in age from two months to six years, and their families. The children were visited at their homes by students who were instructed and supervised to raise parental awareness of the quality of mediation they provide for their children. The families participated in the program for one or two years, depending on their progress.

It was found that all families, regardless of their initial pattern of mediation, could modify the quality of mediation they provided. Families with high, flat profiles, namely, a high frequency of mediational behavior (e.g., focusing, exciting, expending, explaining, encouraging, and regulating behaviors) and families with uneven profiles of mediation, frequently showed more rapid modifiability as compared to families with low profiles (generally low frequencies of mediation, of all criteria).

The length of time it took a family to modify the mediation provided to their children significantly depended on a number of variables, some of which are commonly reported in literature in relation to changes of attitude. However, in the case of DS children, parental motivation to improve their children's cognitive development was clearly present in all homes and was unrelated to parental level of education, income, or ethnic background. It must be noted that there was significant variability between parents with regard to their own belief in modifiability of their children and in their self-perception as agents of this desired change. Assessing these parental attitudes and beliefs may serve as an indicator of the need to spend more time mediating to the parents about their power to affect the children's mind and about their children's potential to change. Parental attitudes or beliefs should not be perceived as indicators that their mediation cannot be affected.

Assessments of preintervention and postintervention conditions in the homes, as well as an assessment of the children, were carried out following one and two years of intervention. Significant differences in parental mediation and in the children's cognitive performance were found between the pre- and postintervention conditions.

Following the intervention, parents were found to initiate more activities directed toward mediating to their children. More of the observed behaviors clearly transcended beyond satisfaction of the children's basic needs, and more affect and meaning were expressed and mediated to the children. Some forms of mediation of competence were affected by the program (i.e., praise and demonstration of the reasons for success).

The following characteristics of a university setting were utilized in the program:

1.   the availability of a multidisciplinary team of experts, and access to new computer and video technology;

2.   access to new research and methodology in the fields of early-childhood development and special education for DS children, including the possibility of obtaining information through a computerized literature search (of U.S. and international data banks), and evaluation and preparation of this information for parents and others caring for young DS children;

3.   availability of a student body that can, with supervision, carry out and assist in the evaluation of the process of intervention tailored to the special needs of DS children and their families.

All the preceding characteristics enable a better awareness of individual needs and ways of optimizing the matching process between children and the world around them, necessary steps for mediated learning experiences to occur.

Young Gifted Children as Mediators to Children with Down's Syndrome

The MISC-DS program includes a project in which gifted children work and play with DS children. Young children with exceptionally high IQs are more sensitive to the needs of other children, more helpful, and more affectionate than children of lower IQs (Abroms & Gollin, 1980). Young DS children tend to be more interested, focus their attention longer, and show that they prefer other young children to older children or to adult models. Parents of children in Western societies, especially parents of gifted children, are highly motivated to push their children ahead, particularly in areas of cognitive functioning, often at the expense of social and emotional growth.

In a program involving two groups of children interacting with each other, parents of both groups must be convinced that their children are benefiting from the interaction. Mainstreaming children with developmental problems with normal children frequently raises opposition from parents, who claim that their normal children are being held back because of this interaction. In the MISC-DS program, the objective is to enhance the development of the retarded and the gifted child, both emotionally and cognitively.

Psychologists and anthropologists have recently begun to inquire into competencies that children might acquire during the time they spend performing household tasks required by their parents. Edwards (1986) focuses on the sociocognitive structures involved in nurturance, specifically, the reasoning about "rational" and "conventional" moral rules that is given a developmental impetus in the caretaking experience. Edwards claims that children in multiage dyads, or groupings, negotiate constantly with one another the rights and wrongs of acts, and who should do what and when. The process through which caretaking children learn rules and social norms is an active one and involves both knowledge that is self-constructed and socially transmitted by others (Schweder, 1982). It has thus been concluded that the responsible, nurturing child becomes not merely a caring and feeling child, but also a thinking child, with special cognitive competence (Edwards, 1986).

The self-learning or even guided learning of social rules and morals of caretaking children are only a fragment of the rich fabric of learning possibilities inherent in an interaction between two children in which one assumes the role of the caregiver or teacher. Such a situation may be especially potent if one can construct an interaction in which young children are motivated to care for and promote the development of other children whose development has been retarded (i.e., their process of learning has been slowed down). A situation like this requires the presence of an adult mediator who *excites* the children with the prospect of helping other children, focusing on the joy in making another person happy, or teaching another person; *reinforces* them in their initial attempts to do so; *focuses* their attention on components of the other children's behavior that have *communicative* value (e.g., "Let's see what he/she is telling us," "How can we tell?").

For gifted children, the encounters with young retarded children who need them, in the presence of an adult mediator, provide fertile ground for various forms of metacognitive learning.

Once a week the gifted and DS children meet on campus at the Baker Center. The meeting takes place in the presence of the parents and an adult mediator (a student or another staff member). The mediator guides the children to focus on each others' signs of communication (smiles, vocalizations, eye contact, head movements, body posture, etc.); and pace and intensity of action, including reaction time, rate, and intensity of response (the latter is particularly relevant for interaction with DS children whose responses may be delayed and may vary in intensity). The gifted children are guided to focus on the thinking processes that occur even prior to simple responses; they are instructed to slow down their own rate of response and adjust it to that of their DS partners. They are assisted to plan activities ahead, set objectives, and test hypotheses regarding the other child. The gifted children become increasingly aware of the need to be active and conscious of learning processes, particularly of the strategies involved in focusing attention and memory. The gifted children learn to be good mediators; they learn how to focus the other child's attention on various stimuli, how to express excitement that will make the other child interested, how to explain and how to expand ongoing experiences for the DS child. In so doing, the young gifted children are helped to grow out of their own egocentric view of themselves and the world around them to become increasingly *more considerate of the other's points of view*, how others do things, understand or think, and of the changes necessary in their own behavior in order to make the other understand or experience what they intend him/her to understand or experience.

The DS children learn to enjoy an interaction with a normal peer and to be active learners. They learn to focus better on stimuli around them, to seek the names and meanings of things, to construct sequences of experiences, and to feel more secure about imitating and relating to other children of their age.

In addition to the cognitive objectives of the MISC-DS program discussed earlier, the gifted children learn to care for and empathize with DS children, to enjoy their successes and the entire relationship with them.

The DS children, through these guided interactions with gifted children who are interested and willing to play with them, gain a unique opportunity for learning through a combination of modeling and mediation. The DS children are the center of attention and receive quality interactions with others. Most other occasions in which DS children are mainstreamed in regular educational settings are lacking in guided attempts to make children better mediators and better learners themselves. The gifted children are not slowed down by the DS children; on the contrary, the interaction between the two provides a unique opportunity for all children to grow as more intelligent yet more feeling and caring individuals.

In order to maximize the effects of the interaction between the gifted and the DS children, their parents are present at the interaction and gain both metacognitive knowledge and mediational skills that can be used in their daily interactions with their children.

The MISC-DS program for gifted and DS children includes the application of a computer program for young children, as well as videotaping and video playback mediation.

Videotaping and Video Playback in the MISC-DS Program

The use of videotaping and video playback is a basic procedure used in the MISC program. It was introduced in the MISC-DS primarily in order to enable the parents of DS children to view episodes of interaction between themselves and their children and between their children and other educators. This technique makes it possible to focus the parents' attention on specific characteristics of their behavior, and to identify the child's specific response or lack of it in various situations.

Parents of children with DS may need assistance in identifying their child's communicative efforts, as do parents of other handicapped children. On several occasions, in analyzing videotaped mother–child interactions, we have noted that mothers repeatedly tried to elicit a certain response from their children, but seemed unsuccessful in getting the children's attention and inviting their response. When the mothers appeared to give up and turned away, the children suddenly responded in line with their previous request. If episodes of this nature are repeated and are not brought to the mothers' attention, the result may be a generalized decrease in the children's responsivity to the world around them and a consequent decrease of parental initiative in such interactions. Awareness of partial responses or approximations of a communicative gesture can also be brought to parents' attention and may contribute to a better understanding of the DS child.

Videotaping became an important technique for improving the capacity of professionals to convey to parents specific feedback regarding parent–child interactions, and for providing rewards for changes in the desired direction. Through videotaping, parents learn about their children, themselves, and the interaction between themselves and their children. The technical capacity to stop the tape, to run it back and forth, allows one to focus on various features of the children's behavior, and on the smallest verbal or nonverbal nuances that make an interaction. A lack of parental understanding of infants' communicative efforts may result in parent–child interactions that are brief and unsatisfactory for both the parents and the infants. These brief interactions may take the form of either overstimulation that is unrelated to the children's rhythm of behavior and needs, or withdrawn and unresponsive behavior.

Available information related to the promotion of more positive interactional styles is collected and modified in line with the special needs of DS children, for example, Fraiberg's work (1977) with blind children, and Field's work (1983) with mothers of at-risk infants. Field taught mothers to imitate their infants' behaviors, repeat their vocalizations, and remain silent during pauses in the interaction. Parents of DS children need special assistance in evoking their children's vocalizations and in "shaping" them through their repetition. They also need to know how to remain silent but attentive during pauses in the interaction, so that it is not broken unintentionally.

One can hardly expect parents to convey enthusiasm and joy to a child about any subject, object, or person, if they do not enjoy playing with the child. Bromwich (1981) described an intervention in which parents first learned to enjoy playing with their infants before specifically working on developmental, skills-oriented activities. Through the analyses of the video-taped interactions, mothers gradually became more knowledgeable about their children's communicative signals, and consequently felt more confident and hopeful about their ability to affect their children's development.

The use of both computers and videotaping were applied in the interactions of the gifted children with the DS children. Combining these approaches increased the interest and motivation of the children and their parents, and enabled the mediators to demonstrate with greater efficiency the presence of the processes of mediation and metacognitive processes in any child–adult or child–child interaction.

Mediational Intervention for Sensitizing Caregivers of Young Gifted Children

Psychologists and educators working with young children, gifted or otherwise, tend to repeat a misconception regarding the evaluation of infants, especially those who are developmentally at risk. Most commonly, these evaluations focus on the infants' test performance, with little or no direct assessment of the quality of their interaction with the environment, particularly the human environment, which no doubt affects development and adds significantly to the predictive power of such an evaluation. In order to identify giftedness in young children, it is necessary to focus both on children's psychological states and on the dynamics of interaction with the important other in their lives.

There is hardly any doubt today that genius does not originate solely from genetic characteristics (Feldman, 1982). Mozart's early musical ability is frequently used to demonstrate the role of genetics in the formation of genius. Yet it cannot be overlooked that Mozart was surrounded from birth by a family of talented musicians. The rate and quality of development of retarded, normal-functioning, and gifted children are determined by a rare and subtle interplay of both genetic and environmental variables. The critical role of the environment and the lack of defined characteristics of the optimal environment for all children are emphasized in the theory of "goodness of fit" (Thomas & Chess, 1977; Lerner, 1982). This notion implies that optimal development occurs in the process of interaction between the children's behavioral style and the environment's response to it.

Very young children today are thrust into independence and self-reliance before they are cognitively and emotionally ready for it. Children are constantly pushed ahead, driven to be competitive rather than cooperative, and grow up with virtually no time to stop and smell the roses or to pause and wonder. At least some of the current stresses are inflicted by parents and teachers who are concerned about the children's achievement and status. Middle-class parents enroll their toddlers and young children in various programs, pushing them to keep up with the Joneses, driving them from one activity to another, with little opportunity for actual mediational intervention.

Elkind (1987) speaks of the evils of what he calls "hurried education of the 1960s" and compares these with the "miseducation of the 1980s." The hurried education consisted primarily of starting school early, rushing to give children what was falsely believed to be an earlier, and therefore better, start. Miseducation includes some types of so-called enrichment courses, training programs, and other extracurricular activities that fill up the days of young children from infancy. This sense of drivenness obsesses well-meaning parents who wish to ensure their children's place in the competitive world and to enhance their own status as parents of these children. Gifted young children seem often to bear a double burden of "hurried education" and "miseducation." Many young children showing precocity in language and thinking skills are placed in formal education earlier, so that they do not waste any more time in kindergarten, and even when reading and other basic skills are acquired, the "enrichment" proceeds in the form of ill-planned make-work and extracurricular experiences.

One growing problem in early childhood education is that gifted young children are sometimes subjected to overintensified compensatory programs, as if they were an undermotivated, high-functioning minority in needing special brands of "remedial" intervention, as do undermotivated, low-functioning children. As a result, "the image of the competent child introduced to remedy the under-stimulation of low-income children now serves as a rationale for over-stimulation of middle-class children" (Elkind, 1987, p. 70). Elkind warns of the dangers of miseducation and suggests a return to a more natural, child-centered, less stressful education of young children. However, it seems unrealistic to expect parents of young children, especially parents who think their youngsters are gifted, to stop the race toward more and more demanding education (or miseducation), simply because it is sensible to call such a halt, even if this common sense were supported by research evidence. Parents feel the beat of time and hear the sounds of competitive crowds pushing their young children onward and upward. What is needed is not merely the suggestion to stop and relax, but a clear definition of what a quality interaction with young children consists of, what parents really want for their children, an identification of distant goals in education, and how to achieve them in a less pressured and less "rehearsed" manner.

Children do manage to learn without adults' direct involvement in the process, but what accounts for much of the variability in cognitive performance is the quality of human mediation they receive. Children's learning how to learn and whether it is worthwhile to do so is shaped by the adults with whom they interact.

Developing a Stress-Free Quality Environment for Young Gifted Children

The MISC program for sensitizing caregivers and educators of young gifted children (MISC-G) is one of a series of MISC programs implemented for infants and young children with special needs.

Judging from our hands-on experimentation in home and clinic settings, it has been demonstrated that high-quality mediation leads to better learning. Most available intervention programs are designed to improve a child's behavior in a number of cognitive domains. The MISC program views improved performance as an objective, but this goal is secondary to one of affecting the child's needs system, creating in the child a greater urge to focus clearly on stimuli, to search for meaning, to associate, relate, compare, and contrast perceptions, to seek explanation, relations, and general information beyond what is perceived through the senses. Other salient aims are to strengthen the need to afford pleasure to others, to summarize one's own behavior, to plan ahead, and to match one's behavior with the tasks at hand. A sample of cognitive and social–emotional needs in relation to basic mediational criteria is presented in Table 3.1.

MISC-G is based on criteria determining the quality of mediation and defining how an interaction should be carried out if it is meant to affect the child. In addition, four general areas of functioning that relate to the question "What should be focused on in the program?" are highlighted. It should be stressed that the specific contents were chosen by the children, with the mediator frequently responding to the children's initiative in the following domains of behavior:

SOCIAL–EMOTIONAL FUNCTIONING

The mediators in the program highlighted ongoing processes of interaction among the children and between the children and their parents or other adults. Prior to the onset of the program, all of the children learned to identify, label verbally, and imitate facial expressions of emotions and what triggers these emotions. They then identified these in drawings and sculptures and in everyday human interactions, devoting attention to their consequences and precedents. The variables that were noted in the mediator's summary card were as follows: (a) showing signs of affection for another person, (b) reacting to another child's distress, (c) helping others physically or verbally, and (d) sharing materials and workspace.

LANGUAGE FUNCTIONING

The use of new vocabulary was introduced when appropriate. Following word introduction, efforts were made to use each word again in different situations. Excitement was expressed with regard to the "beautiful new word," "just the word for it," "perfect word." The children were encouraged to verbalize thoughts. The mediator shared with them his/her own thoughts and feelings. Sentence structure was not corrected immediately; instead, it was duly noted and the correct structure was brought to the child's attention in a different context. A similar approach was used for grammatical closure. Verbal fluency and verbal expression were encouraged in general, and particularly in relation to feelings.

THINKING PROCESSES

Usually, the mediator identified and raised the children's awareness of cognitive processes involved in their own behavior, using metacognitive methods to highlight techniques for focusing attention and memory, sorting out relevant versus irrelevant information, presenting divergent thinking through different people's point of view, pointing out the need to see things clearly, to plan ahead, to assess the challenge of a task or problem, and to consider all aspects of a problem. Raising the children's awareness to the processes of mediation or to the "instructional secrets" was a frequently used strategy to improve children's awareness of the need to plan and regulate behavior, as well as to become familiar with cognitive processes.

AESTHETICS AND ART

The objective of the focus on aesthetics and art was to enrich the children's channels of expression, and to enable them to differentiate and enjoy the aesthetic qualities of the environment. The mediators highlighted and raised the children's awareness of objects that are aesthetically pleasing, giving reasons for, and describing, their aesthetic qualities. The mediators shared with the children criteria for aesthetic choices through joint decisions that required aesthetic considerations (e.g., where to place a flowerpot, or where to hang a picture on the wall). Children were asked to choose works of art, household utensils, clothing, and so on, that they liked, and to say why they liked them.

Based on the outstanding features of the population of young gifted children and their assumed needs, the general structure of the MISC-G program was designed with a focus on the five basic criteria of a quality mediation, suggesting how to mediate to these children, and another focus across four major content areas: social–emotional, language, thinking processes, and aesthetics and art. Following each meeting with a gifted child, the mediator (most frequently an early childhood education student) was required to fill out a summary card reflecting the structure of the program (see Table 3.1). At every meeting different content areas could be dealt with depending on the needs and interests of each individual. Monthly summaries had to include some repeated references to all four content areas and to be carried out through the application of all five basic criteria of mediation. These summary cards were discussed with the parents, who were encouraged to add to the summary table examples from their own interactions with their children.

TABLE 3.1 A GENERAL SUMMARY CARD OF THE MISC PROGRAM FOR GIFTED YOUNG CHILDREN

	What			
	Social–Emotional	*Language*	*Thinking processes (Metacognitive)*	*Aesthetics & Art*
How				
Focusing (Intentionality & Reciprocity)				
Exciting (Meaning)				
Expanding (Transcendence)				
Rewarding (Competence)				
Organizing & Planning (Regulation of Behavior)				

As stated earlier, gifted young children are characterized by their appetite for learning and their unusual capacity to benefit from new experiences. It stands to reason that these children have probably experienced good mediation. Their parents or other adults in their lives have spontaneously provided them with quality interaction. However, in order to ensure continued quality mediation across various situations and time, the MISC-G program was designed to improve parental awareness and the skills for application of the basic criteria that define early enrichment through mediation.

Mediation of Art and Aesthetics for the Young and Gifted: A Sample of Educational Considerations and Mediational Implications

The general criteria of a quality interaction with young children can be applied to various dyadic experiences, independent of their content or context. However, in order to be a good mediator, one has to convey real excitement about what is mediated, a genuine interest in the child, and a general idea of possible educational sequences in the content area in question. Aesthetics education represents still another effort to cultivate cardinal yet neglected areas of learning for gifted preschoolers.

Adults are often fascinated by the freshness and originality of children's art and by the opportunity it provides to look into a child's inner life. Children's art can be viewed as another language for self-expression. However, precocious development of the graphic forms of artistic expression is not considered to be a sign of giftedness until it includes pictorial representations of the environment. There is a meaningful consistency in toddlers' and young children's self-taught art. The artistic creations at that early age appear to follow definite developmental stages, reflecting concern for placement, shape, and aesthetically balanced design (Kellog, 1970). Most parents and educators, however, are unaware of the developmental stages in children's art and evaluate their drawing by level of representation of familiar forms. Before children develop to the stage at which they can produce representational art, they are rarely rewarded for their achievements in their own form of expression. They are not rewarded for using a variety of colors, for using up much of the drawing space on a page, for producing aesthetically balanced designs, or for using artistic nonpictorial representations in creative ways.

Children's spontaneous scribbles become explicitly pictorial at only about the age of three, when they may identify in their scribbles recognizable shapes, label them, and elaborate on them. There seems to be a general lack of awareness of the possible existence of artistic precocity before the age of three. Although Kellog and others suggest leaving children alone to pass through all stages of self-taught art, it is clear that parents could significantly affect children's need to express themselves artistically and to choose a specific mode of self-expression.

It appears that what a young child fails to produce in art, as in other domains, is related to limitations in past experience. It would be more constructive to avoid overgeneralizations based on developmental-stage theories, inasmuch as doing so may lead to closing off exposure to stimulating objects and events. The young gifted child should be provided with art and aesthetics education in order to open a major avenue of self-expression, differentiation, and sensitivity to the environment. Content analysis of children's talk or artistic expression about art and design can provide a penetrating assessment of the way they look at, and respond to, art and design forms. For example, a naive response to, say, a painting or television advertisement characteristically focuses on the literal content or subject matter (i.e., on what is being represented) rather than on how it is represented.

A more sophisticated and educated response would refer additionally to the diverse perceptual properties, such as the colors, tones, textures, organization, and composition. It would also refer to the affective properties, with reasons being given for preferences and dislikes, as well as the inferred or explicit intentions and moods of the artist and the child looking at it. Likewise accessible to the educated, insightful young child is an appreciation of the artist's preferred style, materials, and techniques, and perhaps even something about the period and culture in which the painting was produced. Children, even gifted ones, looking at a painting, for example, can hardly be expected to pass beyond the basic level of reference to the representational content of a work of art (i.e., beyond what their eyes see) unless they are in the presence of an adult who is ready to mediate its meaning to them.

We cannot show the appropriateness of our feelings, even in relation to works of art that fail to move us deeply or passionately. "It is no good saying 'strip it of its associations and look on it purely as a work of art.' For works of art would not affect us at all, if it was not for some associations, however deeply buried: the symbols have to be symbols of something" (Wilson, 1986, p. 96).

Most deliberate brands of "aesthetics education" try to meet only the demand for intellectual initiation, and much of this is, in a way, just a device, almost a cheat. When the person is already in love with a work to some degree, then the critic who knows it more and loves it better can say helpful things: things more closely relevant to what moves us or may move us when we connect what he/she says with what we know of the work already. As Wilson (1986) points out: "Perhaps what we need to know is what makes children really like any kind of good music (plays, books, poems, pictures, etc.) for almost any reason. Given some degree of commitment or love, we have some basis for teaching: not before then" (p. 106).

The young gifted child, looking at a painting, may be able, at an earlier age than expected, to see its content and even derive the emotional message conveyed by the artist. Quality mediation by the adult to this child may involve sharing one's experiences with art and presenting the reasons for liking or disliking it, the emotions it evokes, and some facts about the artist, but all of the above should be presented only if matched with the child's interest, and only if considered genuinely of interest to the mediator. Thus, educators of the young and gifted must be knowledgeable about educational sequences, flexible in using them, and genuinely enthusiastic about the subject matter they teach.

Quality mediation provided to young children incorporates focusing, arousing, and expanding. Focusing the child's attention on detail or stimulating his/her senses does not suffice in creating true aesthetic experiences that may build an appetite for further aesthetic experiences. Arousing the child involves sharing one's own reasons for excitement and expanding beyond the present, beyond what one sees or feels at the moment, into what the artist could have felt, and into the realm of his/her times. Aesthetics can be introduced to children's awareness by pointing out and discussing with them interesting designs of buildings, products, and furniture while sharing decisions as to where to place a beautiful object, how to arrange flowers, which jewelry to choose, and where to place it.

When the center staff suggested to the parents of our Israeli sample of gifted three to four year olds to visit an art museum with their children, they were surprised (although they did visit museums). During the interview held with the parents at the end of the program year, many of them noted taking their children to share an artistic experience that they themselves loved, such as going to a concert, to the theater, to a ballet, or to a dance performance. They could also clearly describe what experiences they wished to share with their children, how much they all enjoyed it, and how this feeling was expressed by and to the children.

A small taste of many subjects, or the "smorgasbord" approach found in elementary education, may not be the best tactic in educating every young gifted child. These youngsters may benefit from bits of information or fragmented episodes of learning, but in terms of long-lasting effects, they require a balance between consistency and novelty presented by a mediator who shows great interest in them and a passion for the area he/she wishes to mediate to the children. One can hardly expect a toddler to remember the contents he/she has learned; however, these experiences may be more effective if they arouse the appetite for more.

One of the four year olds seen at the center, Danny, was a gifted artist. His drawings were considerably beyond expectation for his age and had a strong and fresh expressive message. Looking into Danny's history and background, it became apparent that since infancy, he had spent hours every day with his grandfather, who is an artist and lives with the family. A grandfather who loved his own art and his grandson, and who had the time and patience to be a good mediator, apparently provided fertile ground for the development of the special artistic talents and "artistic appetites" of his grandson.

All parents have the right to their own objectives in their children's development. Most parents, regardless of their cultural background or SES level, want their children to develop into well-adjusted individuals. They may thus be concerned if their children do not do or like to do what other children of their age prefer doing. Danny's mother, for example, was concerned whether she was doing the right thing by allowing him to draw so much. She claimed that he did not wish to engage in any other activity, such as playing with building blocks or watching TV. In fact, Danny's parents did not consider him to be a gifted child (probably because his language development did not exceed the norm for his age). They did, however, realize that he drew exceptionally well. They therefore collected and numbered his drawings, prepared albums, and showed them to all visitors to their home.

At an early stage of development, any content area can be used as a vehicle for educational enrichment, as long as the interaction with the child in relation to the content is meaningful and stimulating. Young artists may learn at least as much about the world around them through art as through playing with building blocks and puzzles, or listening to music. Development in language and thinking can be enhanced through experiences related to children's interest in art. Even social interactions with age peers may be related, directly or indirectly, to art (e.g., drawing a cooperative mural, sharing materials, preparing greeting cards for others, or visiting a museum).

The joy of learning, the eagerness to acquire new skills, knowledge, and understanding, are partially intrinsic as suggested, for example, by Piaget's (1973) notion of the need to operate the schemes of thought as the basis for development of higher thinking processes. There is, however, no doubt that the need for novelty, the quest for knowledge, are largely acquired through the process of interaction between the child and his/her environment. This is true of all children and perhaps more so for children who are more active, demanding, and verbal as toddlers. The toddler years can be a sensitive period for a generalized curbing or encouragement of the appetite for learning. The growing mobility, the newly developed language skills and experimentation of selfhood, bring the young children into many situations that allow them to learn whether it is worthwhile to exert effort, and whether there is something beyond what is seen or sensed momentarily.

4   MEDIATIONAL INTERVENTION FOR LITERACY

A MEDIATED LEARNING APPROACH FOR THE ENHANCEMENT OF LITERACY

Literacy is no doubt an important component of communication and a necessary skill for adjustment and socialization. The technical ability to read and write does not guarantee the benefits or objectives for which literacy programs are designed. Literacy is but a single means (although a very important one) for obtaining new information from the environment and for expressing one's own ideas. Most intervention programs designed to improve literacy focus on the development of abilities and skills necessary for reading and writing.

The MISC approach is designed to enhance the individual's flexibility of mind, his/her general ability to benefit from new experiences of learning (i.e., learning how to learn, regardless of the specific nature or content of the experience), including the acquisition of literacy.

The MISC creates several conditions that enhance the individual's potential for learning and may affect his/her potential for achieving literacy. As a consequence of quality mediation, one acquires the need to focus more carefully on visual or auditory stimuli, to search for meaning, to relate between bits of isolated perceptions, and to seek information that may expend what is perceived by the senses at the immediate present. One can hardly be expected to identify and decode words if one has no need to attend to fine perceptual differences between letters or sequences of letters. One may even overcome the difficulties inherent in the decoding stage, but have no need to search for meaning in any of his/her interactions with the environment, including the experience of reading, which is then reduced to decoding only. The basic motivation to read may be lacking in an individual who has not had a chance to experience the availability of explanations, stories, cause-and-effect relations, and various other forms of expression of information perceived directly through the senses.

Reading and writing as a form of communication should be viewed as part of the larger, more comprehensive process of socialization, and attempts to improve literacy should thus be made as an integral part of mediational process provided to young children within their own sociocultural environment as part of a general attempt to enhance the quality of mediation they are exposed to.

The Mediational Intervention for Literacy (MIL) program has been developed by the author in collaboration with Katherine H. Greenberg from the University of Tennessee. The MIL provides a culturally based, mediated learning approach to helping young children develop an understanding of basic literacy concepts and an enthusiasm for becoming literate. By drawing from common uses of oral and written language within the given family and/or community, the MIL program can provide activities that are culturally relevant to each child. As an extension of the MISC program, the MIL employs strategies for sensitizing adults to the kind of human mediation young children need in order to adjust to our changing world, to benefit from new experiences, and to become caring and intelligent human beings.

The MIL program is designed for implementation in a variety of situations with children and families at risk in a literate world society. It is available as a family-centered program for use in the home and as a school-based program for use in educational settings from preschool through the early grades. Ideally, the family and school program will be implemented in combination. Due to its emphasis on personally relevant activities, the MIL program can be used in communities that do not have schools and/or in homes where no family members are literate when they begin the program.

Unique Features of the MIL Program

The MIL program is unique among early childhood literacy programs in several ways. All aspects of the MIL program are guided by the following principle: We are going your way, to get where you want to go, using your means of communication and what is natural and relevant to you.

All MIL activities for both school and home implementation are selected based on personal relevance to the child and family and the literacy level of those participating. Adults can implement the program at home, even if they are illiterate. Furthermore, the program is designed to help both the illiterate adult, as well as the child, develop literacy skills. The MIL involves a language immersion process with a focus on ongoing verbal modes of interaction including conversation, storytelling, and prayers. The initial stages of the MIL are designed to raise awareness of different types of spoken language (How do you speak to your friend? to a relative? to an important stranger? How do you ask someone for a favor? How would your friend respond if you spoke to him/her using the language of prayer?) The importance of accurate, noneccentric speech is stressed. For example: "Put the butter on the bread." Does it mean placing the package of butter on the loaf of bread? Using humorous examples demonstrates the differentiation in presenting different types of verbal information (different kinds of language in different types of texts, such as the prayer book, a letter, a storybook, etc.). The program begins at a contextualized level, focusing on activities that involve learning to read and write one's own name, as well as those of family members and classmates, and continues to activities that involve reading and writing a list of required chores. Then the activities progress slowly toward a decontextualized level at which participants are involved in reading stories, prayers, and songs well known to those who share a similar cultural background, and eventually reading and writing about events outside their everyday experiences.

Every activity for home and school use relates to real literacy happenings within the community. School activities emphasize family and community uses for oral and written language. Teachers may use isolated skills, drills, and practice activities that are connected to real-life literacy (e.g., sending notes to ask for things or as thanks for them). In turn, home activities provide insight into the differences between school, community, and family uses of oral and written language.

The types of competence mediated to the participants of the MIL are designed to raise their awareness to their specific successes in language-related behavior (i.e., being able to express themselves clearly), the number of new words or phrases they learned, as well as cognitive processes such as focusing and attention, memory, association, and reasoning skills essential for future learning. For example, in verbally responding to a child's successful attempt to recall what he/she had learned previously, one might say, "You learn well, you have a good memory, you remember what you learned yesterday. . . . How do you do it?" then wait for the child to respond and help identify "what other children do in order to remember better" (look, listen carefully, practice, associate, and relate).

The MIL program, like the MISC, is partially based upon the theory of *mediated learning experience* (Feuerstein, 1979), which focuses on the universal and yet highly personalized aspects of relationships between the adult and child. Mediated learning, as distinct from direct learning through the senses, occurs when the environment is interpreted for the child by another person who understands the child's needs, interests, and capacities, and who takes an active role in making components of that environment, as well as past and future experiences, compatible with the child's current level of understanding, needs, and interest.

A growing body of research has clearly demonstrated the important effects of mediated learning on the child's development. And yet, many children, especially those at risk for remaining illiterate, frequently do not receive an adequate quality of mediated learning. When mediated learning is of high quality, children are much more likely to develop an optimistic view of themselves as learners, an appetite for learning (e.g., creating a desire to expand one's understanding and to ask questions), and behaviors that are part of the culture, including the culture of literacy.

Literacy activities that are personally and culturally relevant provide an excellent vehicle for assisting family caregivers and teachers in understanding how to provide high-quality, mediated learning experiences in any situation. As a result, the MIL program is unique among literacy programs because of its emphasis on helping both family caregivers and teachers meet the following MISC objectives:

1. promote a positive conception of the child and his/her potential to develop;
2. increase awareness of the adult's role in promoting development;
3. establish a positive cycle of emotional interaction with the child;
4. promote a more guided and enriching interchange with the child by learning to enhance the occurrence of mediated learning, including such basic elements as focusing, meaning, expanding, going beyond, and building the child's feeling of competence and self-regulation.

In addition, the MIL program—like the MISC—is designed to help adults refine their abilities to convey messages to children, build needs, and communicate scripts—according to the adults' cultural context. The child must receive certain kinds of messages in order to benefit from mediated learning. These include a basic alphabet of communication through affect, smiles, eye contact, turn taking, sharing joy and interest, following the child's initiative, and doing what the child does. As a result, children receive the message that they are good, that the world is good, that it is worthwhile to do instead of remaining passive, and that they are capable individuals. Furthermore, the adult learns to mediate needs to the child, including the need to focus one's attention, to expand beyond what is experienced through the senses, to plan, to connect one thing to another, and in general, to learn to learn. In addition, the adult intentionally shares scripts with the child. Scripts are the sequential steps, plans, or "rules" determined by one's culture concerning what should happen under certain circumstances. Some scripts provide patterns of behavior directly related to literacy, for example,

1. appropriate behavior for "using" a book;
2. how space and time orderings within the family and community are related to reading and writing, or
3. how one's role in the family or community affects the use of language.

As a result, the MIL focuses on language at a deeper level than many literacy programs by building upon a deeper understanding of culturally based communication patterns within the family and/or community.

The MIL System of Implementation

The MIL program relies on an implementation system similar to that used in many countries implementing the MISC program. Paraprofessionals are trained in special workshops to provide three types of services to families. First, they learn to conduct home visits in order to gather information needed to determine the following:

1. the most appropriate kind of literacy activities based on the family's culture, each family member's current level of literacy, and the language socialization process within the family;
2. the relationship between adults and children in the family in terms of affect;
3. the quality of mediated learning interactions within the family.

Indeed, paraprofessionals can make videotapes of the family and then use them to point out, reinforce, and explain various aspects of mediated learning interactions. Finally, paraprofessionals visit in homes on a regular basis to demonstrate specific literacy activities adapted to the family's specific needs, monitor the family's literacy progress, and provide guidance and encouragement.

Teachers who implement the MIL school program participate in special workshops to learn how to enhance mediated learning in the classroom through small-group literacy activities that connect school uses of oral and written language with common uses at home, at work, and in social settings. They receive regular visits from supervisors, who help them adapt the literacy activities to meet specific needs in their classrooms, monitor literacy progress, and provide guidance and encouragement. In addition, teachers communicate regularly with the paraprofessionals facilitating implementation of the MIL programs in homes of children they teach.

A Summary of Special Features of the MIL

- It is designed to enhance *literacy*, as well as *flexibility of mind* in general.

- All activities included in the MIL are meaningful within the home and sociocultural environment of the participants (i.e., include the focus on songs, prayers, folk stories, etc.).

- Activities included in the program are intrinsically motivating. They are worthwhile to the child or adult and are structured to satisfy their needs (e.g., the need to distribute notes to some of the children's mailboxes is related to learning how to identify their names).

- Decontextualization of the language used, starting with human rather than object-related mediation.

- Emphasis on storytelling and listening to stories of the elderly or other adults.

- Involving the entire family in literacy-related activities.

- Strictly guarding the respect barrier in parent–child interaction so as not to destroy any cultural norms. (Parents can help their children develop literacy, even if they are learning reading and writing themselves).

- Use of humor to make the process of learning a pleasant experience for all involved and to create a need to seek additional experiences of enjoyable learning.

- Use of differentiated mediation of competence designed to focus the learner's attention and create an awareness regarding processes of memory and thinking, as well as modes of communication beneficial to learning.

PART 2
MEDIATIONAL INTERVENTION: CROSS-CULTURAL EXPERIENCES

5 A Curriculum for Training Teachers of Culturally Diverse Young Children with Disabilities

Mary McKnight-Taylor and Ruth F. Gold

Introduction

This chapter describes an ongoing process in the implementation of a preservice, early childhood teacher-training program as it incorporates a new curriculum strand. First, a description of the rationale for the inclusion of curricular changes is presented. Then the steps involved in selecting and integrating the new components are reviewed. The impact of the changes will be clarified as we discuss our plans for the future.

The Early Childhood Special-Education program (ECSE) at Hofstra University is a preservice graduate program that builds on prior training in regular preschool and/or primary-level education. The program, which was introduced in 1988, educates teachers to work with young children who have various types and severity of disabilities, from birth through age five. The characteristics of the infants and toddlers may represent noncategorical developmental disabilities, whereas the preschoolers are generally defined by specific disability areas such as mental retardation, autism, language/speech delay, physical disability, and emotional disorders.

Teachers must be equipped to work in a variety of settings. Infants and toddlers may be seen in home-based and/or home/center-based programs. They may be served in hospital settings, day-care programs, or mental health centers. The preschoolers may be found in specialized education centers, developmental preschools, hospitals, or at home. No matter the setting, the special educators must be equipped to work with parents as well as professional service providers, such as occupational therapists, physical therapists, speech therapists, nurses, physicians, social workers, and nutritionists.

Because of the changing compositions of the communities in which our graduates are employed, there is a program emphasis on working with children and families from diverse cultural, ethnic, and language groups. An increasing number of young children with disabilities in New York State come from social, ethnic, and language minority homes. As the numbers of children identified at early ages to have disabilities or to be at risk for disabilities increase, new intervention programs have proliferated, creating a need for teachers who are trained to work with infants, toddlers, and preschoolers from culturally and linguistically diverse backgrounds. The New York State Education Department's plan for 1987–1989, which addressed the need for educating children with handicapping conditions, included among its priorities disabled children below age five who come from low income, minority, and non-English-speaking backgrounds (The University of the State of New York, State Education Department, 1987). These diverse groups include African Americans, speakers of Russian and Spanish, and Haitians. Another priority in New York State is the inclusion of young children with disabilities within regular early childhood and day-care settings.

The purpose of the early intervention programs is to promote engagement and mastery and to facilitate social–emotional development, language and communication skills, gross- and fine-motor skills, and daily living skills. The goals include building social competence and preparing the youngsters for a normalized life experience. Without early intervention, many young children with disabilities are unable to develop needed skills and knowledge of their environment.

In order to meet the needs of young children with different types and degrees of disabilities from varied cultural, language, and socioeconomic backgrounds, several curricula and methods were introduced into the coursework of the ECSE programs. The students were taught to select methods and materials that met the needs of specific children and their families and addressed the specific, individual long-term goals and short-term objectives that are part of the Individualized Family Service Plans for infants and toddlers and Individualized Education Plans for children from three to five years of age. There was no unifying philosophy or theory of intervention within the Master's program that could serve as the scaffolding for the training components.

A search was made for a program that would be appropriate regardless of the age of the child, type of disability, family background, or the program setting. Because we believe that learning should be a natural part of all of the child's environments, we wanted to incorporate an intervention process that could be used within different settings in the school as well as in the home. An intervention was needed that could be used by teachers and paraprofessionals for consistency within early intervention programs and by parents in order to facilitate generalization of learned skills and behaviors. In addition, the program should be applicable to the varied curricula and materials used with children who need early intervention. In developing instructional programs, teachers must answer the following questions:

- What should the children learn?
- How can we motivate them?
- How should the environment be organized so that learning can take place?
- What materials or situations should be used?
- How do we know if the children are learning?

The concept of mediated learning experiences (MLE) as espoused by Vygotsky and Feuerstein to improve the social–emotional and cognitive development of young children appeared to be a compatible intervention process. Vygotsky (1978) described the "zone of proximal development" as occurring in the relationship of the child to a more capable adult or peer in attempting to learn through problem solving. Feuerstein (1979) suggested that mediation of learning is essential for cognitive development. Both intensity and quality of mediation must be considered. The intensity of the mediation will be determined primarily by the child's needs and strengths; the quality, by the style of the mediator. Carew (1980) suggested that intellectual and cognitive development are related to antecedent experiences that do not depend on formal lessons or educational materials but rely upon the provisions of opportunities to build vocabulary, improve perceptual and motor tasks, develop reasoning skills, and engage in artistic and creative expression.

The MISC (More Intelligent Sensitive Child) program developed by Pnina Klein, incorporated the concepts of MLE and appeared to be an intervention/training technique that would meet the needs of the populations we are addressing, as well as a viable preservice/in-service training technique. Klein (1988) examined the natural mediation skills of parents of very low birth weight (VLBW) children (< 1.5 kg) from infancy to age three and noted that "active parental participation in mediating between the child and his/her environment could be beneficial in the process of assessing cognitive performance of special at risk populations such as VLBW children" (p. 82).

The relationship of the quality of mediation and the cognitive and emotional growth of young children was examined in a series of longitudinal research projects (Klein, 1988; Klein, Weider, & Greenspan, 1987b). Included among the infants, toddlers, and preschoolers in the studies were youngsters with Down's syndrome, children from low-socioeconomic-level families, and others who were born with VLBW. A direct relationship was found between child performance on a variety of scales (Klein, 1988) and the level of mediation the child received. Other studies indicated that the level of mediation of the caregivers can be improved with training (Klein & Alony, 1993).

Klein was invited to address the faculty of the School of Education of Hofstra University and representatives of ECSE programs in the Long Island area in the fall of 1989. Based on her presentations, small-group meetings, and the body of research indicating that there is a positive impact on cognitive, social, and creative ability, the MISC program was incorporated into our ECSE training program.

Several additional factors influenced our choice: MISC is process- rather than materials-oriented. Because it does not rely on specific materials and can be used in all environments and with all language groups, MISC promotes flexibility of intervention. With relatively little training, it can be used by teachers, parents, and other caregivers. Although the program and training materials emphasize 1:1 interventions for infants and toddlers, there are applications for the preschool population as well. The four areas (vocabulary building, perceptual motor skills, reasoning, and artistic/creative development) suggested by Carew (1980) as being important for intellectual development can be addressed within the MISC criteria. The child learns to associate activities and to see the relationships between objects in the environment. The use of the MISC criteria teaches the child to question and to link past, present, and future events. Naturally occurring as well as planned experiences can be enhanced within the MISC framework. For example, sponge painting can be used to facilitate the development of the aforementioned areas. Pointing to a purple-colored shape, the teacher may say, "You didn't have this color paint in the jars. Where did you get it?" The child can show how he/she mixed red and blue or may realize that when they overlapped, a new color appeared. "What is the name of this color?" If the child does not know, the teacher provides the name. The child can be given the opportunity to mix different amounts of red and blue to see the differences in the shades. In another lesson, the children may be encouraged to mix other colors to see if they can discover new ones.

The sponge painting may also reinforce perceptual motor skills as the child places the sponge where he/she planned to put it. Individual artistic expression is seen in the use of different sponge shapes, the placement of the shapes, and the choice of colors.

A major value is the fact that there are no specific materials and settings required. Mediation can take place at any time, under almost any circumstances. The very act of mediation serves as a culturally significant intervention; that is, persons from varied cultural backgrounds will extend, reinforce, or teach the child what is important to the mediator, and by extension, to his/her cultural group. When the mediator is socialized into the mainstream as well, the possibility of more global achievement in terms of general functioning is likely to be achieved. Since mediation is a tool for validating culturally linked experiences, a person who values mainstream experiences and skills is able to transmit those values to the child. Someone who knows, accepts, and perpetuates his/her own cultural group's values will be highly successful in bridging the gap between his/her primary group and the mainstream. It is this principle that guides instructional and experiential processes in the ECSE program.

The MISC programs foster a two-way interactive process: the mediator affects the child; the child affects the mediator. The caregivers show changes in their interactions with the children as they learn to attend more to them by watching and listening. This evidence of growth is an important factor in our evaluation of preservice teachers.

In July 1990, Dr. Klein conducted a week-long workshop for Hofstra faculty and students after being keynote speaker at a conference focusing on MLEs for leaders in early childhood education. That fall, the curriculum was officially incorporated into the teachers' training program and became part of the scholarship program funded by the United States Department of Education, Office of Special Education and Rehabilitation. Additional programs (i.e., the Cognitive Curriculum for Young Children [CCYC]) will be introduced into the ECSE teacher training program for use with older children. However, the MISC program forms the basis for the mediation process introduced for the interventions for children from birth through age five.

IMPLEMENTATION

Several important points for establishing an instructional focus exist. The first is the mediational index of entering students. Through observation and interaction with students, it became clear at an early point that some students were already good mediators. The act of mediation involves both linguistic elements and specific interpersonal–interactive components. It involves active listening, inner directedness, establishment of a cultural philosophy, and a certain element of creativity. To these components one should add a knowledge of the learning process and a battery of attention-getting (and -holding) strategies. When these factors exist, instruction in the philosophy of MLE is received and integrated at a more rapid rate. Implementation is highly successful.

The second point is the timing for the introduction, practice, and evaluation of MLE performances in students. The sequence of courses and the field components require additional periods of intensive exposure to and practice in the processes involved in MLE.

The MISC program is included in the first ECSE course, Introduction to Young Children with Handicapping Conditions. The focus is on its use within toddler and preschool programs, with emphasis on the process as described by Klein and Hundeide (1989):

> Mediation is an active process. The mediator acts upon the stimulus by selecting, accentuating, focusing, framing, providing meaning, and locating the stimulus in time and space. The mediation enables the individual to benefit from experience; it prepares him to learn, to become modified. (p. 15)

The importance of belief in the child's ability to learn and grow was emphasized. The students were encouraged not only to use what was in the environment, but also to think in terms of enhancing what was there and/or to introduce materials or activities.

Five criteria of an MLE interaction (focusing, expanding, meaning, rewarding, and organizing/planning) were discussed using a series of sketches based on real teaching situations. Each student was required to do a field observation in an ECSE classroom. The students were encouraged to give examples from their own observations of each of the five criteria. From the students' comments, it became apparent that some of the teachers they observed were natural mediators."

> The children made ice sculptures using cubes of different sizes. The teacher asked each child to think about what his/her sculpture would look like. "Will you make it high or wide? How many cubes high will it be? How many cubes wide?"

> After having the children feel an ice cube, the teacher asked how it felt. "Cold?" "Hard?" "Slippery?" She then suggested they put on their snow gloves and see which way was better for the project.

> The children put sparkles over their shapes when they finished sculpting. They were encouraged to compare their sculptures. After a few minutes, the teacher asked them to see what was happening to the sculptures. "They are melting." "Why?" "It's too hot in here." Another child offered, "Let's work outside next time."

Other teachers appeared to have little understanding of what children needed to learn.

A new child, Jeremy, came into the class. The teacher introduced the students, one at a time, by name. Two of the boys were named John and Joseph. The teacher did not make any comment on how their names began with the same sound.

The teacher planned a lesson on colors and showed three squares of red, blue, and green. She asked the children to name the colors. She had each child take two crayons, name them, and then color a picture with them. She did not relate the colors to objects in the room or to the clothes the children were wearing. Afterward, the children played a game with balls of different colors. The balls were referred to by size. The color names were never used.

The teacher planned to read *The Three Bears* to the class and have them do an art project. The children sat around the table with the teacher at one end. As she read the story, she sometimes showed a picture and infrequently asked a question about the story. Of the seven children, only two appeared to pay attention for the whole time. The rest appeared bored. There was intentionality but little reciprocity.

She didn't use good questions to get the children to understand what was happening in the story. She did not link this lesson with past lessons. She didn't discuss anything about going into homes without being asked or using people's property without permission. The "art" project wasn't art and it wasn't used to teach. Since I have been introduced to MISC, I have become aware of lost opportunities to expand thinking, show connections, and build vocabulary.

A common factor appeared to be that, in many settings, although the teacher intended to share an experience, the children in the group did not respond to this intentionality. This realization led to a lively discussion of the differences between large-group, small-group, one-to-one teaching, and the utilization of MLE.

In a follow-up session, vignettes from the MISC training manual (Klein & Hundeide, 1989) that had been modified for ECSE settings were introduced. Applications that promoted active involvement of individuals and small groups of children were stressed. For each vignette, the students were asked, "Given this setting or situation, what would you mediate? Why? How would you focus on the topic, introduce meaning, transcendence, feelings of competence, and/or regulation of behavior?" The students worked in pairs to develop their responses. The group then shared and discussed their recommendations. All students did not focus on the same aspects of the vignettes for their instructional plan. The reasons for their choices of what to mediate became apparent. The difference in focus appeared to be related to perceived goals for the children. For example, in Vignette 3 (p. 94), some students focused on the content of the snack, while others stressed the sharing aspect.

Major emphasis in our ECSE program is on developing reflective practitioners. Reflection is an integral part of successful action plans. Students are engaged in the reflective process in all courses and seminars. The value of reflection has been demonstrated in working with parents of children with special needs. An examination of the various types of interaction between parents and educators immediately highlights the positive gains to be achieved through teachers' modeling of reflective and mediative behavior.

Children with special needs profit from mediation by adults who are skillful in mediation and who are convinced of its effectiveness in achieving student growth. Children with physical, mental, or emotional disabilities require external structure for sustained periods of time. The ability to engage the children in an interaction process (intentionality and reciprocity) is an important skill for parents and teachers.

Reflection begins with a personal journal and continues in seminar sessions. Gut reactions, questions, and analyses of successes and failures provide the grist for our educational mill. The MISC curriculum provides scaffolding for reflection on the selections of appropriate methods and materials for teaching infants and toddlers with a range of disabling conditions.

The first step, intentionality and reciprocity, highlights the necessity for acquiring strategies to entice youngsters to attend and to respond. Because children with special needs may have severe deficits in attention or in expressive areas, early attention to alternatives for reaching children must be identified and practiced.

Some children are likely to respond indifferently to incoming stimuli, as in the case of children with autism or those with emotional problems associated with abuse, neglect, or isolation. In such instances the mediator must adjust the timing, structure, content, and method of delivery to actions designed to get and maintain attention.

Initiation of interactions between mediator and child should be scheduled for short, intensive periods. Observation of the child enables planning for times when the child's energy level is sufficient to maintain activity. To help break periods of tantrums or severe withdrawal, interactions may be attempted. Mediation activities including only intentionality and reciprocity are appropriate for attempts to help children regain control when they are in crisis or having a tantrum. Mothers do this when they introduce a favorite toy or a new experience with expressed feelings of excitement, curiosity, or pleasure. For example, a child drumming her heels on the floor and crying may be left alone until the agitation subsides, or the caregiver may sit down next to the child with an appealing toy, a favorite food, and so on, to gain the child's attention and a new response. Optimal times are periods of rest (wake-up time from naps) or change of activities.

Ideal structure for interactive sessions includes ways to shut out or downplay extraneous stimuli. Methods of establishing boundaries for activity include placing tape on the floor, around session space, desks, or chairs to indicate limits.

A great deal of emphasis was placed on helping students to identify potential management problems related to the children's developmental level or their particular disability. Attention deficits in young children with special needs are exacerbated by the additional energy-outlet demands that are typical for young children. Motoric development is contingent upon frequent opportunities to use large muscles. Thus, structuring the environment so that children have permitted energy outlets is an important part of the MISC curriculum. Students were asked to plan and analyze lessons for appropriate pacing of instructions, the level of participation for students, and the types of activities in which they engaged. Sedentary activities (listening) were alternated with movement. Both activities were carefully structured so that support could be provided according to the level of the children's attention, perceptual motor development, and social–emotional functioning.

For example, in moving from one activity to another, definite breaks were established. Transition was begun only after established cleanup, storage, and a return to established seating patterns had been made. Verbal reinforcement from teachers was paired with hugs, handshakes, or a high five for approximations of expected behavior or the behavior itself. The fact that wait time should be brief was reinforced. Young children should not have to wait for long periods before becoming involved in activities. Students were encouraged to prepare all necessary materials with (backups) before beginning one-to-one or small-group lessons.

Structuring Seating to Manage Social Behavior

Children with low-impulse control, or those who require a great deal of personal space because they fidget, can be helped to participate in a group by establishing early a sense of personal space, privacy, the rights of others, and a response to a central focus or teacher's direction. A small mat establishes the child's base spot; the proximity of another child's mat establishes boundaries. An example of a teacher's good judgment in this area was shown during transition from a tabletop group activity to story time. The teacher went to the library corner with the mat, and after placing one mat at the beginning of what was to be a semicircle, she called the child's name.

When that child was seated, the second mat was placed opposite the first. This was done on alternate sides until all children were seated in the semicircle.

```
        1           2
        X           X
  X                       X
        X     X     X
```

Verbal reinforcement was given for appropriate movement, waiting, posture, staying in one's own space, and attending. The order of the selection of children was based on their ability to wait or stay attuned until all the children had made the transition. The order may be decided based upon whether or not a child needs to be in the next lesson site early to welcome the others or whether it is important that he/she join the group later and *be* welcomed.

Transcendence seems to be a combination of extension of concepts and elaboration using probes to elicit further thinking and response and a sort of turn-taking strategy in which ideas are shared. Parent's or teacher's talk provides information and/or feelings as fodder for new thoughts and responses in the child.

For example, a mediated learning experience may occur when a caregiver engages a child's attention using a rag ball. Even if the child does not make a verbal response, reciprocity could be achieved if he/she looks at, touches, or holds the ball when it is offered. Transcendence may occur in this exchange: Caregiver is naming the "Ball" then she Transcends—"Soft" (squeezing the ball while showing it to the child); "Soft" (hand over hand with the child, physically prompting squeezing); rolling the ball—"You can roll it" then, "Roll it to me" (with gesturing to indicate the child should roll the ball).

Another level of transcendence is to throw the ball or show that it will not bounce. Having two balls, one rag and one sponge, adds still more information. Depending on the child's age, physical intactness, and cognitive level, comparisons can be made, the properties of each enumerated, and activities that are possible may be listed. Eliciting responses to the teacher's sensory information is a transcendent act as well.

The interactions that have just been described illustrate the bases for and possible implementations of the following MLE processes for Kyle and Joey.

Kyle is a youngster with autism. His vision is limited. Acuity is not affected, but he is unable to lower his gaze. He lies on his back, lifts objects with his feet to eye level, and plays with them that way.

Kyle also turns his back to the speaker, shakes his head from side to side, or does whole body jumps and hops while listening. In one session students were attempting to get him to be actively involved by looking at or handling the toy. Kyle would repeat the name of the object, express pleasure with the activity by smiling and rocking or roaming away from it, and returning, but he did not sit or look at the student teacher or the object.

What was needed was regulation of Kyle's behavior, structuring the environment so that however briefly he did address the activity, the teacher could determine that intentionality and reciprocity had been achieved. Reinforcement for this directed attention should be both verbal and concrete because Kyle responds well to praise and affection. By specifying the act for which he was being reinforced—looking, holding, pasting, or whatever was required—Kyle will begin to recognize how desirable it can be to sit still and look at the teacher-held objects.

Joey is severely retarded and autistic. He always works with his gaze averted. Tasks like pegs and a pegboard are done in random order, with no specific pattern. The teaching sessions are structured by having the teacher in close proximity, sitting next to Joey rather than facing him. Joey permits contact shoulder to shoulder. The teacher is thus able to physically prompt him to pick up pegs and place them without triggering a tantrum.

Other opportunities for mediation within home- or center-based programs can be seen in the following activities:

1. Allow the child to choose a photo or a catalog picture. Point out the objects in it. Introduce a story about what happened before and or what will happen later. Find out how the child feels about your story. Does it remind him/her of anything?

2. When a child comes into class, take a Polaroid picture of what the child is wearing or draw it on the board. Discuss what the picture shows. Have the child look at, hold, name, or talk about the function of a piece of clothing (e.g., a hat or coat).

3. Initiate associations between objects (i.e., "The hat keeps your head warm. The coat keeps your body warm.") Compare and contrast things around you.

4. When a child attempts to put an arm in a sleeve or put on a hat, reinforce the actions verbally or nonverbally. Relate it to more general concepts, such as "You are growing up. You can dress up by yourself."

5. Tell the child where to place outer clothing, how to fold, how to hang up, or roll them. Set a time for hanging up or taking down items. Describe the order of dressing (e.g., "Put your hat on first, your sweater next, your coat next, and then your mittens").

IMPACT AND PLANS FOR THE FUTURE

To date, thirty-five students in the ECSE teacher's training program have been trained to use the MISC process. Each of these students has implemented the process within a student-teaching situation, thereby sharing this knowledge with the cooperating teachers. Of the thirty-five students, fifteen are currently working with young children with disabilities.

The impact of the training in the MISC process has not been formally evaluated. We have not gathered data to examine changes in the students' teaching styles and have not been able to compare their teaching with that of others in their programs. Because the MISC process is introduced before the students are actively engaged with children, we have not been able to obtain pretraining data. We are planning to develop and implement a research design that will enable us to focus on differences between teachers trained in this process and teachers who have not been trained. Informal evaluations indicate that the students trained in the process have found it to be effective. As we observe them in the field, we ask the following questions:

1. Does the student teacher demonstrate the ability to engage infants and

toddlers in a communicative exchange using basic objects found in most homes?

2. Does the student teacher's manner and physical and facial appearance communicate acceptance, enthusiasm, and approval?

3. Does the planned interaction between the student teacher and the children reflect such planning?

4. Does the student teacher demonstrate flexibility and creativity in responding to unexpected challenges in the interaction?

5. How does the student teacher demonstrate his/her ability to spontaneously mediate to children who have varying degrees of impairment?

We are also restructuring course content to reflect MLE and MISC components. In a course that covers Assessment and Diagnosis in Early Childhood Special Education, we introduce observational checklists and strategies around MLE as a part of a section on ways of obtaining information about children's functioning. Counseling Parents of Children with Disabilities includes MLE as a part of the strategies to be used when working with parents of exceptional children. The course, Crafts and Allied Skills for Children with Disabilities, provides an additional focus on the value of mediation in relation to materials and art processes for developing curiosity and a feeling of competence in children.

As part of the practicum for teaching young children with disabilities, we plan to introduce videotaping as a feedback mechanism for student teachers. Currently a written transcript of observations is provided with concrete examples of various mediational techniques that were observed. A weakness in this format is that the student's recall of the situation may be diminished/tempered by the stress of observation. A review of the taped performance helps the student see the whole process more clearly and learn to mediate more effectively.

The authors have developed a model in-service training program for Head Start personnel in Nassau County. Head Start is a day-care program for children three to five years of age, who come from low socioeconomic level families. At least 10% of the enrollment includes children with disabilities. We hope to obtain funding to train the staff and the children's parents to use the MISC program.

A high proportion of youngsters in these programs come from minority and culturally/linguistically diverse backgrounds. In addition to training the staff to understand different types of disabilities, a major focus of the project is to introduce the MISC process to the teachers and professionals who staff the programs. It is also a goal of the project to have the staff work with parents and other caretakers to use MLE in their own settings.

The need to help staff provide parents with training is demonstrated by this excerpt from an in-service teacher's log.

> I met B's mother and she was very thankful to me. She told me that B often talks about the sizes and shapes of objects at home. She has become aware of this for the first time ever in her life. B's mother said, "I just don't have the time to work with her on these things, so I thank you."

This in-service teacher had not received training in the MISC program and did not realize that there are many natural home situations that can be used to review the concepts introduced in the school setting and that she could have helped the parent to do this. We are planning training sessions to teach our preservice and in-service students ways to encourage parents to use the MISC process in their homes.

Additional collaborative exchanges have been established with Head Start in East Harlem, New York, and two Brooklyn, New York, sites for preschool children who are developmentally disabled. Workshops were conducted with staff and parents in each setting. Feedback forms indicated understanding of the five basic principles and an increasing recognition of opportunities for using them.

Several students have referred in-service teachers to us to learn more about the MISC program in particular, and MLE in general. Based on our experience, it appears the MISC program has application in the training of staff in early intervention and preschool settings. The teacher/caregiver learns to be a skilled observer who uses the available environment and creatively prepares and arranges suitable activities. Because the mediator's role includes assigning value to what is being presented to the child, as well as to the child's responses, training is conducted in a culturally sensitive mode.

Sample Vignettes

1. You are in the school yard with a child during recess. You both witness a fight over a ball.

2. A parent or supervisor is expected in your classroom. You are getting the room ready. One child keeps trying to get your attention.

3. It is time to prepare the midmorning snack for your class of three-year-olds.

4. A child in class fell and hurt his knee.

5. The first snowfall of winter is falling and the children are not paying attention to your lesson.

6 MEDIATIONAL INTERVENTION FOR SENSITIZING CAREGIVERS: ETHIOPA

Tirussew Teferra, Lakew Wolde Tekle, Teka Zewde,

Fantu Melese, Zelalem Fekadu, Henning Rye, and

Karsten Hundeide

The overall objective of implementing the MISC in Ethiopia was to explore the possibility of enhancing the quality of mediation in early mother–child interactions and consequently to improve the cognitive and emotional development of Ethiopian children. The Intervention program was based on the MISC program. It is tailored toward promoting the quantity and quality of infant–caregiver interactions, both in home- and institution-based settings. A special attempt was made to integrate the psychosocial intervention within the existing primary health-care services in the local community.

Prior to implementation of the intervention, local professionals surveyed the health status and ethnographic characteristics of the children and the families participating in the study, in order to reach a "preliminary community diagnosis." Most of the local research staff participated in a two-week training on the MISC program, conducted by professors Pnina Klein, Karsten Hundeide, and Henning Rye in June 1990, at Addis Ababa University.

IMPLEMENTATION OF THE PROJECT

The following criteria were used to select the project site:

1. families with very low socioeconomic status and mothers with hardly any schooling;
2. a culturally homogenous population;
3. families with children between six months and three years old.

In addition, it was preferred that the project site be located at a reasonable distance from the University of Addis Ababa.

Accordingly, Kechene community of Kebele 15 and Kebele 18, located in the northwestern part of Addis Ababa, about three kilometers away from Addis Ababa University, were selected as project sites. These communities are considered among the most congested urban slums in the city of Addis Ababa, with overcrowded households and poor sanitation. Most families in these areas lead an impoverished life, down to the lowest limit of subsistence. The dwellers of this community are self-employed and culturally homogenous. Almost every household earns its living through weaving, clay work, and other home-based handicraft activities. The educational background of most of the families ranges from literacy to primary-school education. The living quarters are extremely overcrowded because they are used not only as the family's living room, bedroom, and workplace, but also because of the number of family members (ranging from seven to nine persons) dwelling in this one room (rarely two rooms), the size of which rarely exceeds six square meters.

There is hardly any space for children to play at home. Children spend most of their time playing in the streets. There are no books in the homes or any stimulating play objects except for balls made from old cloth. Children commonly enjoy interacting with the animals (i.e., chickens and dogs) found in almost every household. There are no liquid and solid waste-disposal facilities in the community, and waste is therefore left in the open. Fathers have absolutely no role in child care, which is the sole duty of the mother and the elder siblings, particularly the girls. When the mother is out shopping, children are left at home and are usually attended by older girls or by the grandmothers.

The MISC program was also implemented in the Kechene Children's Home, which is a residential institution for homeless children ranging from one to eighteen years of age. The children in this home are orphans gathered from hospitals or off the streets of Addis Ababa. The institution is run by the Ethiopian government's Children, Youth, and Family Welfare Organization and is located near Addis Ababa University.

THE PILOT STUDY

Twenty-six families from Kebele 15 and Kebele 18, and thirteen children from the Kechene Children's Home participated in the pilot study. The objectives of this project were as follows:

1.   to investigate and map out the existing needs, local conceptions, and childrearing practices of parents and other caregivers in the participating families;

2.   to adopt the MISC intervention program to the local needs, conceptions, and traditional childrearing practices;

3.   to implement the MISC in Ethiopia and examine its application and consequences;

4.   to build up the competence of local educators, supervisors, primary health-care personnel, and the staff of the orphanage.

Project Implementation Strategies

COMMUNITY APPROACH

In order to assume access to individual households in the community, the local research team contacted the leaders of the Urban Dwellers Association in the community. It was not an easy task to convince the community leaders about the importance and relevance of the project for the community. Actually, they were more interested in a concrete and visible development project geared to the satisfaction of their immediate needs related to building or receiving something concrete, rather than a program designed to enhance the future development of their children. However, following a number of group and individual meetings, the research team succeeded in convincing them of the practical benefits of investing in their children's development. It should be noted that only after permission to start with the intervention was granted by the community leaders, did the team approach the individual households. The research team did not dare go and knock at the door of each household and interfere in the privacy of individual family affairs. Indeed, the consequence of such an act would have jeopardized the overall implementation of the project. Therefore, the team preferred to approach the selected families through the community leaders, an approach that was found to be practical and effective. Through the office of the community leaders, a general meeting of the selected families was called and held in their respective communities, that is, Kebele 15 and Kebele 18. These meetings presented an introduction to the program, tailored to the needs of mothers or caregivers. The objectives of the project were described in very simple language, including concrete examples that could be easily understood by the participants, and clarified the essence and potential impact of the program. The initial session improved the parents' understanding of the program and their feelings toward it. The success of the introductory phase may be attributed to the objective of the intervention program, which was to promote the value and belief system of the traditional family that considers the child as an asset for the future of the family. Even after reaching such an understanding, the research team did not go from door-to-door to the households of the selected families on their own, but with an "insider" from the community who shared their problems and spoke their language.

The research team did not approach mothers with an attitude of "We know it all," as experts, but with due respect to parents' opinions and an openness to learn from them. This strategy enabled them to break through the sociocultural barriers and successfully undertake the project.

The effort to convey the objectives of the MISC to the officials of the Kechene Children's Home was less complicated. The officials were more professional, with some years of college education and backgrounds in child psychology and development. Unlike a natural home environment, the children's home was a structured environment in which older orphaned girls and young orphaned children were kept in different buildings on the same compound. As a rule, girls were not allowed to enter the young children's house or contact them in any way.

SELECTION OF TARGET GROUP

Using a systematic random sampling technique, 15 of the families from Kebele 18, and 15 of the families from Kebele 15 were selected for the experimental and control groups, respectively. The age of the children ranged from six months to three years. In the course of the study, 3 families dropped out from the experimental group and 2 from the control group for reasons such as a child's death or change of residence.

Regarding the orphans in the children's home, 13 children, ranging in age from one to three years, were selected for the intervention program. Thirteen adult caregivers as well as 13 older girls from the orphanage were included in the study. The objective for involving older girls was to establish a 1:1 caregiver–infant relationship by matching one child to one older girl, so that each girl had "her own baby" with which to interact. This type of interaction promoted an intimate and individualized relationship that could not have been attained by the adult caregivers alone. There were only four adult caregivers on duty per shift for 16 children, that is, a 1:4 ratio. Furthermore, these caregivers had to carry out a number of tasks, such as dressing children, cleaning the rooms, making the beds, and cooking. Data available for final analysis regarding the children's home were based on 11 subjects only, because 2 children were adopted by families and left the home.

BASELINE OBSERVATION

Mother–child interactions were videotaped for about thirty minutes for each mother–child dyad. These recordings included natural feeding, bathing, and play episodes. The recordings were analyzed using the Observing Mediational Intervention method described earlier. In addition parents were interviewed using the Parental Mediation Questionnaire (as described later in this chapter) as a guideline for the interview.

Intervention Procedures

HOME-BASED INTERVENTION

A combination approach of three group meetings and three home visits were employed alternately every two weeks. Each group meeting lasted from two to three hours, whereas the home visit took one and a half hours: The home visits as well as the group meetings included the following procedures:

• The basic criteria of mediation were explained through the use of demonstrations from the videotaped sessions.

• Mothers were invited to demonstrate their understanding of mediational criteria by role playing as mediators in various situations of interaction with their children at home.

• Presentation of videotapes of good and bad mediation and asking mothers to comment.

• Presentation of pictures depicting different ingredients of mediational criteria and asking mothers to identify the criteria and explain what is going on.

• Pointing out positive elements in mothers' own interaction with their children and explaining these elements in relation to their children's future development.

• Beginning every meeting with a summary of the major theme discussed in the previous meeting.

• Ending every meeting with specific questions presented to the mothers pertaining to the nature of their interactions with their children and asking them to think about possible answers and ideas for the next meeting.

The Sequence of Intervention Procedures

AN INTRODUCTORY GROUP MEETING

The first group meeting was an introductory and brainstorming session designed to familiarize mothers with basic concepts of child development, with the general content of the MISC intervention, and with the setting and time schedule for the home visits and the group meetings. There was a certain degree of flexibility in scheduling the home visits. Rescheduling was also possible in case the mothers were not able to keep an appointment for different reasons (sociocultural variables such as funerals, religion-related holidays, weddings, visiting sick persons, or marketing).

HOME VISIT 1

The first two criteria of Mediated Learning Experience (MLE), focusing (intentionality and reciprocity) and transcendence (providing information beyond the concrete experience), were demonstrated and discussed at the first home visit. Interestingly, some of the fathers participated in the intervention program alongside the mothers while involved in their weaving and other related activities. It was also not uncommon to find a number of siblings quietly and attentively listening to the visiting mediator. It is therefore clear that the intervention was not directed exclusively to the mothers but rather to the entire family. At the end of the meeting the mothers were presented with the following questions:

1.   How does your child show that she/he likes or wants to do something?
2.   How does your child express her/his feelings of happiness, hunger, fear, or discomfort?
3.   How do you show your child that you have understood what she/he wants or needs?
4.   How does your child react when you make eye contact with or smile at her/him?
5.   How do you direct your child's attention toward something in the environment?

Mothers were asked to think about these questions as they interacted with their children.

Group Meeting 1

This meeting started with a review of the previous home visit and the mother's reaction to the questions handed out during the home visit. Short video recordings and sketches were shown to illustrate specific MLE criteria and trigger group discussion. Parents were encouraged to evaluate the films and sketches in terms of the MLE criteria and present their own suggestions.

Home Visit 2

The second home visit started with a discussion of the previous group meeting. During this meeting the remaining three criteria, that is, mediation of meaning, competence, and regulation of behavior, were explained in relation to specific episodes of mother–child interaction. At the end of the session several questions were handed out to the mothers to be discussed in the following meeting. Examples of these questions are as follows:

1.   When do you praise your child?
2.   How do you show your child that you are satisfied with what she/he is doing?

3.   How does your child react when you show a positive response to her/his initiatives?

4.   How do you teach your child to plan (before doing) certain tasks? Give examples.

5.   How do you interact with your child while feeding him/her?

GROUP MEETING 2

This meeting started with the discussion of the questions that were handed out to the mothers during the home visits. After everybody was encouraged to talk about each question, discussion about the previous presentation continued. Mothers were asked to explain specific MLE criteria and demonstrate how they would use them in their day-to-day interactions with their children. This meeting was accompanied by video recordings depicting both good and bad mediation. Mothers were encouraged to identify parental behaviors that, in their opinions, represented good or bad mediation.

HOME VISIT 3

This was the final session of individual meetings during which all MLE criteria were reviewed in detail. Mothers were asked to relate to an episode of either feeding, bathing, or play, and to demonstrate how they would apply the MISC principles to enhance mediation in this episode.

GROUP MEETING 3 (CLOSING SESSION)

During this meeting general issues pertaining to the MISC training program were raised by both the trainers and the participants. Questions pertaining to MLE criteria, relevance of the training, effects on the quality and span of mother–child interaction, observed behavioral changes of both the child and the caregiver, and the attitude of the caregivers toward the MISC were raised and discussed. In short it was the mothers' " talk session" and practically everybody expressed their own experience and view.

The same procedure was applied for the Kechene Children's Home. The only variation from the home-based program was the setting in which the intervention was undertaken, as well as the involvement of both older girls and adult caregivers in the training program.

Postintervention Evaluation

After three months of the intervention program, a postassessment was launched in all sites, that is, the home-based (experimental and control groups) and the Kechene Children's Home. The postintervention evaluation was based on thirty-minute video recordings of mother–child interactions during bathing, feeding, and play (a ten-minute videotape for each situation. There were variations in the duration of these episodes in different families; those variations were noted).

Findings

PARENTAL ATTITUDES

Parents were asked to identify what they considered good and bad characteristics of their children. Characteristics relating to being obedient, respectful, peaceful, carrying out errands, being duty-minded, considerate, and polite were mentioned as desirable by 60% of the mothers and by all of the caregivers at the children's home. The parents were also asked about the childrearing practices they used to foster the positive traits they identified. Ninety percent of the mothers and 69% of the caregivers reported that advice, reprimand, and physical punishment (e.g., pinching and spanking) were used to instill and promote desirable behaviors.

The mothers and caregivers were further asked to describe what they did when the children refused to obey (e.g., take medicine); 58% of the mothers and 7% of the caregivers indicated that the child should be forced to take it. The rest of the respondents indicated that persuading, cuddling, and giving medicine with a sweetener like sugar was advisable. The actual practice, as observed by the research team, particularly in the children's home, was harsh treatment (i.e., hitting, shouting, ridiculing, and threatening children).

Almost all of the respondents indicated that having a child is an asset that God has given to the family. The benefit of having children was unequivocally stated by all mothers. Children, during their childhood as well as adult years, were perceived as helpers and supporters of parents. A similar attitude was expressed by 85% of the caregivers in the children's home. The utilitarian value of bearing a child seems to be rooted deep in the Ethiopian traditional society. Following the introduction of formal education in the country, educating children was considered as a means of securing a job for them, which in turn ensured a social and economic advantage to the family. Families were not worried about the number of children they had, but rather about the expenses or difficulties encountered at times when a child is ill, aggressive, or has nothing to eat.

CONCEPTUALIZATION OF CHILD DEVELOPMENT

A number of questions were posed to explore the conceptions of mothers as well as other caregivers about child growth and development. Some of the questions drew upon the knowledge of issues, such as the approximate age when children can identify their parents, begin thinking, understand spoken words, relate differentially to people, understand stories, and begin "using" their first book. Based on parental replies to the aforementioned questions, it may be concluded that most parents shared the following assumptions:

- Children discriminate between their parents and others at the age of four to six months.
- Thinking begins at one to three years of age.
- Understanding of spoken language begins at the age of one to two years.
- Starting at three months, it is worthwhile to speak to a baby.
- The child is able to understand stories and may be ready to handle the first book at the age of three years.

Most of the caregivers in the children's home viewed these developmental landmarks as occurring relatively earlier than indicated by mothers. Both mothers and caregivers described an intelligent child as an active, conversant child who is quick in grasping ideas. *Most of the mothers and caregivers believed that keeping the child clean and providing appropriate nutrition and medical care were the essential ingredients of childrearing.*

In answer to the question about what parents need to know about child development, 33% of the mothers and 23% of the caregivers mentioned exclusively child management and the capability to foster desirable behavior.

HOPES AND EXPECTATIONS

In response to the question of what determines the child's chances to succeed in life, 53% of the mothers and 85% of the caregivers chose "good education," whereas the others mentioned the predestined fate of every individual. Providing children with a good education was viewed by 60% of the mothers and 54% of the caregivers as necessary in preparing children to support their families. Both mothers and caregivers viewed appropriate feeding and hygiene as the most important needs of a growing child and, consequently, as the main obligation of parents.

We found the psychosocial component of childrearing to be the most neglected aspect of childrearing practices in Ethiopia. Surprisingly this held true also for parents who were professionals. The child mortality rate in Ethiopia is high, and child survival is considered the first priority. Parents had to be convinced that in order for children to become assets to their family and to society at large, survival is not enough. The objective of the intervention as presented to the parents was to raise children who are active, responsive, and intelligent, and who could be self-supportive, help the family, and contribute to the society in which they live.

OBSERVATIONS AT HOME

Based on the observations carried out at the homes of the participating children, the following general statements could be made:

- Physical proximity between the mother and the child were most commonly manifested during breast feeding or when the child was carried on the back of the mother.
- Intimacy was noted through the expression and sharing of joy and through "turn taking."
- Mothers were observed drawing the attention of their children to things (or persons) and naming them.
- Praising the child was quite rare in the process of mother–child interaction.
- Explaining things beyond the immediate, concrete experience was hardly observed.
- Mothers were not observed to mediate regulation of their children's behavior.
- Parents were observed to use some types of restriction, reprimands, and verbal and nonverbal cues of disapproval of misbehavior (i.e., when the children engaged in "messy" play or when they were exposed to dangerous situations).

Quality of Interaction Following the Intervention in the Homes

Focusing, as defined within the MISC framework, is a two-way process that can be triggered either by the mother or by the child. The Ethiopian mothers in our study tended to be the initiators of the interactions with their children. The frequency of mother-initiated focusing that was met by a response indicating reciprocity on the part of their children, was raised from an average of 10.5 (during a thirty-minute observation) at the preintervention assessment to 29.6 at the postintervention. Mothers almost tripled their successful attempts to focus their children's attention (see Table 6.1).

The sharp increase in the frequency of focusing may be related to the fact that the intervention reinforced in this case an already existing pattern of behavior. Mothers did, however, become more conscious of this type of behavior and increased its frequency. The following examples represent some of the mothers' attempts to focus the attention of their children:

"Look at this! This is an orange! You will eat it soon!"
"Look at this! This is a ball! You will play with it!"
"Smell! This is bath soap. It smells nice!"
"Taste this! It is a piece of bread for your lunch! It is delicious!"
"Touch! The stone is rough."
"Listen! That is your father's voice! He is coming!"
"Look at the cat! It is eating something!"

Although these examples are initiated by an attempt to focus the child's attention, they include components of mediated meaning or even transcendence.

TABLE 6.1 MEAN FREQUENCIES OF MOTHERS' MEDIATIONAL BEHAVIORS DURING THIRTY MINUTES OF OBSERVATIONS AT HOME, IN THE CONTROL, AND IN THE EXPERIMENTAL GROUPS, BEFORE AND AFTER THE MISC INTERVENTION.

MLE Criteria	Preintervention		Postintervention	
	Control	Experimental	Control	Experimental
Focusing	11.5	10.5	20.0	29.6
Expansion	—	0.1	—	4.8
Meaning	11.4	5.7	12.4	39.7
Competence	4.0	2.0	1.9	12.4
Regulation	4.0	5.4	7.5	21.7

Transcendence (i.e., expanding the information presented to the child beyond the child's concrete experience) was almost nonexistent at the preintervention assessment. The frequency of transcendence has increased from 0.1 at the preintervention to 4.8 at the postintervention assessment. The ability to expand, to explain, and to relate to what the child experiences requires knowledge about the environment and related subjects, as well as communication skills and the intention to mediate to the child. In comparison to the other elements of MLE, transcendence presented a challenge for most of the mothers. Another difficulty observed in most of the homes was the limited number of objects in the immediate environment in which mother–child interactions were taking place. Consequently, repetition of the same subject or issue in an attempt to transcend was commonly observed in most homes. Some of the examples of mothers' attempts to mediate expansion include the following:

"This bag contains many biscuits. Biscuits are made of different things like wheat powder, eggs, milk, and sugar."

"The cup is yours! You will drink milk, tea, and water from it."

"This ball is made of plastic, rubber, and pieces of cloth. You can play with it alone or with your friends."

"The tea is hot! You should cool it first! It is sweet because sugar is added to it."

"This is a box. It is made of wood. The person who made it is called a carpenter. He used different tools such as nails, a hammer, a saw, an axe, and nails to make it. We use it to put our clothes and other things in. It protects the clothes from becoming dirty or from being easily damaged."

While feeding their children, most of the mothers described the steps and the ingredients used for baking *injera*, a type of bread used in Ethiopia, prepared from a special kind of grain called *teff*.

Mediation of meaning is, namely, introducing the child to the meaning of objects, people, and events through expressions of excitement, naming, or associating them with other meaningful experiences. With regard to this variable, a marked increase was found in the frequency of mediating meaning following the intervention. Mediation of meaning increased from an average frequency of 5.7 to 39.7.

Mediation of competence refers to the expressed approval (verbal, nonverbal, or combined) communicated by mothers in response to their children's behavior. The tendency to praise children, especially when they follow parental orders, was apparent at the preintervention assessment at home. Following the intervention, the frequency of rewarding increased from 2.0 to 12.4. Children were rewarded for a wider range of behaviors that were not related to following parental commands only. Interestingly, mediation of competence in the control group had shown a marked decrease in frequency and included negative comments about the children's behavior rather than praise.

The following are examples of maternal behaviors of mediating competence following the intervention:

"Good!"

"Well done!"

"You can do it!"

"I love you."

"I will buy you candy!"

"Go ahead!"

"That is right!"

Hugging, caressing, nodding, and patting.

Parental behaviors that involve cultivation of self-control and fostering of planning behavior in the child are considered as mediating *regulation of behavior*. The preintervention assessment revealed the presence of certain ingredients of regulation of behavior in the mother–child interaction. A significant increase in the occurrence of these behaviors (from 5.4 to 21.7) was noted in the comparison between the pre- and postintervention assessments.

Mothers frequently used mediated regulation of behavior in the following situations:

- mediating dining manners before and after meals, seating arrangements, drinking or eating hot foods, and so on;
- regulating interaction with adults and peers (i.e., style of greeting);
- behavior patterns for dressing, bathing, and going to bed;
- where, when, and how to play.

According to our findings there is a clear indication of improvement in the quality of maternal mediation following the psychosocial intervention. The effects of the intervention may be attributed to many factors, but the motivation and interest shown by the mothers and children need not be underscored. Furthermore, other family members, including siblings and some fathers, had the opportunity to attend the MISC training, which consequently enabled them to create conducive conditions for promoting episodes of quality interaction with the children.

Findings for the Children's Home

The educational approach of the caregivers at the children's home was regimental in nature. Children were required to line up and wait while going to eat, to bath, or to play in the playground. In the dining hall, they were required to sit still and remain quiet until the meal was served. They were also instructed to sit "orderly" by folding their arms. Instructions of this nature caused psychomotor strain and psychosocial stress. If children did not fully follow instructions, they were either threatened or hit by the caregiver. This adversely affected the relationship between the children and the caregiver, as well as the children's self-esteem.

In order to promote interactions between caregivers and individual children, older girls (volunteers) from the same institution were assigned to care for younger children (one- to three-year-olds). The involvement of the older girls in this project was an accomplishment in itself, because there were strict regulations prohibiting older girls from visiting the younger children in the orphanage. At the onset of this project, the adult caregivers did not like the idea of bringing older girls to interact with young children. The research team discussed the potential contribution of such interactions for the development of the older girls as well as the young children, and finally convinced both the administration and the adult caregivers to allow the older girls to play with the younger children. However, even then, the older girls were permitted to contact "their" respective children only during the play session.

Following a comparison of the videotaped interactions before and after the intervention in the orphanage, the following findings were noted:

1.   An increased tendency to pay attention to the children's initiations and requests.

2.   Less frequent use of harsh disciplining behaviors that were regimental in the provision of information and explanations.

3.   A marked reduction in excessive usage of commands: for instance, in the preassessment, the bathing situation was particularly characterized by high-toned commands such as "Come here," "Sit down," "Stand up," "Close your eyes," and "Hold the wall." In the postassessment, a friendly and more humane relationship was clearly noted.

4.   Prior to the intervention, there was a general understanding among the caregivers that educating a child does not occur during simple caregiving activities such as feeding and bathing. Following the intervention, certain ingredients of mediation of competence and naming were frequently observed, particularly in the bathing sessions, as well as in the play situations.

5.   Following the intervention, young children behaved differently in interactions with adults as compared to their behavior before the intervention. Among the most noticeable changes was the tendency to approach people and initiate interactions, the tendency to request mediation, and a general increase in activity level and responsiveness.

Based on the initial observation in the children's home, the children could be described as having a low level of activity, and being introverted and fearful. Following the intervention (with both the older girls and the adult caregivers), these characteristics were no longer typical of the children's behavior. The role played by the older girls in promoting the quality of interaction with "their babies" was significant, despite the fact that their access to the young children was limited to play situations only. In comparison with the adult caregivers, it was the older girls who were highly interested and motivated to mediate to the children. They had succeeded in learning and applying the MLE criteria in their interactions with the children. It must be noted that some of the babies showed avoidance behavior, and it was initially difficult for the girls to approach them, let alone manage a quality interaction. Later on babies were observed seeking the physical proximity of the older girls with expressions of affection and elation.

CONCLUDING REMARKS

Based on the findings of this project it may be concluded that the MISC can be applied within the framework of the Ethiopian culture. As it was identified in the baseline assessment of both the home-based and the institution-based settings, the psychosocial component of children's development was undermined. One can safely speculate that this has happened most likely out of ignorance. Parents hope to provide their children with a good education so that they might be able to support the family in the future. Parents believe that this hope can only be achieved by sending children to school. This is of course true. However, it excludes the family environment as the basis for subsequent learning and limits the perceived role of the family to provision of health care only. The family sees to it that the child is well fed, well dressed, and clean. If parents were aware of the fact that they can enhance cognitive and emotional development of the child through interaction, they would most probably do it with dedication. This is especially true since it does not involve any expense and has no foreign, "imported" components. The size and composition of the average family seem to create a conductive ground for the enrichment of mediated learning experience; that is, family members other than the mother (i.e., siblings, grandmothers, or other relatives residing with the family) could become assets when sensitized to share their experiences with the young children in the family. Thus, the findings of this study suggest that the MISC seems to have the potential to be efficiently and effectively implemented in the Ethiopian setting.

THE MAIN STUDY

Objective of the Study

The objective of the main study was to examine psychosocial intervention strategies that could improve childrearing practices in the community and promote the cognitive and emotional development of children. Other specific objectives included the following:

1.   to implement the newly adapted methods and strategies for early intervention in mother–child relationships, with the special intention of integrating these methods into primary health care and health education;

2.   to assess and evaluate the effects of the intervention procedures on the quality of mother–child interaction and on the child's psychosocial and cognitive development;

3.   to disseminate the knowledge acquired following the initial MISC project to relevant institutions and organizations in Ethiopia, and possibly to other African countries;

4.   to develop competencies of the participating team in the area of early psychosocial intervention.

Assessment and Intervention

The assessment and intervention methods and procedures applied in the main study are generally the same as those used in the pilot study. A number of modifications were made. The number of participating families in the main study was 96, including 49 families in the experimental group and 47 in the control group. In both sites, that is, Kebele 15 (control group) and Kebele 18 (experimental group), the ages of the target children ranged from one to three years.

Training of the Trainers

The selection and training of twenty-one paraprofessionals for the psychosocial intervention was an important landmark in the main project. The paraprofessionals were selected from the site of the project as well as from the neighboring communities. The group of paraprofessionals included 52% health workers and others who had completed twelve years of schooling and were employed by the community (62% of the paraprofessionals were females). The fact that paraprofessionals were health workers and community workers facilitated easy access to the participating families. The training of the paraprofessionals lasted two months (one meeting per week). The training was based on the MISC method and followed the procedures employed, and contents used, in the pilot study.

Following the training, the paraprofessionals were divided into four intervention groups (with five paraprofessionals in each group). One group leader was selected by the trainers in each group. Moreover, the four groups were further divided into two subgroups and were assigned to work with specific families throughout the intervention period. In other words, two paraprofessionals were working together. Every group leader was responsible for his/her group with regard to filling weekly report slips, checking the weekly session plans, and substituting for each other if necessary.

The duration of the intervention was three months. During this period a home visit and a group meeting took place every other week, alternately. The intervention procedure followed the same outline as that of the pilot study, with four group meetings instead of one general meeting for all the mothers. The group-meeting approach (with no more than twelve participants) was found to be very effective and practical for sharing views and feelings. The fieldwork was supervised by members of the local research team and a physician who was one of the twenty-one trainees.

The baseline assessment as well as the psychosocial intervention was carried out prior to the intervention. The postintervention assessment started three months following the MISC intervention.

Effects of the Intervention in the Main Study

In order to have a general idea about the effects of the main study, both paraprofessionals and mothers were asked to comment about the effects of the MISC on the quality of mother–child interactions. The following observations were made by the paraprofessionals:

"At the beginning of the intervention, most mothers did not feel comfortable to suggest anything, to ask, or comment. Gradually, mothers' active participation in the training sessions increased and became more consistent."

"Most mothers developed a positive attitude and interest in the activities and affairs of their children. The change of attitude was exhibited in their manner of communication, eagerness, and concern for their children's education."

"It was observed that those mothers who used to force and punish their children when they refused to eat have begun persuading and soothing them."

"Mothers have begun giving more time and attention to the affairs of their children."

Some typical comments of mothers were as follows:

"After the training, I have started to talk to my child like an adult person."

"I have only one son among other daughters in the family. My child was very aggressive, but after the training, I succeeded to cool him down through soothing and explaining."

The mother of a child who was unable to sit by herself at one year and eight months and was carried around by her mother, commented: "After the training I have started to bring her down from my back. I interacted with her and observed some signs of progress. She started to sit with support, to smile and to play with her siblings."

"Children have begun asking a number of questions and demand explanations whenever they come across strange things."

"We accumulated a body of knowledge for ourselves regarding the essentials of interaction."

Finally, one mother commented that she gave advice to three families in the neighborhood on how to interact with their children. According to the comments of both the paraprofessionals and the mothers, there is an indication that there are a number of concrete achievements in the mother–child interactions following the MISC intervention. A complete analysis of the outcome for the main study is scheduled as part of a comprehensive follow-up study.

New Beginnings

As a spin-off effect of the MISC project, two other small projects have been initiated in Ethiopia. These include (a) preventing the risk of early school dropouts, and (b) training pediatricians in the MISC method.

The first project is funded and has started in one of the primary schools near the community in which the main project is going on. In this project, twenty first-grade repeaters (potential dropouts) were identified and psychosocial treatment based on the MISC method was carried out with the children and with their mothers. This project is carried out by trained mediators for a period of three months. In addition, literal and numerical skills have been introduced in a very simplified way. A number of positive behavioral changes have been observed following the intervention and a follow-up of students' school achievements will be carried out for two consecutive semesters.

ACKNOWLEDGMENT

Teka Zewde, Fantu Melese, and Zelalem Fekadu are from the Department of Educational Psychology, Addis Ababa University, Addis Ababa, Ethiopia. Henning Rye and Karsten Hundeide, Center of International Health, University of Bergen, Norway.

7 FACILITATING CULTURAL MEDIATION: INDONESIA

Karsten Hundeide

> *Deprive children of stories and you leave them unscripted, anxious stutterers in their actions as in their words. Hence there is no way to give understanding in any society, including our own, except through the stock of stories which constitute its initial dramatic resources. Mythology, in its original sense, is at the heart of things . . . (MacIntyre, 1981, p. 201)*

DIFFERENT CONCEPTIONS OF MEDIATION

In Vygotsky's developmental theory, mediation refers to the acquisition of cultural tools, such as the use of physical tools or symbolic tools (e.g., language and literacy) that later become internalized as tools of thought—what were external interactions become internal operations (Vygotsky, 1978). Similarly Feuerstein (1980) refers to formal features of good interaction between caregiver and child that he specifies as certain mediational criteria which are intended to promote cognitive development and flexible minds. But what is the sense of a flexible mind when there is nothing to live for, to strive for? What is needed in addition are structures of meaning and social networks that can make life worth living, such as a supportive network and conceptions of life that promote an identity that can use a flexible mind for a meaningful life. If we focus only on developing flexible minds and cognitive skills, we ignore a dominant problem of our time, namely the loss of meaning and the alienation and meaninglessness that seem to be an increasing problem in the Western world (Bronfenbrenner, 1975). We can see this in the rising incidence of suicide and violence among children and youngsters. This problem was raised by an American Indian participating in an international conference, when he emphasized the need for "healing our conceptual worlds" that had been destroyed through a process of demoralization and alienation due to the impact of modernization on traditional cultures. He also emphasized that the most important point in this connection was "how we conceptualize inner life," which includes the spiritual and psychological aspects of life, what we believe in, and what gives us a conception of ourselves that generates self-confidence and courage to face life.

This point of view has quite radical implications for most developmental theories such as Vygotsky's or Piaget's, and most enrichment programs, because these theories tend to isolate human development from human goals, social reality, identity, and existential meaning. Such theories become irrelevant in practice because they do not face the dominant problems relating to socialization and development of our time, namely, the *loss of structures of meaning that can provide a basis for meaningful lives and prevent the deterioration of social caring networks.* The problems of meaning, values, and identity are key questions in any theory of human development that faces current problems of our time (Giddens, 1991). Splitting up cognitive development from these issues implies taking away the motivation behind cognitive development. Even programs that try to promote the development of altruistic behavior in children tend to be too narrow from this point of view, because altruism is part of a wider pattern of human values within a society and should not be promoted as a "skill" apart from this wider conception and context (Zahn-Waxler, Radke-Yarrow, & King, 1979).

In a poor, uprooted environment full of hopelessness and despair, which we sometimes see in shanty-towns and in refugee camps all over the world, the revival of conceptions of hope that support the process of coping, promote self-respect, empowerment, and mediation of meaning, is more important than the promotion of isolated cognitive or social skills. Such skills will only be sustained if they are in some way instrumental to attaining certain life goals. If these are missing, I am afraid that there is no motivating force to sustain them when the intervention is over. We are talking here about mediation or socialization of "worlds of value," or value-oriented conceptions of life. It seems that these macroconceptions or contexts have to be restored or reactivated in some way if interventions at a microlevel are going to be sustainable. Feuerstein (1980) touched upon this question and included the promotion of an optimistic outlook on life as one of his criteria of mediation.

The implication of what has been stated previously is that we need to have a broader view of human development and mediation, in which the emphasis is not on the development of skills, tools operations, or even cognitive structure as such, but on *the mediation of a framework for skills that are our shared cultural conceptions of the world, of life, values of persons, identities, and human relationships within which individual coping becomes meaningful and worthwhile.* The current tendency to detach skills or cognitive structures from the broader framework and content of human life is misplaced because our skills, cognitive or not, are by nature instruments for living; therefore it must be of prime importance to revive the cultural framework of values and meanings that make the development or "appropriation" of cultural tools worthwhile and plausible.

By doing this we see human development not only in its cultural and situational context and variability, as most Vygotskians do, but in addition, see it within *a framework in which meaning, values, and commitment play the key organizing role.*

Mediation as Part of a Cultural Practice

Mediation in the sense indicated before is something that is necessarily present in any culture that reproduces itself: mediation of knowledge, values, and norms that guide the child into a world of shared social knowledge, meanings, and skills. The question is not whether there is such mediation, but rather: *How does mediation (or guided participation) take place typically within this culture?*

The natural way in which mediation takes place in many cultures is through storytelling and dramatization of events and features in the child's surroundings. A friend of mine who stayed for many years in New Guinea told me how the children used to gather around the mother in the kitchen while she was preparing sweet potatoes and at the same time singing stories about the history of the village, the mountains, the animals, and how the first human beings arrived in the valley from a hole in the earth. The children were enthralled and participated in the refrain while the mother added new topics in the narrative between the refrains. These children knew all the stories of how and why things in their surroundings were as they were. Singing and storytelling to children were part of a cultural practice involving caregivers and children. Early education was, so to speak, an implicit part of activities that all children enjoyed and took part in (Hundeide, 1991).

The point is that natural forms of mediation are always content-related. We tell stories to children about things in the environment, about persons, actions, and events, and the more we are able to present our knowledge in a personalized story or dramatic form, the more interesting it becomes. Our minds seem to be more like mechanisms for assimilating stories and dramas than for manipulating logical operations, and it is a serious mistake when we try to turn education the other way around to focus on operations and leave out the content and the meaning of our social world. This is like leaving out the essence of culture, namely our storied traditions, mythologies, and folklore. Bruner (1990) makes the same point when he states that our capacity to render experience in terms of narrative is not just child's play, but an instrument for making meaning that dominates much life in culture—from the soliloquies at bedtime to the weighing of testimony in our legal system.

If narratologists are right in assuming that the primary mechanisms for creation of meaning are the story and emplotment (Sarbin, 1986; Bruner, 1990), I suppose one consequence of this view is that we should use more stories in our interaction with children and through stories create contexts and incentives that make the acquisition of cognitive and social skills relevant, stories that convey the values that we feel are important, using characters that children can identify with and which embody such qualities (Sutton-Smith, 1986; Meadows & Cashdan, 1988).

Life Narratives

In the narratologist tradition (Sarbin, 1986), one would say that we tell stories to ourselves and others about our lives, and these stories have trajectories and projections into the future in line with what happened earlier. Our lives unfold in a plausible way through what happened before and by what we believe is reasonable, not necessarily logical in the narrow sense. Life narratives, life "theories" or "scripts" are like structures of meaning inside which we find both solutions and direction to our individual acts.

In other words, we seem to live our lives according to "scripts," some of which are open to introspection and reflection, integrated with our everyday common sense. Others, however, can be more hidden, partly outside, and in some cases, in conflict with our everyday commonsense understanding of ourselves and our lives (Berne, 1964).

For this reason I prefer to make a distinction between the "scripts or metaphors we live by" and the theories we tell ourselves (Lakoff & Johnson, 1980). The scripts we live by need not always be represented as theories; they can be outside and, in some cases, difficult to integrate with our more personal life theories. Such scripts are generally viewed from the observer's position. Personal life theories on the other hand, are viewed from the agent's experiential position—how we understand our lives and explain our choices. And, as mentioned before, these explanations and theories may not necessarily coincide with the patterns of action we call scripts that an outside observer, a therapist, or a biographer may discover.

In our everyday life such "theories" are taken for granted to such an extent that we are seldom aware that we have such conceptions. It is only when there are variations that we become aware of their existence—when somebody expresses hope and courage when most other people give in, such as in a concentration or refugee camp. Such attitudes do not appear out of nowhere, in isolation, but are part of a more general conception of life inside which such attitudes appear plausible. Stories that explain why a person is in a particular position, how he/she may get out of it—stories that give hope for improvement or convey some human values—are in fact important for psychological survival.

There are numerous examples of prisoners of war, living under the most demoralizing conditions, who felt that they had been able to survive due to the memory of a simple poem emphasizing the value of human dignity. Through invocation and repetition of such "value narratives" they were able to redefine and transform their deprived and demoralized situation into a situation of challenge and fight, mobilizing their moral and emotional commitment for a goal that was congruent with their basic values. (This shows, in fact, the close relationship between cognitive beliefs and emotional states. It also shows that it is possible to control negative states of hopelessness through mediation of positive conceptions and attitudes.) Therefore, *it is the story that is important, not the objective situation as such, because it is through the story that a definition is produced that can be interpreted and evaluated in accordance with some shared standards or honor system that one must assume is the basis for any civilized human life.*

Different Cultural Forms of Mediation

Through seminars and discussions with educators and parents in different traditional societies, I have found that there are different forms of cultural mediation, some of which may be just as informative and important for us as ours may be useful for them.

THE ANALYTIC–INQUIRING MODE

This mode is implicit in many intervention programs (i.e., High Scope, Instrumental Enrichment) and seems to be typically associated with the Western scholastic style of promoting "school intelligence." There is a special framing or contextualization of this type of mediation and discourse (Edwards & Mercer, 1987; Walkerdine, 1988) that seems to be part of Western educational tradition and that is not automatically part of any culture's way of communicating. For example, when we interviewed some beggars in one of the slums of Jakarta, they seemed to be unable to answer questions if those questions were not part of a story, a natural response to what had been presented in advance. In other words, it was not possible for them to answer a question out of the narrative context.

Similarly, as Cole and Scribner (1974) have pointed out, in many traditional societies, questions are normally considered as concrete requests for information, not as tests of competence. In other words, in our school- and achievement-oriented culture, children are required to get used to dealing with questions within the context of control and competence. These are usually questions with a double meaning; at the same time as they refer to some realistic situation, their answer presupposes looking away from that context and considering the question in a purely formal, deductive way. This "decontextualized" style of answering questions and solving problems is quite alien for most traditional people, not that they are incapable of deductive reasoning; rather, they misunderstand the framing and take the questions to be a request for concrete situational information. (Cole & Scribner, 1974; Donaldson, 1978).

In addition, asking a teacher questions in a traditional society would in many cases be considered as a sign of disrespect, challenging the authority of the teacher.

STORYTELLING—THE NARRATIVE MODE

As pointed out earlier, this seems to be the basic, possibly inborn, mechanism for "making sense" (Bruner, 1988).

In most societies there is a treasure of stories with a moral-heroic content. The hero goes through all kinds of difficulties and temptations and finally wins and gets the appropriate reward (i.e., the princess) for his virtue and endurance. Moral virtues and values are conveyed through a typified employment represented in the storytelling. In most traditional societies in the Third World, parents seem to be more concerned about promoting moral values and good behavior in the child than about conveying knowledge and intelligence. When parents are asked what are the qualities they would like to see in their children, the usual answer is obedience, respect, and good behavior. This is also reflected in their storytelling, which is about good and bad characters and human virtues.

In a way storytelling is an indirect way of conveying knowledge. Through the example of the hero or the protagonist, a message is conveyed but not always explicated.

Storytelling can also take on a more personalized form in which caregivers tell children about their childhood: "When I was a kid like you we used to . . ."

According to Burke (1945, cited in Bruner, 1990) a well-formed story contains an actor, an action, a goal, a scene, and an instrument—plus an imbalance between any of the five elements. It is this deviation from the normal that creates the dynamism of the story (Bruner, 1990).

DIALOGIC STORYTELLING

I first experienced this form of storytelling in Zimbabwe, where a preschool teacher demonstrated how they used to tell stories in the traditional way. She collected all the children around her and started to tell a story about a well-known topic, a child who had been taken by an animal. She told it with great dramatic expressivity and passion. As the tension of the story rose, the children were fascinated and completely absorbed in the way she expressed and partly demonstrated the main features of the story.

As the story progressed, new items were introduced and for each item the storyteller stopped and had a dialogue with the children: "Do you know what that is? . . . Yes, that is right, it is a . . . What do you use that for? Have you seen that before?" and so on. Then the story progressed further, and at each new item she stopped and had a dialogue.

She also stopped and asked the children *to predict what they thought would happen next.* In this way the children became like coconstructors of a narrative line for which they had to adjust and revise their expectations to the unfolding story. Mediation in this case was naturally embedded in the dialogue that took place as the story progressed.

DRAMATIZATION AND ROLE PLAYING

This is also a basic form of symbolization and mediation that seems to develop particularly in the interaction between children. In fact, this seems to be the usual way that children learn social knowledge: Roles, norms, typical routines, and characters of everyday life are exercised over and over again in preparation for participation in adult life.

When caregivers join in and use this interactive form as a tool for mediation, it can be a powerful way of mediating knowledge about significant events, actions, and happenings as an alternative to storytelling. In addition, when contents related to cooperation, fair play, and moral aspects between children are going to be communicated, this can be done quite effectively through dramatization and role playing. This form of mediation is also used in order to promote language acquisition (i.e., with minority children). Dramatization, role playing, and songs can be used by inserting recurrent phrases in dialogues representing typical forms of interaction from everyday life (Hundeide & Naeshagen, 1988).

Another variation of this is *telling a story through the use of a puppet.* This is another powerful, dramatic way of attracting children's attention and interest. This can be done by introducing a particular character who plays the role of the "wise man" or the "hero" who can be asked for advice. The storyteller modulates his/her voice so that it fits in with the character of the "wise man." Through this approach, even shy children can come forward and start asking the puppet questions that they would not dare to ask the preschool teacher or the mediator.

Music, Songs, Dance, and Gestures

These more artistic expressions could also be characterized as forms of mediation, although their messages may go beyond representation of external states of affairs to the deeper, expressive feeling qualities that are shared within a culture.

These emotional–expressive forms of mediation are generally part of the cultural traditions of most societies and they play an important role in socializing children into the shared feelings, memories, and aesthetic standards of their society. Javanese dancing is an example of how quite young children are being introduced into the graceful, balanced, and controlled expressivity of the Javanese through dance.

Not only stories, but also music, songs, and dance are the typical ways in which most people express their shared feelings regarding memories from the past and of special occasions in which these artistic expressions have been used. These forms of mediation seem to be underestimated in modern approaches to socialization and mediation.

Graphic and Iconic Forms of Mediation

The iconic imagery and symbolism is another aspect of culture that is expressed in pictorial art, in graphic representations, and also in children's drawings. As Goodnow (1977) and others have pointed out; these graphic forms vary among different cultures. Each culture seems to have its own characteristic graphic or pictorial world of representations that reflects in some way typical features of this culture. Through apprenticeship under a "master" in different arts and handicrafts (Greenfield, 1989; Rogoff, 1990), children become socialized into the pictorial aesthetic world of their culture. Like music and dance, this is another way of mediating the expressive, aesthetic, feeling aspects of a culture.

The Cultural Repertoire of Metaphors and Prototypes

Stories, sayings, poetry, mythologies, significant events, heroes, or typical characters, typical life careers, and so on—all these shared, typified forms of representation may constitute *a collective narrative–dramatic employment repertoire* that participants within a culture can directly or indirectly refer to or use when they communicate. This creates an interpretive background or basis for metaphorical use of language, double meanings, allusions, and symbolisms that may be difficult to penetrate for an outsider who does not share this collective interpretive background of stories, persons, and events. Being competent within a culture consists to a large extent of mastering these tacitly shared references.

When Cultural Mediation Breaks Down

As Bruner (1990) points out,

> When there is breakdown in a culture . . . there is also a breakdown that results from sheer impoverishment of narrative resources—in the permanent underclass of the urban ghetto, in the second generation of the Palestinian refugee compounds, in the hunger-preoccupied villages of semipermanent drought-stricken villages in sub-Saharan Africa. It is not that there is a total loss in putting story form to experience, but that the "worst scenario" story comes to dominate daily life. (pp. 96–97)

Under conditions of extreme poverty and cultural change, the normal process of enculturation through mediation and guided participation may be disrupted. In such situations children may be deprived of the typical cultural ways of making sense, such as the stories that constitute a frame of reference or background for interpreting typical situations in their everyday lives.

We know from studies of families under conditions of extreme survival pressure and cultural change that this process of enculturation may collapse and the children may then be deprived not only of "stimulation" and affective contact, but may be even more seriously deprived of the shared cultural "capital" of meanings, frames, values, and ideals that are contained in the typical stories and dramas that are tacitly transmitted from one generation to the next. These also include the scripts or recipes that we tacitly live by, the life theories and the values that we take for granted. Under such conditions, children become "unscripted and erratic," living in a here-and-now world, dominated by the attractions of the moment with little future orientation and planning (Feuerstein, 1980).

When Children Are Helped to Die

Even worse than the condition described earlier are the conditions described by Scheper-Hughes (1990) and others, in which the pressures of survival may prevent even the normal process of bonding between mother and child, which is a precondition for normal mediation and care. Scheper-Hughes describes some extreme cases like this from her experience in one of the slum areas in Recife in North Brazil:

> A high expectancy of loss can produce . . a decisive "under investment" in these infants seen as poor risks for survival which may further contribute to the spiral of high fertility, high mortality in a kind of macabre lock-step dance of death. . . . The Alto women mocked at my efforts to save "Ze" and cautioned that it was playing with death, that a child who "wanted" to die as much as this one did, should be left alone. I managed to save Ze, but I worried about the ethics of returning him to Lourdes in her scrap material lean-to, where she had barely resources to care for herself and her new baby. . . . Would he face a longer, more painful death from starvation at a later date? (p. 113)

This mother may, perhaps, need to protect herself emotionally by withdrawing her attachment in order to prevent the suffering related to the mourning process that naturally takes place when an attached infant dies in a society in which mortality rates range between 30% and 50%. When a child is not wanted, it is considered another competitor for the family resources that reduces the family's chances of survival. At the same time, mother's love is a richly elaborated theme in the poor Brazilian culture and society. Still the gradual selective neglect of certain ill-fated children is also common and is not criticized by other women. Part of learning how to mother in the slum includes learning how to "let go" of a child that "wants to die."

This death diagnosis was given to children who looked "ghostlike." They were allowed to die, or they had no chance to survive through the self-fulfilling process of their death diagnosis—another example of how crucial the mother's theory of the child is.

But neglect of children is not only a phenomenon linked to poverty in developing countries. There are also indications that it is just as serious a problem in Western countries.

The question then arises: *Is it possible to intervene in some way to promote the human care that infants and young children need for normal development inside their culture?*

EARLY PSYCHOSOCIAL INTERVENTION IN A NON-WESTERN CULTURAL SETTING

As the MISC Program seemed more flexible and adaptable to non-Western settings than more content-oriented programs, International Child Development Programs (ICP) started to use the MISC in our work in different developing countries.

The following discussion includes a summary of the intervention effects and some of the challenges we have encountered when we tried to implement the MISC program in a slum area in the outskirts of Bandung, Indonesia.

The Bandung Project

Sixty-four families participated in the experimental group of this project. Half of them came from poor rural areas outside Bandung, and the others came from a poor area in Bandung itself. The MISC program was implemented by first training a group of professional psychologists and anthropologists at the University of Padjandjaran who "translated" the program into Indonesian. They have created booklets of examples and illustrations that grow out of the Indonesian cultural context. The program was then implemented in a community-based manner. Local resource persons or *kaders* were trained as home visitors. Following the training they visited the homes of the target families every fortnight over a period of three months and implemented the program. All kaders were supervised by one of the professionals at the university.

A pre- and postintervention design with an experimental and a control group was used. The effects of the intervention were evaluated based on videotaped mother–child interactions in three situations: feeding, bathing, and play. In addition, mothers were interviewed and questioned about their conception of the child, of good caregiving and development, and about the extent to which they thought that child development could be modified through learning.

OUTCOME OF THE STUDY

The outcome of the MISC intervention is to a large extent dependent upon how the principles or the criteria of mediation were communicated to the mothers. In this case it was done by the paraprofessional kaders, many of whom were experienced in health-oriented projects. In line with their general cultural orientation and based on their reports, it seemed that they used a rather instructive, nonfacilitative, and authoritarian approach in their communications with the mothers in the experimental group.

EFFECTS ON MOTHER–CHILD INTERACTION

Figure 7.1 summarizes the main results focusing on the comparisons of the experimental and control groups, before and after the intervention, on each

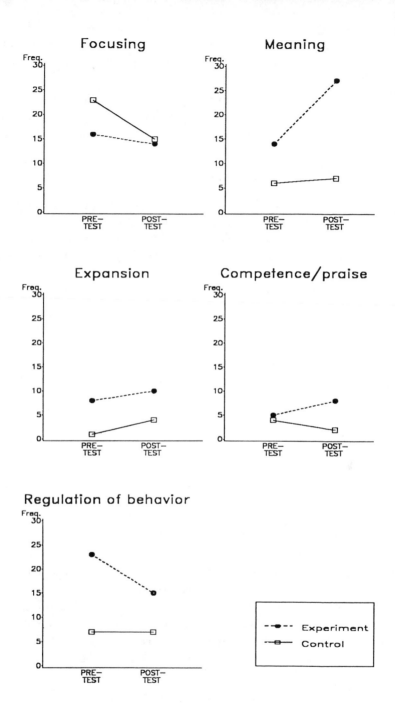

Figure 7.1. Mean frequencies of mediational criteria in mother–child interactions during feeding, bathing, and play.

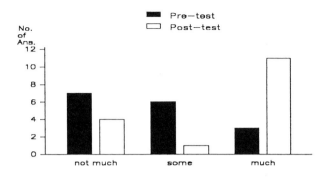

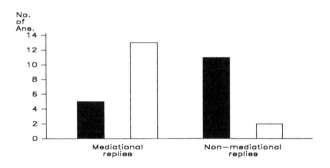

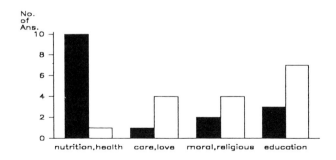

Figure 7.2. Distribution of mothers' answers to questions on their conceptions of child rearing.

of the mediational criteria that were used for scoring the videotaped mother–child interactions.

The control and experimental groups were compared prior to the onset of the study with regard to demographic variables but not with regard to mediational criteria. There were initially clear differences between the two groups in the preintervention assessment. For this reason, the effects of the intervention are estimated, based on the change that occurred, that is, the differences between the pre- and postassessments.

As can be seen in Figure 7.1, there was a significantly greater increase in mediation of meaning in the experimental as compared to the control group. There was also a slight increase in mediation of competence in the experimental group, with a comparable decrease in the control group. The experimental group showed a decrease in frequency of regulation of behavior. No difference between the two groups was noted on expansion/transcendence, and a decrease in focusing behaviors was noted for the control group.

Regulation of the children's behavior was fairly high before the intervention as part of a typical authoritarian, low-mediational profile (Klein, 1985a). Thus it is not surprising that the intervention led to a reduction in frequency of this criterion. More emphasis on conveying the significance and meaning of things and events, as well as praising the children for their behavior, was found following the intervention. No increase in frequency of expansion was noted. This may be due to the fact that this criterion is more difficult to understand and communicate (in its original form) to simple-minded caregivers than the other criteria.

EFFECTS ON MOTHERS' CONCEPTIONS OF THEIR CHILDREN'S DEVELOPMENT

Mothers perceived "development" as a physiological phenomenon. Thus, in answer to the question "What can be done to help the child develop?" there was no difference between pre- and postintervention; they all tended to give nutritional replies, "good food, vitamins," and so on. However, in reply to the questions "How far can you train the child to become more intelligent? and "How would you train the child?" there were clear differences between pre- and postintervention: The postintervention experimental group had a stronger belief in the modifiability of intelligence with training.

The postintervention experimental-group mothers gave consistently more mediational-type replies in answer to the question of how they would train their children to become more intelligent. This result is not surprising, because it coincides with one of the initial messages of the MISC Program. This tendency is further substantiated by the increase of "educationally oriented replies" in the experimental group in answer to the question "How do good parents bring up their children?" (see Figure 7.2).

These effects of the intervention should be attributed not only to the nature of the program, but also to the way in which it was implemented and communicated to the kaders and the caregivers. Findings regarding the effects of the intervention on caregivers and children have been reported in other studies as well. In this context it is interesting to examine how the cultural background of the participants influenced the way they acquired the different criteria and how they perceived the teaching situation and the messages conveyed through the MISC program.

The Interpretation of the MISC by the Indonesian Recipients

It must be noted that there were several steps of "cultural translation" before the children could benefit from the MISC intervention. These were as follows:

1. Presentation to Indonesian psychologists and adjustment of the program following their recommendations.
2. Their translation and exemplification of the program to Indonesian paraprofessionals or kaders.
3. The kaders' assimilation of the program and its adjustment for training of the mothers.
4. The mothers' assimilation of the program and their understanding of how it should be put into practice in relation to the children.
5. The children's perceptions of mothers' interactive behavior toward them.

In order to get more detailed information on this process of cultural translation, both kaders and mothers were interviewed on their conceptions of the program and the messages they had received. Most of the mothers (62%) accepted the MLE messages of the program without any comments, while some (23%) responded with objections or comments and dialogue, and only a few (3%) actively resisted the program. According to the kaders' reports, most of the mothers had understood and accepted the message after the third visit.

Further analysis of both mothers' and kaders' reports led to the following conclusions:

1. For some mothers, the program was assimilated or categorized into *the domain or world of modern fashionable knowledge,* in opposition to traditional, routine knowledge. By participating in the program, the moth-

ers felt they participated in the modern trend, which had a clearly positive and prestigious quality.

2.   Similarly they felt *privileged to be associated with the university.* Some of the mothers called themselves "children of the university" and this was experienced as promoting their status in relation to nonparticipants.

3.   Finally some felt privileged because they had *access to some knowledge that they, in line with some Eastern traditions, thought was nonpublic or esoteric* and not available to anybody else.

4.   The criterion of mediation that was most difficult for the mothers to accept was praise or mediation of competence. "In Indonesia it is not usual to give open praise to our children," they said, and this was confirmed by the psychologists at the University of Padjandjaran who directed the research. Somehow explicit praising of a child seems to interfere in the authority/respect relationship between parents and children. This has been confirmed by other studies in traditional societies (Hundeide, 1991, p. 104; LeVine & White, 1986).

5.   Another criterion that was difficult for some mothers to accept was expansion or transcendence, and this may be one of the reasons why there was no increase in frequency of this behavior during the intervention. When examples of expansion were presented to the mothers, some of them would say, "This is not the way mothers speak; this is the way teachers speak." They seemed to make a distinction between the caring role of the mother and the didactic role of the teacher.

The points that were mentioned before can be summarized in a more general model of metacommunication as can be seen in Figure 7.3.

This model needs further explication. (In addition, there are, for example, the caregivers' conceptions of the world, of values, of the child, of the caregiver's role, etc.) Whether we are aware of it or not, there is always a *metacommunicative, contextual framing when something is conveyed or communicated.* The way this framing takes place will influence how the message will be understood, remembered, and used. This framing can be analyzed through a focus on the following components:

1.   *Domains of meaning.* Knowledge is always conveyed within "worlds of meaning" or "intentional worlds" (Schweder, 1991), or "fields of activity" (Wertsch, 1985). This creates the frame or the context for how the message or knowledge is interpreted. This answers the question: *What kind of knowledge is this?* In the case of communicating the MISC program, it was clearly conceived as modernistic rather than traditional knowledge.

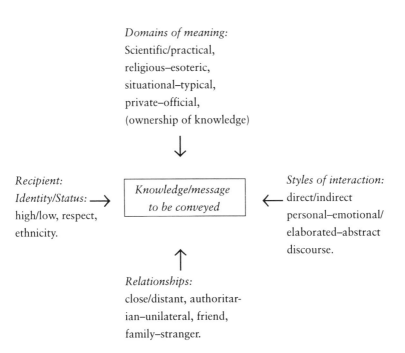

2. *Styles of interaction.* Any message is conveyed in a certain discourse style or style of interaction. For instance, when the mothers say, "This is the way teachers speak," this refers to their awareness of what is an appropriate style of communication. Suggesting that they speak like teachers may not be so easy. In addition, style or "genre" may be situational; one speaks differently in a formal situation as compared to a informal one.

3. *Kind of relationship or "contract" between caregiver and child.* The way a message is conveyed and understood is also related to the *type of relationship* that exists between caregiver and child—which again is related to the style of interaction.

As mentioned earlier, a mother who has a warm, spontaneous, and joking relationship with a child, may have difficulty in taking on the more formal role of an instructor who patiently scaffolds, guides, and evaluates the child's problem-solving performance.

So style of interaction and relationship between interlocutors are closely related, because a relationship is usually expressed in a particular style of interaction. Sometimes the nature of the relationship may be related to deep values within that society, such as respect and obedience in most traditional societies. Under such circumstances an expressive style of carelessness and lack of respect may strongly interfere with the expected relationship of respect and even fear between father and child in some traditional societies.

4.   *Identity and status.* The way one communicates with or addresses a person, may also indicate one's perception of him/her as a person, his/her status in relation to you, and his/her identity (Giddens, 1991). In some societies, like the traditional Javanese, status is clearly indicated by the way the person is addressed. There has to be a decision on this before any further communication can go on. Not only the way of addressing a person, but simply *being selected as a subject for participation* in a scientific project directed by the university may be perceived as something special that gives status. In our case, being selected for participation in the project was perceived by them as an indication of being "at a higher level" as "children of the university." This strongly facilitated their commitment and willingness to participate as compared with other health-oriented programs that were not perceived in this way.

Who do they think I am? This is a question that is answered indirectly and metacommunicatively by the way the person is addressed and by what the participant reads into the mediator's comments. The answer to this question may be decisive for how the participants respond and how willing they may be to continue in the project (Braaten, 1991).

SOME CONCLUDING COMMENTS ON THE IMPLEMENTATION OF THE MISC PROGRAM IN A NON-WESTERN SETTING

There is no doubt that the intervention had several clear effects on both the quality of interaction between the mothers and the children who participated in the MISC program and on mothers' conception of development, particularly in relation to the modifiability of intelligence. It is equally clear that the effects of the intervention could have been expanded with further consideration of each of the variables described in the mode of metacommunicative framing. To improve the chances of sustainability of the intervention effects, we believe that it is necessary to assure that the messages conveyed to the mothers in the intervention are *congruent with the typical cultural-discourse style between caregiver and child in the local culture.*

Before we intervene with an early intervention program, however adaptable it may be, we should try to examine the typical forms of childrearing, the styles of communicating with children, and the metacommunicative frames, values, conceptions, and relationships into which childrearing and interactions with children are embedded. In addition, we need to know about the typical problems in the household that prevent a sensitive, mediational relationship with the child. Some cultural research along these lines is needed as a basis for more sensitive early intervention (Braaten, 1991; Hundeide, 1992).

The Use of Mediational Criteria for Cultural Reactivation

The mediational criteria (Feuerstein, 1980; Klein, 1985a; Klein & Alony, 1993) specify certain general conditions for mediation that are implicit in the concept of socialization itself, and for this reason the criteria are conceptually universal (Smedslund, 1984). Still, the way these conditions are implemented or practiced is a matter of cultural variation. For example, I cannot imagine any culture or any socialization taking place without a shared focus of attention in any interaction between caregiver and child. Similarly, I can see no socialization taking place without some intentionality on the part of the caregiver to transfer meaning, expansion, and regulation of behavior. The question is not whether these criteria are present in the cultural communication between the caregiver and the child; it is more a question of how useful it is to view the interaction this way, and how useful it is to use these criteria as guidelines for facilitating different cultural ways of mediation (e.g., How do you achieve shared attention or intersubjectivity in your interaction with your child within the framework of your culture? How do you focus your child's attention to an object? How do you mediate meaning, expand, regulate a child's action, confirm, and mediate competence to a child?). Answers to these questions open a rich field of cultural research that has not yet been explored—namely, the subtle ways in which these criteria of meaningful communication are implemented in the caregiver–child interactions in different cultures, and how they can be used to facilitate and activate indigenous childrearing practices and interactions. Instead of teaching these criteria in an instructive way, they may instead serve as conceptual vehicles to focus, facilitate, and activate those qualities in the indigenous practices that seem important according to the mediational theory. This presupposes an open definition of the criteria that allows for cultural variation in how they are specified in different cultural settings. Observing video recordings of mother–child interactions and interviewing mothers helps identify the typical cultural patterns of interaction and the typical forms of mediation within that culture. This knowledge represents a basic prerequisite for any facilitation or sensitization that is to take place.

If we consider the criterion of *intentionality and reciprocity, or focusing* in Javanese childrearing, for example, we will find that most mothers seem to play a relatively passive role in relation to their infants, mostly following the initiative and activity of the children, especially when they are infants. When mothers are asked about this, they explain that according to their tradition, infants are still close to God, and for that reason their activity is still guided from within, from their souls, and so on. In a similar way, when babies are making sounds when they are alone, this is interpreted as communication with a spiritual being with whom the infants are still in contact (Timor, 1993), and for that reason, one has to show respect and follow and support the infants' initiatives and activity. *It is the infants' intentionality that is guiding the interaction,* and reciprocity of attention is achieved by the mothers' adjustment to the children's activity. Even after infancy we can see in our videotapes how the mothers follow two- to three-year-old children into the street with a bowl of rice trying to feed them—when they please.

For this reason, mothers' initiation of interaction would be in conflict with their traditional conception of how good interaction with infants should be. If we accept this conception and practice as a baseline, then it is possible to facilitate mediation by emphasizing the positive side of this—praising mothers for good reciprocity with their children and pointing out how they can learn to select and support those initiatives that are important for the children's social development. *This is how mediation is facilitated by operating inside existing childrearing practices.*

Similarly, with regard to mediation of competence, most Javanese mothers claim that they normally do not praise their children. This would, so to say, break the natural discourse style and the tacit contract of authoritarian respect that normally exist between parents and children. Taking a closer look, however, we could see that competence is mediated, but in a much more indirect and subtle way, by an approving nod, touch, or smile, or even by communicating to a neighbor how good the child is. If we believe that praise is important for children's self-esteem and motivation, it is possible to facilitate this aspect by *pointing out and praising the mothers for those features in their natural interaction with their children that correspond to our conception of mediation of competence,* without suggesting open praise in the typical Western style.

The typical form of expansion as it occurs in Western culture seems to be quite different from the Javanese traditional mode of expansion. The latter is more like telling a story, very often with a mythological content that may frighten the child. In fact, this is quite frequently used to regulate the children's behavior so that they operate within the limits set by the parents (Geertz, 1959). In the traditional Javanese society, children learn quite early the typical mythological dramas of the Wayang and the Hindu tradition, and these are sometimes used as metaphors for understanding people and episodes from everyday life. Expansion and transcendence are therefore closely linked to the worldviews and values contained in the cultural repertoire of myths and stories that are transmitted from one generation to the next.

In summary, I started this chapter by emphasizing the importance of seeing both child development and early intervention in the context of worldviews, values, and construction of persons and identities within a culture. It was assumed that congruence or conflict with these, very often tacit, cultural macrocontexts, could be decisive for whether intervention at a microlevel of skills, operations, and interactive patterns would be experienced as meaningful, plausible, and therefore also sustainable over time.

Forms of mediation that are different from the typical, inquiring analytical mode that is characteristic of Western academic culture were explored as different modes that could enrich our own conception of life and our understanding of factors that must be taken into consideration prior to intervention in non-Western cultures.

The implementation of the MISC program of early intervention in an Indonesian cultural context was used as an example to illustrate how this program can be used to explore the typical features of interaction, by using the criteria of mediation (MLE) as guidelines for observation.

ACKNOWLEDGMENT

This research has been made possible by a grant from the Golden Cross Foundation, Ottawa, Canada.

8 MEDIATIONAL INTERVENTION FOR SENSITIZING CAREGIVERS: ISRAEL

Pnina S. Klein

Since the MISC was designed in Israel for use within a multiethnic society, some of the basic empirical studies described earlier were carried out in Israel and will not be repeated here.

Israel has been considered a melting pot for immigrants from all over the world, especially since the establishment of the State in 1948. Despite the common denominator of those immigrants being primarily Jewish, they differed considerably in physical appearance as well as cultural and educational backgrounds. Among the poor and deprived populations in the country, immigrants from African and Asian countries tended to be found more frequently than those of Western origin. Their general level of education and average income per family was lower. They tended to live in poor neighborhoods, and their children's school achievement was lower, with a higher number of school dropouts. Although differences between the immigrants from the East and West tended to decrease with time, many of them, as they integrated into the core culture of the country, tended to leave behind their parent's cultural and religious values without properly replacing those with others, leading to breakage points in cultural transmission to the young. Immigrants are still flowing into the country, primarily from Russia and Ethiopia. As professionals attempt to assist the immigrant families in dealing with their new world, they also transmit the tacit message: "We are locals. Do as we tell you. We know better." When this type of message is conveyed in relation to childrearing practices, it may have a devastating effect on the parents, reducing their trust in their own ability to help their children grow and develop. In addition, because many different approaches were attempted with the same populations, feelings of resentment surfaced. Some parents clearly verbalized their concern: "We do not want another program for the poor." The objective of the MISC in Israel was to empower poor parents, immigrant parents, or parents of children with special problems to help them regain confidence in their ability to raise competent children through their own philosophy of childrearing. Parents were assured that this program is not just for the poor; rather, it is designed to improve any child's flexibility of mind.

The program identifies for the parents those components of childrearing practices within their own behavior toward their children that are potent factors in enhancing children's development along the objectives desirable to them. The MISC focuses on parental needs as well as children's needs. At times mothers' immediate needs may not be beneficial to future child development. In those cases mothers are helped to realize their own long-term objectives for their children's development in the future. For example, a mother may be content with the fact that the baby sleeps a whole day, leaving her more time to rest or carry out her work. She may actively attempt to prolong the baby's sleep by darkening the room and keeping the house extra quite. When this mother is helped to become aware of her long-term objectives for the baby, namely, normal development and in direct relationship to her own needs—that the child would be able to play with toys on his/her own—she may be more willing to act in line with her own objectives.

Within the framework of the Jewish culture and the State of Israel, children are viewed as our main natural resource and there is no question as to the centrality of the child in governmental decision-making processes. In Israel there is no lack of intervention programs for young children. Quite the contrary, there has been a proliferation of early intervention programs that are implemented for short periods of time, only to be replaced by others. Most of these involve structured instructions to parents to do things with their children in a specific way or to use predesignated toys. These programs may develop in parents a tendency to depend on specific toys or materials but a lack of understanding that may be generalized to other activities with the child as he/she grows older.

The MISC in Israel is carried out through mother–infant health-care centers and through the educational system in preparatory training of day-care workers, kindergarten teachers, and primary school teachers.

The MISC in Training Public Health Nurses

Close to 98% of the entire population of infants and very young children in Israel are seen by public health nurses. There is a network of mother–infant health centers across the entire country. The nurses provide services that include periodic health checkups, immunization, information about feeding infants, and a general developmental assessment. Through the initiative of Nira Baram, National Director of Ongoing Programs for Nurses' Continued Education, the MISC was adopted by the National Board of Health as a requirement in the training of all nurses working with mothers and infants. The nurses have been trained to look at the quality of mother–infant interaction, using a modified form of the OMI (Observing Mediational Interaction) and other variables of the MISC approach. In addition to recording the children's physical characteristics and general level of development, they now assess the children's potential for future learning and development through an assessment of the mediation to which the children are exposed. In cases in which there is extremely poor mediation provided to the children, the nurses are trained to intervene directly (using the techniques described in the MISC) or to suggest that mother and child be referred for further help. Because health services provide a network reaching all mothers and infants in the country, it is a most efficient way to improve mother–child interaction. This approach may bridge the service and communication gap between health and educational services and help the parents develop mediation skills that will lead to more academic readiness and academic success for their children in school (which is the prime objective of most parents in the country. Poor parents feel that educational success may be the only chance their children have to break the cycle of poverty). In addition, the program helps reduce the feelings of alienation and inferiority felt by parents toward school authorities and helps parents become better consumers of educational services.

The MISC in Israeli Early Education

The most apparent effect of the MISC approach on Israeli early childhood education is inherent in the fact that teachers' colleges across all sectors of the population—including the kibbutz educational system, state colleges for teacher training, and teacher training institutions for the religious sector—include the basic mediational approach in their training. The book *Promoting Flexibility of Mind* (Klein, 1985c) has already appeared in its fifth edition in Israel. The program has been adopted for national use in training teachers and other caregivers within hundreds of kindergartens and day-care centers, especially within the Public Religious Kindergarten System. The objective of adopting the program for active implementation within this educational framework is to improve transmission of cultural and religious values.

Despite the fact that there is a national educational program designating the specific content areas, programs, and general educational objectives to be covered by the teachers (who are all certified), there are considerable differences in the level of education provided to the children and in the transmission of cultural values occurring within different kindergartens. It is through a direct focus on the quality of mediation that an increase in quality of education and transmission of values and religious aspirations is hoped for.

The implementation of the program started with a series of workshops for all the teacher supervisors, followed by training for teachers and parent meetings conducted by the teachers. The workshops and parent meetings focused on the identification of parents' and educators' own perceptions of various individual children, educational goals, ways of improving a positive cycle of expressive, affective communication, and achievement of better mediational interactions with young children.

The latter are achieved through minilectures, role playing, and other exercises (described in this book), and primarily through analyses of episodes from everyday life in kindergarten, collected on video or in verbal vignette form. These episodes are analyzed first with regard to the actual situation, identifying the criteria of mediation within the interaction, and answering sample questions such as the following for analyzing teacher–child interactions in kindergarten:

- What is the intention of the teacher in doing, saying, showing, what he/she did?
- What is the intention of the child initiating the interaction?
- Is there reciprocity from the children (or teachers)?
- How can you tell?
- Is the teacher mediating affect? (Is it a warm, pleasant atmosphere?) Can excitement be detected?
- Do you think the children understand the relationship between the concrete present situation and the idea the teacher attempted to express?
- Was the teacher mediating expansion or explaining beyond the immediate experience?
- How many children were "with" him/her? What happened to others?
- Is the teacher responsive to children's signs of distress, interest, boredom? How do you know?
- Does the teacher use spontaneous occurrences and expand on them if they seem interesting to the children?
- In what way does the teacher reward or encourage children?
- What aspects of children's behavior are rewarded by teachers?
- Is there an attempt to encourage behaviors that may represent cul-

tural values or religious beliefs?

- Are there any stories, songs, or dances that could have been used in the lesson?

Following the initial discussion, parallel questions are answered that refer to what could have been done, said (or avoided) to improve mediation in the situation discussed.

A follow-up of the training workshops is carried out nationwide through the use of questionnaires that are sent out to all participating teachers, asking them to identify within their daily contacts with children the components of quality mediation and criteria of mediation that they find most helpful or difficult, and to share one or more case studies of children for whom a change of mediation led to positive outcomes. Many of these cases are shared with all other teachers in subsequent meetings and workshops.

Most teachers respond to the presentation of the mediational prerequisites and criteria of mediation by an expression of their general agreement regarding the importance of these factors in their educational interactions with young children. They seem to enjoy the fact that "We have been doing it all the time, but now we know what it is." Following the initial lectures, many teachers express their guilt feelings for not mediating enough to their own children. Following the training and videotape analyses, teachers often become over-self-conscious and most frequently *overmediate* (trying to practice what they have learned, to the fullest). To reduce overmediation, it is necessary to repeat and stress the importance of *congruency* with the children, of following the children's initiative, and of matching what one does with the children's needs at any given moment.

Following training, teachers report a growing awareness of what they choose to do with the children and of the preferred way of reaching their goal. They become aware of the need to redesign the educational environment in line with both the children's needs and their own. Teachers express more satisfaction with their jobs and with their personal relationships with the children. Similar effects on the teachers were noted in the United States, Sri Lanka, and Sweden, and are described in other chapters in this book.

One of the basic areas of concern within the MISC intervention in the kindergartens is related to enhancing social values such as *kindness, respect, concern, tolerance, acceptance*, and *assistance* in interpersonal relations in the kindergarten milieu. These involve both relations between children and between children and adults.

Teachers were helped to identify and encourage children who expressed verbal or nonverbal empathy for another child or behaviors that reflected attempts to help or express concern for another person (visiting a child who was unable to come to kindergarten, preparing a present for someone, sharing a sandwich with someone who does not have anything to eat). They focused children's attention on the joy involved in making someone happy, and on questions such as "How do you know that Johnny is sad (happy, excited, angry, etc.)?" or "What could you do to make him feel happier?"

The Use of MISC in Computer-Assisted Education

Computers have entered almost every aspect of life in Israel, including education. Computers have been placed in schools and kindergartens and used with various programs. However, the effects of computers on the education of young children is as yet unclear. It is clear, however, that when children use computers in the presence of an adult who is focusing their attention, exciting them, conveying meaning and expanding around what is seen on the screen, learning is more efficient. In a recent study (Shani, Cohen, & Klein, 1993a), the effects on kindergarten children of using a computer were assessed. The experimental group in this study was divided into two subgroups. In one of these groups, children were expected to work with the computer without assistance from an adult (except for an initial introduction to the program). In the second group, the children were using the computers with an adult who followed their work and mediated to them throughout all the sessions, as needed. When the two experimental groups were compared with the control group, it became apparent that the children in the second experimental group, namely, those who were assisted by an adult, did considerably better (obtaining higher scores on a series of cognitive measures) as compared to the other experimental groups as well as the control group. The MISC approach is used to define the types of behavior that could be enhanced in an educational interaction between adults and young children working with computers.

In another study (Klein & Nir Gal, 1992) involving Israeli kindergarten children, an attempt was made to design a computer program with several basic features of mediational behavior, as defined earlier. The program was designed to enhance analogical reasoning of young children, including features that mimicked human mediation (i.e., flashing arrows indicated relationships that should be kept in mind). Children were directed to the next frame, following an individualized program based on the type of response they gave to the previous question (not just on the basis of right or wrong answers). Competence was mediated by presenting a smiling face and a musical tune following correct responses. However, in addition, the reason for the response being considered correct was also identified. The latter was achieved through the use of "the smiling clown." The clown presented the concepts that were kept in mind in giving the correct or partially correct answer. For example, if the correct answer was a big red square, then the clown appeared to hold the code for color, form, and size.

It was found that introducing some of the mediational criteria into a computer program for young children raised the effectiveness of the program. The analysis of mediational behaviors and their effects on educational gains achieved by young children through the use of computers is still a major issue in educational research. Attempts are made now to design the optimal balance between independent and adult-assisted work with computers. The MISC can be used in training good mediators to help young children learn better, enjoy more what they learn, and transfer their learning more readily to other areas of their schooling and everyday life.

9   Child Focus through Mediated Learning Experience: Sri Lanka

Andreas Fuglesang and Dale Chandler[1]

From Facilitation to Mediation

The concepts of facilitation and animation have been central in discussions of development, especially human resource development. In our view, these concepts are frequently inept in their implicit, liberal value assumption that through their practice and application something good always emerges from the depths of the people. With the recognition that development is not value free, *mediation* may become a more powerful practical and theoretical concept. In what has been called the cognitive revolution in human sciences, Chomsky (1964) pointed out the mediated nature of language acquisition in infants. At a very early age the child acquires the capacity or skill in the "rule-governed creativity" of language in action. This is learned through an exposure to speaking practices mediated by mature others of the culture. Not only language, but also beliefs, values, knowledge, skills, traditions—in other words, culture as a whole—is communicated from the old to the young in this guided way. Mediation is the means by which societies ensure their survival. Also it is the means by which desired change takes place. Mediation is what caregivers do in all cultures. What matters for the child is its quality.

Toward a Collapse of Caring Capacity

It is a dictum in all human resource development to build on people's own strengths and capacities. The starting point is that caregivers of all cultures are competent at what they are doing. The issue is that caregivers are now, however, under increasing and sometimes unbearable stress. Research bears evidence to the gravity of this situation. Modernization brings with it a general devaluation of children and a consequent increase in child abuse, neglect, and deprivation of basic cultural experience. It erodes the kinship and extended family system that formerly ensured the children's status as resources invaluable to the community while the new forms of social organization are not capable of compensating for the loss in caring capacity. The Kilbrides (1990), who spent twenty years researching this process of erosion among the Baganda and Abaluya of East Africa, characterize it as an economic, social, and moral delocalization of the control of childrearing from the immediate social environment of the child, the family, and village neighborhood. In general, as community structures and cultural mores dissipate, the status of children as well as the status and traditionally ensured protections or power of women diminish. Similar concerns are raised by the LeVine (Korbin, 1983) in a chapter on child abuse in the region of sub-Saharan Africa. When childrearing was a concern of the community, the standards were guaranteed. When it becomes exclusively the responsibility of parents, and as more and more women become single parents, the standards deteriorate. Today, parents do not have the family and communal support they once had. Confronted with this problem, *Childwatch*, the official organ of The African Network for the Prevention and Protection against Child Abuse and Neglect in Nairobi, defines the momentous task ahead as follows:

> We must focus on strengthening these weakening and important networks in order to help our families through the transition of modernization. Our task requires that we integrate the traditional frameworks with our contemporary problems and professional training to provide a network that acknowledges both the strength of our communities and the very real stresses of surviving modernization. (Nowrojee, 1991)

Considering the magnitude of this task and its wide economic, social, and cultural implications, including its geographic and demographic scale, one cannot sensibly attempt a narrow clinical, psychosocial approach. It is necessary to think in comprehensive community development programs in which child development is set in focus. The realization of such a scheme is further premised on an organizational development conducive to profound people's participation. The issue is not to run small successful pilot schemes that we know can be implemented and replicated. The issue is to achieve cost-effective quality impact through a large-scale organizational outreach mobilizing community capacities. The ideal is the emergence of self-selected social support groups within the community. Unfortunately, community development is an avenue of action in which one easily stumbles into conceptual confusion, contradictions of terms, and partisan equivocation of predominant paradigms. It is necessary to survey the field.

Some time in the 1950s colonial administrators began to turn a limited attention to the human aspects of economic development. Community development departments became institutionalized. The emerging projects were a mixed bag of activities such as home-economics and homemaking, horticulture, health education, and literacy that very often took place in women's groups. Since Dr. Cecely Williams "discovered" infant malnutrition in Ghana in the 1930s, nutrition education and child care became increasingly important. As the concept of primary health care evolved in the 1960s, it was added. Coordinators were employed with the idea of forging a well-functioning development process out of the many inputs. Coordination proved practically difficult and a yearning for integration arose, as it always does, in a multidisciplinary context. Integrated community development programs (ICDP) are today being practiced all over the world, mostly by nongovernmental organizations. Prominent among these are the International Save the Children Alliance (ISCA) organizations, which include U.S. and U.K. Save the Children, the Scandinavian Redd Barna, and others. A variety of sector activities are implemented, such as sanitation and water supply, health care, infrastructure (e.g., roads, schools, clinics, and community halls), improvement of housing, adult education, agriculture, credit and income generation, and cultural activities. Often, preschools and child/youth welfare activities are central. These programs can point to considerable achievements, especially in infrastructure and school buildings, but it is doubtful if credit can be taken for an overall uplift in the quality of life of the communities concerned. Some nongovernmental organizations (NGOs) advocate an advanced view on the involvement of people, much in line with community-based integrated responsive development (CBRID), described in great detail by Chambers (1983). This concept is akin to what is now frequently attempted by governments with the assistance of bilateral development agencies, the integrated rural development programs (IRDP). Although the concept is interesting and even sophisticated, evaluations document that its practical implementation is heavily flawed. The failures evolve around the issues of people's participation and social organizing. There is need for an analysis of the practical field situation.

Community Participation So Far

The brief history of implementing community participation programs reveals that they suffer from feeble conceptualization of very concrete and practical issues. *Integration* is a nice word, the meaning of which is rarely achieved. At best what is being operated are multisectoral community development programs that are badly coordinated. If integration is impossible, the pursuit of effective coordination in the face of practical obstacles is equally elusive. This situation emerges partly from expert pedantry, and partly from a failure to understand what motivates village people to action. There is the delusion that in dialogue with people one can construct and catch community reality in an analytic factorized grid, a preconceived conceptual framework that mirrors people's needs and, by summing up the many parts or factors, one can identify and recreate a functioning social whole. Such approaches, which are at intervals attempted in various guises, ignore the elementary insight of epistemology that fail-safe action plans are not deducible from data, but are products of our inductive, creative faculties and, ultimately, of leadership. It is a form of problematizing academicism that remains oblivious to a long and well-documented experience in community activism, notably, Saul Alinsky's (1972a) organizing of black communities in North America (1946–1972). Recognizing the need for a people's program, Alinsky maintains that if you have faith in people, you should have faith that they will evolve a people's program. If it is not a program to your liking, remember that it is to their liking. From such a viewpoint, it is folly to start a community dialogue with the knowledge of an academic discipline rather than with the knowledge of the people themselves. The evolution of a program goes hand in hand with the organization of people into a people's movement. Program and organization are opposite sides of the same coin. To Alinsky, organizing is the creation of a set of circumstances through which an educational process will take place. The educational goal is a community's understanding of its place in the general mosaic of communities in the nation and in the world.

One of Alinsky's strengths was his analysis of the duality and complementarity of social problems. It is in these contradictions and their incessant, interacting tensions that creativity of the dialogue begins and the social-knowledge product emerges. This is what participatory action research (PAR) is all about. The notion of complementary factors allows us to see every problem or issue in its whole, interrelated sense. It leads to political understanding of the issues.

People themselves have the capacity to think out actions and solutions. It is only when people feel they do not have the power to change a bad situation that they do not think about strategies of change. Thus, the starting point for any community development effort is people's self-image and empowerment. Whereas Alinsky argues for a more confrontational style, Paulo Freire has developed his thought in a more process-oriented direction (1970, 1973, 1978). He joins Alinsky in identifying practical or political issues as the only relevant starting point for community development. People do not act on dispassionate factorial analyses, but on issues that they have strong feelings about. Motivation to act is strongly linked to people's emotions. All community development projects should therefore start by identifying the "hot issues," the issues that people in the local community speak about with anger, fear, anxiety, hope, or excitement. The essence of this approach to people is that the researchers do not work from a ready-made questionnaire or from a predetermined grid of factors they want information on, but seek people in situations in which they feel relaxed. Whereas prearranged meetings place the researcher in the limelight, people are more at ease and conversant in familiar milieus such as local markets, bus stops, bars, and the community water pump. The task of the community organizer is to help people to identify what they are doing and how they can control a change of their behavior. Real learning and radical change take place when a community is emotionally upset and dissatisfied with an aspect of daily life and becomes determined to change it. In essence, such a process of powerful conscientization is undertaken by mediating; in other words, the mediator responds to the intentionality of the community, clarifies meaning and expands on it, and reinforces the link between meaning and feeling in a turn-taking cycle in which regulation of behavior, planning and organizing, action plans, and modification of action plans are recurring features.

DOMESTICATION OR MEDIATION

A few activist voluntary organizations, especially in Latin America and Asia, have been able to facilitate over time such process-oriented work (Fuglesang & Chandler, 1986). Private development associations, Huancavaelica (ASINDE) in Peru, Process for Social Change in San Miguel, Mexico, Proshika and Nijera Kori in Bangladesh, and People's Institute for Development and Training (PIDT) in India, are some examples.

International NGOs have a much poorer record. In fact, much in line with the World Bank and other similar agencies, they are prone to ideological rhetoric. Although the funds and the goodwill may be there, the kinds of skills that emerge from a strong political commitment are not yet manifest. By and large, these NGOs do not fulfill their stated mandate of reaching the poorest sections of the community, especially women and children. Already in their initial benchmark studies one will find that community development projects are oriented toward the better-off in the community for several reasons. The staff members who prepare implementation do not seem to recognize the complexity of intracommunal life, aggravated as it is by the social transitions to modernity. The community is generally perceived as an "entity" and subjected to little or no analysis. When development workers call a village meeting, those who attend are normally male elders and local politicians or officials. Their opinions of the community's needs are elicited and the community is then considered to have been consulted. One may generalize the situation in several indicative directions. The richest people do not attend meetings because they have their own access to resources and little to gain from an NGO. The poorest do not attend because they have no good clothes to wear for the meeting and because their self-image of poverty prevents them from perceiving that they have the right to attend. The people who do attend meetings come from above-average socioeconomic groups, have more self-confidence, are a little more literate and articulate, and represent their own needs rather than the needs of the poorest. Frequently those who participate by contributing labor on a school building are the poorest women, and those who benefit are the children of the better-off families who can afford school fees and uniforms. What starts out as a well-meaning exercise in participation ends up widening the social stratification in the community. Moreover, it becomes a gross and unjust taxation of the poorest and most vulnerable group.

In a study of seventy-five evaluations of projects operated by NGOs, Tendler (1982) concluded that what these organizations refer to as participatory processes are better described as decision making by the NGOs themselves and/or the local village elite. Esman and Uphoff (1984) followed up with a study of 150 local organizations, finding that NGOs perform a little better than governments judged according to participation in decision making. Both studies found that NGOs are no guarantee of participatory development involving and benefiting the poorer strata of the population. In an overview, Gezelius and Millwood (1988) pointed out that there is a gulf between large government and NGO donors on the one hand, and advocates and practitioners of self-reliant development on the other. The two do not speak the same language, even if they use the same words. For example, when both advocate participation, the latter think in a nonproject, process-oriented way of proceeding.

These are some of the reasons that support the criticism that international NGOs mandated with child orientation operate under a myth as far as people's participation is concerned. It is an illusion that they reach children effectively. Just as there is maldistribution of resources within the community, there is maldistribution even within the family, especially in situations of stress when the adult breadwinners are likely to be favored at the expense of the smallest children. In community development, a great need exists for an approach that can bring children better in focus.

Welbourn (1991) presents a similar experience and points out how such elementary initial false steps can be avoided. Rapid Rural Appraisal

(RRA) is a participatory action research approach now coming to the fore that can be used for training of development workers in an analysis of intracommunal difference. Several axes can be explored: age, gender, ethnic/tribal, adult–child, clan background, poverty. These will hardly ever be clear-cut, but they all carry the implication of stratification, oppression, exploitation, and lack of access to opportunities. Such a mediation of social analysis and meaning to the poorest is fundamentally important for any community development effort. On the background of this problem in community development, we now analyze the predicament of the child and argue why the MLE approach offers an opportunity for resolving it.

The Poor Self-Image

In a comprehensive analysis of both the local and international context of power, Gran (1983) emulates the interconnection. Those in control present their ideology in the form of scientific accuracy. Business, government, and aid agencies have their own agendas. For the international NGOs it may be an unwitting involvement. Nevertheless, the fundamental question remains whether their efforts work to create a community development process that adds to the empowerment of the people or, conversely, facilitates a co-opting process wherein elites more smoothly incorporate previously marginalized people into their fold on the local level.

The issue of marginality goes beyond its purely material implications. Poverty erodes human relationships. Under severe stress even parent–child bonds become marginalized. The situation of poverty is aggravated by the process of modernization and party politics. The rural village is becoming today a social ruin, factionalized by vested, economic, ethnic, or political interests. What was once a fairly well-working system of horizontal loyalties and communal support has become vertical loyalties to strongmen and moneylenders. The village is disturbed by constant bickering and violence between such competing factions.

An action research project among youth in Sri Lanka, some of whom sympathized with guerrilla participation (Fuglesang & Chandler, 1989), revealed the destructive impact of such a social environment on the self-image of the young. Failing at school and in finding meaningful employment, incapable of acquiring the conspicuous consumption offered by the media, they have little feeling of agency, of being able to do and achieve. In such a situation, violence easily becomes an expression of personal meaning and feeling. In an age where violence is close to being the only language, the young have to learn to talk—to use words—anew. In our work, we have sometimes met fifteen- to sixteen-year-old boys who may be literate in the mechanics of a T-56 gun, but who are not familiar with elementary mechanisms in their own language. Poor youth who leave school by grade three or four also have poor vocabularies. The most disturbing psychological characteristic is that they are not really capable of articulating their feelings or giving voice to their inner states in words. They are literally trapped in their emotions. What appears to take place is that this poverty of expression and lack of release of mental energy in meaningful activities builds up an explosive emotional state over time. In daily life this leads to helplessness, negative self-image, and lack of creative effort. In politics, it leads to increased dependency on the more inventive and articulate elite. Poverty reproduces itself. Our experience in counseling indicates that one way to break this vicious circle is for the young to learn to control their anger by venting it through an articulation in words. The young need someone to talk to about their problems—someone who can listen to them with empathy.

However, along with emotional care, there is the need for mediation of meaning, joining meaning to feeling, and planning for the future. The fundamental challenge in a situation of poverty and deprivation is the reconstruction of the emotional and cognitive self. In an analysis of the development of the social self, self-esteem, and self-image, Shotter (1984) elaborates convincingly how selfhood is established in a person through a process of increasing social accountability and mediation of meaning. People, children and adults, learn how to mean, and learning how to mean is learning many different, practical skills. By accounting for their actions, children learn whether an action has been or will be intelligent or pointless, effective or ineffective; thereby standards are instituted. By using their ideas and theoretical accounts to formulate a plan for their actions, children learn to extend their acquired social practices into other areas than those for which they were originally developed. Shotter concludes,

> For if people are ever to be self determining, and act as they themselves require rather than as their circumstances require, they must develop the ability to deliberate before they act. That is, they must develop the ability to decide courses of action in theory before executing their choice in action. (p. 76)

People make progress in their lives when they have learned to plan and organize an effective utilization of the resources they control. The capacity for planning and organizing is a scarce resource among the poor in the Third World. Attempts at collective action or joint enterprises fail as a rule for the lack of such management skills. This is the point at which the MLE approach has an essential contribution to make. Community development approaches must be seen over two generations. This is the ultimate aim of the MLE approach in childrearing.

THE OBSTACLES IN ADULT EDUCATION

Freire (1970) has voiced exactly the same concern in relation to adults with his terminology of conscientization and empowerment in his *Pedagogy of the Oppressed*. What has emerged over the years, however, is the experience that adult education is complicated to implement on a large scale, and it takes a long time. General literacy rates are stagnant or in decline. Female enrollments at the primary- and secondary-school level are declining in most sub-Saharan countries. In Africa, where rural women are the main cultivators and food producers, 95% of people still cannot read or write. The predominant male migration to urban areas increases the labor demand on women who already have a work week of sixty-five hours. Under such circumstances, adult education is exceedingly difficult. The developmental predicament is aggravated further by other well-documented facts. Literate women with some degree of primary education are more capable of benefiting from various community development initiatives, perform better as food producers, and care more proficiently for the health and nutrition of their children.

Closely connected with this adult-literacy problem is facilitation of community participation. Case studies on participatory processes in communities indicate that these are much longer-term endeavors than first anticipated when the concept of participation took hold in development thinking. Project periods of two to five years are irrelevant. A sustainable participatory process in a community emerges only through long-term facilitation following a prior development of the organizational basis for it. One should rather plan and act on the basis of periods from ten to twenty years (Fuglesang & Chandler, 1986). Operationalizing the concept of *conscientization* on a large scale in an adult population raises insurmountable logistical problems. Since Freire (1970) introduced the concept, it has had an enormous influence on development thinking, but its successful practice has been less conspicuous. MLE is akin to conscientization. In our view, it can be more fruitfully applied as a vehicle for development because it is directed toward children.

ACCESS THROUGH THE CHILD

In this long-term perspective, it makes eminent sense to focus community development on children under age five years, who become adults in a decade and a half. This, in turn, demands a strong focus on the parental role in childrearing, in addition to special training connected with the operation of preschools. The role of parents should be focused on in classes for functional adult literacy and other community-development activities. Strengthening the role of parents must include strengthening of the social-support network available to them. Grandparents, older siblings, and the wider kinship structure have a vital role to play. The child provides the development worker with a rare access to the community and with an ideal starting point for the facilitation of participatory processes. Dialogues with the community quickly reveal that issues concerning their children are the issues that people feel most strongly about. Parents can readily unite and participate in activities for the benefit of their children. Politicians and local power brokers are not likely to oppose or obstruct communal initiatives for children's welfare. In a community full of conflict, the child frequently represents the least controversial issue and, if sensibly facilitated, a focus on the child becomes a means of conflict resolution. In this particular situation, the MISC approach bears the promise of reviving community development.

CHILD DEVELOPMENT THROUGH ORGANIZATIONAL DEVELOPMENT

There is no doubt that the parents and other caregivers in the family are the primary partners in the efforts to introduce child-oriented intervention in the community. It should be recognized however, that one cannot reach many parents without an appropriate organization for an outreach project. To reach twenty families is not very cost-effective if there are 2,000 families in the project area. The real challenge is to organize child-development networks on a large scale, with the ultimate objective of strengthening the childcaring capacities parents already have. In order to build a solid foundation for future work in the field, one must first focus on the issues of staff and organizational development. There is also the challenge of promoting understanding of the importance of early childhood education among the surrounding government institutions and local authorities. Some of the fundamental organizational issues that should be addressed in community development programs that have a mandated child orientation, are as follows:

1.   All staff members should be trained to become thoroughly familiar with the stages of child development. They should learn to observe children and develop a capacity to interact positively with them. This includes administrative staff members such as accountants and clerks, as well as drivers and storekeepers. The organization as a whole should be imbued with a sense of mission.

2.   Several senior staff members who display particular talents should be selected for more thorough training as master trainers and supervisors.

3.   When master trainers are available, the organization should start strategizing its outreach and train various groups of field-workers, for example, preschool teachers, primary-school teachers, community workers, relief and rehabilitation workers, or home visitors. In this connection it is important to recognize the ratios for outreach based on experience from general community-development work. One community worker can manage to work effectively with 50 households or families only, and for each cadre of 10 community workers, there should be a field coordinator for continuous professional feedback and backup. In an area of 2,000 households, 40 community workers and 4 coordinators would be required. The workers should be selected from the community by the people themselves in consultation with the coordinators. Considering attrition, sickness, and failure to attend, a number of 40 would necessitate starting the training with 50 to 60 workers.

4.   Both coordinators and community workers should be trained in social organization of support groups. People's involvement does not happen unless there is a social frame of reference established within which participation can take place. Some form of social organization should represent the end stage in the process of organizational development of outreach. Depending on the situation in the communities, such organizations may already exist or should be created from the ground. There are often a number of options: sports clubs, women's clubs, adult education classes, income-generating groups, parents' associations, mothers' societies. Optimally, these organizations should not comprise more than thirty to fifty members because larger social entities are prone to internal conflicts.

Although the process is still ongoing, these ideas have largely been implemented in Redd Barna's Sri Lanka program.

Development work cannot be made child-focused unless development workers are given the tools they need to focus on children. The MISC program with its focus on mediation provides such tools.

AUTONOMOUS SUSTAINABLE SUPPORT SYSTEM

Only within social frameworks established through people's own volition does social action acquire meaning. Above all, they are groupings for mutual social support in which issues can be discussed and decisions taken by people who face similar situations. These are also the forays where professional inputs and advice by specialists such as agriculturists or educators can be evaluated by the people. Anchored in the support group, Participatory Action Research (PAR) can be undertaken successfully on issues of concern to the members. The groupings must have rules and regulations if they are to function effectively, and officials should rotate yearly to prevent entrenchment of vested interests. From the point of view of early childhood education, it is ideal that the groupings are formed as mothers' or parents' societies around the issue of preschools and general child welfare in the community. The preschool concept has several important contributions to make in community development. It provides the object for a concrete focus on child welfare. It is the anchor point for the spreading of an early childhood–education message through home visits or family meetings. Experience indicates that extensive work through visits in the households does not succeed without such a professional support basis or center where training can be repeated and backup discussions can take place. Before one can reach the parents, and especially the mothers, at all, one must have established such a professional base in the community, and it must be supported by an organizational base in the form of a mothers' or parents' society. The next issue is the problem of facilitating the development of sustainability in such groupings. This can be done by combining them with systems for credit and income generation (see Fuglesang & Chandler, 1993).

The Story of the MISC (MLE) in Sri Lanka

Redd Barna–Norwegian Save the Children has worked in Sri Lanka since 1975. It has evolved quite extensive and comprehensive community development projects in Colombo, Batticaloa, Hambantota, Hanguranketa, Kilinochi, Maskeliya, Matale, Mullaitivu, and Puttalam. All nine projects, which in 1987 comprised over 9,000 families in 184 of the poorest village communities, were serviced by 536 staff members and volunteer community workers. Of these, 61 were highly qualified, experienced community coordinators and 134 were preschool instructors operating in 103 established preschools. At that time 2,448 children were registered in these schools. The projects were engaged in the standard community-development activities such as health, nutrition, maternal and child care, water and sanitation, agriculture, animal husbandry and fishing, adult education, and a great deal of infrastructure and house building. People's participation in these activities was mostly limited to physical labor connected with building. There was, however, some participation connected with the preschools. Various revolving credit schemes had not succeeded very well.

Although Redd Barna is a Save the Children organization, it has had difficulties in practice to make its community development programs sufficiently child-oriented or, indeed, child-focused. In most project areas, staff members have been oriented to general development and dealt directly with the problems of children in a limited manner only, the assumption being that whatever was done in development would directly or indirectly benefit the children. Several evaluations confirmed that this did not occur and community participation was limited.

The poor communities in which Redd Barna works suffer not only from lack of opportunities to meet their basic material needs, but also from factionalized conflict and drug abuse or alcoholism. Concomitantly, both adults and children are mentally marginalized. The poor children have a poor self-image and this negative self-perception is aggravated by the social environment, frequently turning young children's development into a downward spiral. Schooling is inadequate in these communities. If they attend school at all, children usually drop out at grade three or four, unable to cope with the challenges, or because their labor is needed at home.

This general situation of marginalization of the communities is further aggravated by the continuing uncertainties of the ethnic conflict in Sri Lanka. Staff members have been murdered and kidnapped. A general malaise and demotivation characterizes staff attitudes. From a leadership point of view, a work environment of this nature may be approached in several ways. Rather than promoting a soft and lax line, we chose to challenge people to perform as professionals in spite of all their personal or social problems and adversities. It became necessary to launch fresh ideas and find ways of focusing people's attention on professional issues as a matter of mental hygiene, creating a sense of common purpose and achievement.

Conditions at the Preschools

The conditions at the preschools reflect the general situation of poverty described earlier. Motivation of the preschool teachers was low. Children spent most of their time sitting passively around the walls. There was some repetitive dancing and singing, but the quantity and quality of the general interaction between the preschool teachers and the children was minimal. In spite of their good intentions, they clearly lacked knowledge and were in need of training and professional guidance. To supplement this overview, a study in traditional childrearing practices was undertaken (Consortium, 1989). It confirmed the favorable attitudes that the poor in Sri Lanka hold toward preschool education and education in general. It also brought to light several problems related to parental attitudes. Children were not supposed to speak in the presence of adults. Some parents thought it impertinent if children asked questions. A box on the ear occurred frequently. Both parents and preschool teachers might refuse to allow children to play with new toys, because these could be destroyed. Some parents did not want their children to play with materials such as sand, water, or clay. Learning to read and write was the uppermost value held by the parents.

Training involves theory and practice—classroom work, observation of mediation and mediation with children in the preschool situation. Often preschool teachers are young girls with a grade six or seven education who would otherwise be unemployed. The coconut is the center of life in Sri Lanka.

Mediating in nature or with homemade materials is a prominent feature of the MLE program of Redd Barna. Utilizing whatever is available in the environment is a must, and seizing on opportunities for mediation in everyday situations is a principle.

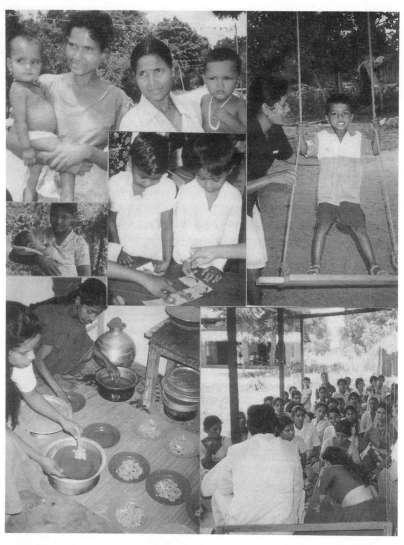

Nutritional status is not entirely as it should be. Involving parents and older siblings in preparation of a balanced meal, "Kola Kanda," and in active mediation are all part of the day's program.

This story, reported by one of our preschool teachers, illustrates the situation vividly.

> A boy who was a fairly normal pupil suddenly started to stammer and act differently. When the teacher discussed this with the mother, she said there might be a growth in the boy's throat. She took the boy for examination at the clinic, but the doctor said there was nothing physically wrong with him. The doctor requested that the preschool teacher inquire about the home situation. Sure enough, the visit revealed the cause. The father, a fisherman, used to come home drunk and beat the mother. In disgust and despair, she attempted to commit suicide by drinking insecticide, but was saved. The boy witnessed with horror his mother's suffering and started stammering. The preschool teacher helped to change the home situation and the boy returned to normal and stopped stammering.

> Such incidents are not uncommon in the preschools.

Searching for New Approaches

In light of this background, our attempts to reform the program started by searching for an appropriate child-development approach, rather than a community-development one. From the context of our work, it was clear that the educational approach would in this case have to meet the following criteria:

1. It should focus on the interaction between caregivers and poor children, and promote children's cognitive and emotional development, particularly enhancing flexibility of mind and the capacity to cope with stressful situations.
2. It should be conceptualized in a manner simple enough to communicate throughout an organization, utilizing the various levels and categories of staff members to create a child focus in all work with community members, and simple enough to be understood and used by the community members themselves.
3. It should fit within the cultural and environmental context of everyday life in the community.
4. It should not incur any extra costs beyond training, but be based on existing staff with the educational limitations they had (including staff of the then 103 preschools operating in Redd Barna project areas, some of whom had a level of formal education below grade seven).

In response to this, the MISC (More Intelligent Sensitive Child) approach was evaluated by Redd Barna leadership and staff members and found appropriate. There was, however, a discussion around the name, which appeared to have undesirable cultural implications. The more neutral, generic term, Mediated Learning Experience (MLE), was chosen instead, and has since been used consistently within Redd Barna.

A training program for all staff members was conceptualized. Its goals and overall implementation were seen in three phases:

Phase I—Training of all staff members, including accountants, clerks, and drivers in the skills of seeing, observing, and responding positively to children and upgrading the general quality of early childhood education in preschools through the MISC approach.

Phase II—Training of parents and/or caregivers in the five MLE criteria and related dimensions in early childhood education.

Phase III—Wider training and orientation for primary school teachers and other members of the community involved in education.

To some extent, the goals of Phase I and Phase II overlap informally and naturally in the everyday situation.

Training Strategy

Training was pivotal to the implementation of this program and seven senior staff members were sent to attend a MISC training seminar. On the basis of this seminar, staff acquired the basic theory and skills of the MISC approach and received documentation and tools to assist in developing their own program. Two master trainers were identified, one for each of the two main language groups of the country, Tamil and Singhalese. The master trainers developed the training curriculum for the preschool instructors and their assistants, taking into consideration the variability in formal-educational level and previous training of the caregivers, as well as variability in the local conditions of the educational settings. The senior staff were assigned research tasks such as (a) to assess and identify the kinds of mediation taking place in the preschools, and (b) to interview preschool teachers and mothers. The information and experience obtained through this preliminary research were used in developing the training program and its curriculum and as baseline data for later monitoring and evaluation of the preschools. Some baseline videos were made for the purpose of training and monitoring.

The following three overviews illustrate the implementation of the program in terms of objectives and training sequence. Some case studies are included to illustrate the effects of the MISC in terms of change of attitude and approach. The following overviews are based on a recent evaluation report (Ferdinando, 1991).

OVERVIEW 1: PROGRAM OBJECTIVES–PHASE I

The baseline survey revealed that the quality of Redd Barna Sri Lanka (RBSL) preschools was very poor, starting with the physical appearance and condition of the children and their school accommodation, and ending with the pedagogical insight and attitudes of the preschool teachers.

During Phase I our objective was to raise the overall quality of the preschools from very poor to average (according to our grading system). We realized that both the home and the preschool are important factors in the development of young children. However, since Redd Barna has a strong community-development network across the country, we decided to use the preschools as an entry point and reach the parents and the entire community during Phase II.

During Phase I our main objective was to train all RBSL senior staff, field staff, and all our preschool teachers, and to continue follow-up programs with them. Our specific goals were as follows:

- to enhance the quality of RBSL staff as supporters of the preschool teachers through supervision, monitoring, and evaluation of the general Early Childhood Development program, including the MISC component;
- to enhance the performance of the preschool teacher as an immediate caregiver as well as a primary caregiver;
- to enhance the quality of mediation provided by preschool teachers to the children;
- to enhance the quality of activities planned for preschool children;
- to enhance the creativity of the preschool teacher, particularly with regard to the use of environmental resources utilized when mediating to children;
- to identify and enhance the status of children with problems, (i.e., malnourished, physically handicapped, mentally and emotionally disturbed);
- to enhance parental participation in preschool activities and their responsibility for the preschool;
- to assist in developing societies of the Savecred[2] income-generating centers;
- to enhance the development of basic physical facilities in preschools.

Master Training Seminar
7 Senior Staff Members
_____ |

Training |
additional |
senior staff members

| Selection MLE training team --- → | Training middle-level and other --- → staff members | Training preschool teachers --- → | Informal discussion with parents' groups by MLE team and field staff |

↓   ↓

Introductory   Follow-up
training in batches   training
All staff members   in the field
2 weeks residential   project areas
at RB Training Center

↓

Outline Training Curriculum Based on the MISC Approach

Part I   Understanding the preschool teacher as a mediator

Part II   Understanding the child as a person

Part III Mediational Curriculum

1. Early emotional/expressive relationship between the mother and the child
2. Introducing five criteria of mediated learning
3. Preschool activities in an MLE way
4. Health and nutrition of preschool children

Methodology

Brief lectures—discussions—exercises—(individual and group)
Demonstrations—role plays—video films—transparencies—handouts
    workshop—preparing teaching/learning materials
Observations in other preschools
Evaluations (oral and written)

Objective: To extend more training on MLE and general upgrading of preschools
following the Introductory Training

Means: To carry out a follow-up through monthly correspondence exercises and
personal field visits.

Overall Approach

Monthly exercises mailed to teachers from RBSL office $----\rightarrow$	Follow-up training in the field $----\rightarrow$	Monitoring and evaluation by field staff
	$\downarrow$	$\downarrow$
Exercises 1 to 6 with guidelines	• Visit preschools • Make observations on teachers' practice of MLE • Discussions	• Feedback to teachers
• Introduction of activities for children in small groups (Time spent on each activity— fifteen to twenty minutes) • Play ideas, language skills, health messages etc., all presented in the MLE way, encouraging use of environmental resources.	• Reinforce and deepen the understanding/practice of MLE • Feedback of the exercises from RBSL office • Other aspects of upgrading the preschools • Evaluations • Identify pilot preschools in the field project areas	

The next few pages include an example of the follow-up training program
with instructions to the preschool teachers as well as the first exercise in
a series that was mailed to the preschools on a monthly basis. (Due to the
eruption of unrest in Sri Lanka, mailing substituted for some field visits).
These exercises consisted of a pictorial theme and a written guide, and
served to support and maintain motivation among the trainees while field
visits were interrupted. It proved successful in itself and continues to this
day as part of the follow-up field approach, along with direct preschool
observations and focused workshops. Emphasis was placed on curriculum
content available in the immediate environment: flora, fauna, food staples,
and customs. The idea is to use the existing cultural base, material, and

symbolic representations for the specific and enriched focus of MLE interactions that were integrated into the morning's activities.

The Redd Barna Sri Lanka Preschool Follow-Up Training Program

Objective: To extend more training on MLE to the 150 preschool teachers who have participated in the two-week introductory training on MLE and general upgrading of preschools in Colombo.

Overall Approach:
1.   Monthly exercises mailed to preschool teachers from Redd Barna Sri Lanka head office.
2.   Short training sessions carried out periodically on site.

Instructions for the Mailed Exercises:
1.   Every month a simple topic will be introduced.
2.   A set of lessons developed for each of the chosen topics, together with guidelines, will be sent to you.
3.   Spend about twenty minutes on each lesson.
4.   Every lesson should be presented using MLE criteria to create learning experiences for the children.
5.   Carefully preplan all lessons, following the MLE guidelines.
6.   When planning the lessons, include play activities and focus on language and social skills, and so on, as you have learned in the Introductory Training Program.
7.   Make use of your own creative ability when planning and implementing the exercises.
8.   When you mediate to children, use examples from the environment.
9.   Maintain a separate file for the follow-up training exercises.
10.   You need not return the completed exercises to the secretariat or project office. We will discuss them with you when we come to visit you.

It is difficult to travel when a civil war is going on. As follow up after the training courses, exercise books with examples of mediation were mailed to the participants. These were again followed up with field visits when the opportunity for travel came.

MLE EXERCISE I—THE STORY OF THE COCONUT

Name: .... Pre-School: ....

Date: .... No. of Children: ....

Location: ....

Approximate lesson time: 20 minutes

(Prepare the mediation according to this exercise guide BEFORE you carry it out with the children. All the work is to be kept in your own notebook for this purpose.)

1. What do you intend to mediate?
2. Where do you intend to mediate the topic?
   e.g., in the classroom, the compound, a paddy field,
   on a nature walk.
3. How many children do you intend to reach in this mediation?
   - one
   - a small group (5 to 8)
   - all the children
   - a combination of the above
4. How will the children experience this mediation?
   - by touching
   - by smelling
   - by hearing
   - by seeing
   - by tasting
   - by doing an activity, e.g., puzzle, sweeping the floor
   - a combination of the above
5. What will the children learn?
   e.g., shape, size, color, weight, difference in shapes
   or shades of color, a moral such as cooperation, the name
   of a flower, a feeling such as joy, better motor control.
6. Describe how you intend to mediate the topic applying the MLE criteria
   a) Focusing and Reciprocity:
   b) Naming and Meaning:
   c) Expanding:
   d) Praising:
   e) Helping to plan:

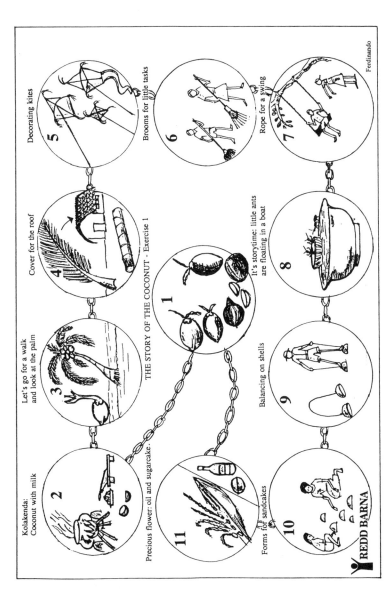

The Story of the Coconut: Sample Exercise 1. This drawing is based on an illustration in the MISC manual.

How Did the Children Respond to the Mediation?
(Complete this section AFTER you have finished the mediation with your preschool children.)

1. Were the children interested, bored, feeling distracted, attentive, etc.? Describe their reactions in your own words.
2. What questions did the children ask you? Try and list all of them.
3. Which part of your mediation do you think the children enjoyed best? Why? (See the drawing previous page. It offers ideas for mediating with or without a coconut at hand. Some or all of the five criteria can be included in the mediation.)

Two Case Studies

Training the teachers and establishing the practice of MLE in the existing preschools was the first step toward reaching the mothers and fathers. It provided a powerful demonstration and basis for the work with parents, grandparents, and siblings to be undertaken both by the preschool instructor and Redd Barna's other field staff.

SUNETRA NUGEPITIYA IN HANGURANKETA

Sunetra is one of the 150 preschool teachers who participated in the MISC project in Sri Lanka. She tells about her own experience and the effects of her training on her pupils.

I have been working as a preschool teacher since 1983. It is very correct if I say I conducted the preschool as a small classroom in the formal school during the period from 1983 to 1989, before I received the MISC training program of early childhood development. I really didn't have a proper understanding of the value of a preschool. I thought children come to my school to read, write letters, and numbers only. That was what the parents also wanted from me. So I did what they wanted. Parents did not like play activities in school or at home. They thought it was just a waste of time.

I did not allow children the freedom to play; even the little play I allowed, I structured the way I wanted. Even a drawing or a creative piece of work, I used to draw first on the blackboard or in their books and I expected the children to do it in the same way. I did not know the developmental stages of the child or that each child is a unique person. I was not aware of the fact that age differences play a big role in organizing activities. I just used to give work, mostly numbers, letters, to all the children and I used to hold the child's hand and force him to write. Parents wanted me to give maximum homework for children on numbers and letters. I still remember I gave long sentences to copy and difficult letters to write. Now I realize their older siblings must have done difficult homework I used to give. I was not aware of it, I used to make a big OK sign in their books.

I tried to discipline children to become very obedient by using very strict methods, but they became more and more stubborn. I sometimes got very angry, I remember, but I did not understand them, their needs, and how I can change them. Those days I thought a good preschool should have a big nice-looking building with painted walls, with painted tables and chairs, with expensive toys and materials. I never thought, free play with sand, water, mud, and imaginary and constructive games are good for children. I never allowed them to do so.

I didn't have a proper work plan. I really did not know that thousands and thousands of opportunities for children are found around the preschool in the natural environment, available for them to get learning experiences.

The valuable training changed me for the better. Now I really know the value of early years. I understand the child as a unique person. I can think of activities according to age differences and understand real needs and the rights of children. Now I know I really feel for children. The kindness, the love, the interest I have toward children are genuine feelings which come from my heart. I know how much time I invest on my preschool children, but I am happy about it.

I am proud of myself. I feel I am strong—I am confident—I can change little children for the better, even parents.

I now preplan my work. I have developed lots of toys/educational materials for children and I love to observe children. I realized the improvement in my mediation. I realized the dangerous effect of strict discipline on children.

I give opportunities to children to explore the environment. They ask nice, interesting questions. I give them enough time to think, to talk, which I didn't give earlier. During story time, some days the children tell stories and I listen. I give enough praise with warm feelings and explanations.

Earlier I used to neglect children who had problems, children who were isolated or withdrawn. But now I give them special attention. I have experienced that love, body contact, praise, kind words, warm feelings can do wonders with children who have problems. They develop positive emotions quickly.

I do not dream now of a preschool with painted walls, with expensive materials. I am equipped now with plenty of materials free of cost and I know what learning experiences the children can get from those.

My parents and my sisters are also interested in the school. My father is a carpenter. He has made an improvised see-saw, a wooden ladder for my school. I make use of the wood cuts, etc. for constructive games for the children.

Parents' participation has improved. Parental attitudes have improved. They prepare balanced meals for the children. They now do not hesitate to provide play materials for their children.

I am now quite better as a mediator.

JAYANTHA BANDARA (FOUR YEARS OLD)

Jayantha was first brought to my preschool by his mother, but then onwards he used to come with his older sister. Jayantha did not like to come to the classroom or play with other children. He used to sit on a stone step in the garden and just watch the road. He did not talk to anybody; he had a blank look. I talked but he did not respond. One day I gave him a ball and he took it, but did not talk. Then, everyday he came very early, before other children came and he wanted the big ball. He kept it till the end of the day. I did not know where to start with him until I went through the (MISC) training. It helped me understand Jayantha. I was inquisitive and I spent much time with him until his sister came to take him home. I used to talk and talk with him after school. I tried to be friendly with him, but he did not respond; not even a smile. But I did not give up. After one and a half months, he started responding. Earlier he refused the midday meal too, but I managed to take him inside and I introduced him to a little friend.

A few days later I observed him speaking only to that little friend; I was happy. I managed to send him home with the little friend as the friend too lives close to his house. Slowly Jayantha started talking. In the meantime, I visited his house and listened to his mother. According to her, the father was severely addicted to alcohol; he used to come home very late and hit her. She prepared dinner early and forced the children to sleep before father comes. Some days the children woke up and cried in fear. Early in the morning she sent the children to school before her husband got up. The children went to sleep in deep fear and got up in fear. They had no freedom at home. Jayantha slowly got friendly with me and I used to teach him little songs and encouraged him to recite them in front of his mother. I encouraged him to be polite to his father in the morning before he comes to school. It took a few months to change Jayantha and his home situation. I made frequent home visits, met the father, and encouraged him and the mother to come for the monthly meetings. I encouraged him to get involved in the preschool development work. Jayantha's father contributed his time happily and his attitude toward his family changed. I am happy now that Jayantha comes to school happily; he is talkative, active, very good in art and creative work. I am proud of him and of myself too.

Leena Swarnalatha's Story
This is the story of another preschool child, as told by her teacher Kalyani Indrani.

When Leena was an infant her mother committed suicide due to a problem with her husband. Leena lives now with her grandparents. They have told Leena that they are her parents. Leena's real father has remarried and lives in the same household, but the child is taught to believe he is her elder brother. The grandparents did not allow Leena to mix with other children in fear that some of them might reveal the truth about her real parents. When Leena came to the preschool she was very ruthless, fought with the other children, and did not want to listen to me. I knew the child's background and with my MLE approach I tried to win the attention and affection of the child.

I did not give up. After about six months Leena slowly turned to be more attentive and less aggressive.

Effects of the MISC on the Preschool Teachers

In a situation of warfare, one of the unexpected effects of the systematic MLE training was the improved mental hygiene of the staff members. They responded with enthusiasm to being addressed as professionals and were eager to demonstrate good performance in their preschools in spite of all adversity. The following is verbatim what some of them said during an evaluation:

> Sunethra: I have realized I am an important person for the preschool child. I have understood that children should be directed to be creative and that time should be allotted for them to think, explore, and get learning experiences.
>
> Indrani: I am happy about my self-image. Now I have a good understanding of the qualities of a preschool teacher.
>
> Lokumenike: After the course on MLE, I have confidence and strength to work in a more systematic way. I have learnt that mental and physical development of the child are equally important.
>
> Wasanthie: I have realized that I used a wrong approach—my weaknesses in dealing with children during the years I have been teaching. I am now able to understand children and their needs.
>
> Sriyani: As a preschool teacher I used to get angry sometimes with the children. Now I know it is important to mediate to them in a sympathetic way, like a mother. I feel there is a positive change in me after following the MLE program.
>
> Podimenike: As a woman I feel the training is beneficial to me for my future life. When I have my own children I will be able to bring them up to be healthy and intelligent. The training cannot be valued in money, as I gathered such a vast amount of knowledge.

The Cultural Implication

The MISC presents a powerful approach to childrearing. It has definite effects. It is bound to run into objections that it changes social mores and is culturally impervious. On the other hand, to argue that it is "culture-free" is hardly correct. It is, however, culturally amenable and adaptable. Only "nothing" is entirely culture-free. No idea, new technology, no health measure, no methodological approach introduced into one culture from another can be argued to be culture-free. For better or for worse, they have implications in the short or long term. The ethical task for those in development work is to attempt to assess what is "for better" and what is "for worse." Decisions and judgments have to be made based on values, social and economic analyses, and future implications, and these should be clearly stated in the principles, mandate, and approaches of any development organization. At this juncture in history, fostering capacities to cope with modernity may be as critical as authenticating cultural traditions. Both aspects should be addressed. The imperative consideration is that change is inevitable in the world reality of international capitalism and the communications industry. We cannot stem this tide; perhaps we can attempt to manage it humanely for some of the most vulnerable groups; perhaps we can go a little further by forging past, present, and future in the meaningful context of people's own culture so they become more effective agents of change. MLE is an approach to early childhood development that may start a process of generating such potentials. Through the practice of its five simple criteria in the situation of a collapse of caring capacity, a meaningful continuum of past, present, and future is reestablished in the child's mind. MLE that is concentrated in the five MISC criteria has the potential of cognitively and emotionally integrating the wisdom of tradition with the skills and capacity required to cope with modernity. Culture encompasses the material, linguistic, and spiritual foundation of people, which they use to manage their daily lives, to interpret their experience, and to raise their children. The material world of a culture is not separate from the spiritual realm. This is a dichotomy we make to satisfy our need to differentiate and define. Usually, the material base of a culture is infused with meaning, and everyday artifacts often are accorded different values when related to special events. Language is the medium that specifies and integrates culture, particularly by linking the past to the present. In Africa and elsewhere, the rich oral traditions in polite daily communication, public speaking, and storytelling testify to this.

Mediating from Tradition to Modernity

Based on our experience in conducting MISC training workshops in both Asia and Africa, it can be concluded that participants, most of whom were parents of young children, responded positively to the approach from an intellectual point of view, while at the same time absorbing it emotionally into their own cultural modes. Given tasks of mediation in role play between caregivers and "children" participants from Sri Lanka, Nepal, Ethiopia,

Sudan, Uganda, Kenya, Zimbabwe, and Mozambique, we resorted to a wide variety of ways of using their own proverbs, riddles, storytelling, dances, or cultural artifacts, from musical instruments to masks, whisks, mortars, clay pots, or combs. The general experience in early childhood education confirms children's need to identify with their own culture, but it also underscores in these times of rapid change the need to mediate meaning beyond that culture. MLE training in the tradition-rich cultures of Asia and Africa needs to integrate this particular point and make it more explicit. An example will illustrate the case. The task may be to mediate the concept of "light" to the child. For an adult caregiver from Africa this story from the folklore will easily come to mind:

> Once an old father who wanted to test his three sons said, "Here is one shilling for each of you; go to the market and buy something to fill my room." The oldest boy thought this was an easy task. He went to the market and bought straw. The second son, who also thought it was easy, went and bought feathers. The youngest boy sat down and thought for a long time and said to himself, "What can it be that costs only one shilling and fills a room? What is it my father wants?" He thought very hard. Then he went to the market and bought a candle and a match. The father rewarded the youngest son. When the light filled his room, he was so pleased that he gave the youngest son all his land and cattle.

Mediating such wisdom from the past is certainly a fundamental cultural requirement, but there is also a need to mediate and expand meaning as it relates to a concrete present, and to the advent of modernity:

> Have you seen the poles and wires along the main road? They carry electricity. Soon we shall have light all over the village. We shall go and buy a light bulb together. When the bulb is connected to the wire, the electricity makes it glow like an ember. That is how we get light.

And there is a need to regulate behavior:

> Electricity can also be dangerous. It can kill people like lightning. You must never climb the poles and touch the wires.

To illustrate the point further we are including two training exercises based on traditional objects commonly found in the African village environment.

We have found these particularly useful in spurring dialogues or role play among the trainees.

Exercise 1

Look at this comb and bear in mind the hair dressing salons in the towns. How could a caregiver expand on meaning? How could the comb be used to mediate feelings of competence?

Create a dialogue between two children and their mother or mother's sister.

Exercise 2

Look at this finger piano *(mbira)* and bear in mind radio or tape decks. How could a caregiver expand on meaning? How could feelings of competence be included?

Create a role play between grandmother and grandchildren. You may include also other characters if you wish.

Considering the common experience that in poor traditional communities mediation of meaning and regulation of behavior tend to be predominant, we promote training exercises that emphasize mediated expansion of meaning and feelings of competence. Above all, poor children are starved for praise.

Certainly all cultures are mediated from adults to children, but this should not imply just incessant repetition of whatever wisdom was gained by the forefathers. Children need the mental capability of coping with the events and adversities of their future, particularly the feelings of competency and agency. Interviews with community development workers from the aforementioned countries about positive and negative aspects of traditional childrearing revealed the following information.

A prominent negative feature of parent–child interaction was that parents rarely verbalized praise directly to a child. Whereas displeasure with children's performance would be expressed through reprimands, satisfaction would, at best, be expressed by silence. Sometimes praise would be given by talking favorably about a child when he/she was not present. Fathers in polygamous marriages would frequently favor the children of the preferred wife and would generally not pass on to their children the knowledge they had regarding social issues. On the positive side, the trainees pointed out that parents trusted their children a great deal by giving them work tasks and responsibilities, such as conveying confidential messages. Parents would give small gifts to their children as incentives for good behavior or doing well on exams. They would frequently use traditional stories to teach them.

On the background of the general observation mentioned earlier, namely, that tradition-rich cultures are also rich in mediation of meaning and regulation of behavior, but poorer in expanding meaning and mediating feelings of competence, there is reason to discuss the issue of praise extensively with trainees. It is too simplistic to assume that traditional childrearing is unenlightened in this respect. Yet it is hardly disputable that children are in need of good self-images and feelings of agency. An analysis and discussion on another level is required. Geertz (1983), using the following statement, intimates the direction in which we should focus our attention:

> The Western conception of the person as a bounded, unique, more or less integrated motivational and cognitive universe, a dynamic center of awareness, emotion, judgment, and action organized into a distinctive whole and set contrastively both against such wholes and against its social and natural background, is, however incorrigible it may seem to us, a rather peculiar idea within the context of the world's cultures. (p. 25)

The high-performing individual, with his/her uniqueness as a person, is a notion that has evolved probably quite exclusively in Western culture. In the West it is desirable to compete with others and be the best. The disciplines of pedagogy and psychology, including the MLE approach and the ideology of individualism, have all emerged from the core of that civilization, the Judeo-Christian tradition. Among the Abaluya in Eastern Kenya it is rather a shame to be better than others. The community expects a person to overcome weaknesses through her/his own efforts, but if one has an exceptional talent, displaying it should be contained. It is not right to make others feel inferior. A good person is a person who competes not with others but with him/herself to become better. There is a price to pay for the harmony and survival of the community as a whole. This is so not only in the Abaluya tribe. It is remarkable that in Swahili and other Bantu languages there is no word corresponding to the notion of the *unique individual* in English. Some further thought should be devoted to these issues.

THE POWER OF THE CHILD

Our task is to facilitate opportunities for parents, families, and communities to voice their concern over issues concerning their children and to articulate the solutions they wish to implement to resolve these issues. Our task is to strengthen the capacities people already have to rear their children. However, it is very naive to think that under the extreme stresses of poverty and modernity this will happen on a large scale without the presence of an organized effort to facilitate and mediate the process. It is true that parents would always do more for their children—if they only could! The issue is that they so frequently cannot. Faith in people alone is not enough, because the presence and pressure of other powers are so overwhelming. Yet, perhaps it is wrong to emphasize always the vulnerability of the child. The child is in fact very powerful and controls to a large extent his/her own environment. Fairly recent research (Oudenhoven, 1992) indicates that babies, for example, enhance their own chances of survival by *de facto* preventing the mother from becoming pregnant. There is evidence that mothers who breastfeed their baby on demand do not get pregnant as long as they allow suckling, whereas mothers who breastfeed on a fixed schedule do. In other words, the baby controls the mother's hormone production, preventing her fertilization. The fact that babies also control and shape the behavior of their parents is evident for any concerned observer. There are many good reasons to believe that given thoughtful responses to their endeavors, children may also have the power to revive and unite communities.

ACKNOWLEDGMENT

Acknowledgment is due to our Sri Lankan colleagues and master trainers, Malini Ferdinando and Getsie Shanmugam, with whom we trained colleagues in Africa. Our master trainer in Africa is Lucilia Salbany.

NOTES

1. The authors have been in charge of Regional Office Africa for Norwegian Save the Children–Redd Barna since 1989. The MISC program in Sri Lanka was initiated in 1988. The opinions expressed in this chapter are ours and do not necessarily reflect the views of our organization. The chapter is based mostly on our experience in Sri Lanka, where the program has progressed quite far. Also included are examples from our African experience with trainees from Ethiopia, Kenya, Mozambique, Sudan, Uganda, and Zimbabwe. Throughout we use the acronym, MLE (mediated learning experience), although it is the MISC approval our programs practice. This designation was chosen by our participants themselves and we like to be consistent with their wish.

2. Savecred is a savings, credit, and income-generation scheme for women in Redd Barna project areas. The point of the scheme is to make the preschools sustainable through regular savings in a Children's Welfare Fund. The money is used for payment of preschool teachers' salaries, equipment, materials, and a supplementary meal during school hours.

10 UPGRADING THE QUALITY OF EARLY CHILDHOOD EDUCATION: SWEDEN

Ingrid Pramling

SOCIAL BACKGROUND

In Sweden there is a long tradition of early childhood education, because a major part of the responsibility for preschool children has been assumed by society. Today, parents share fifteen months' paid parental leave from the time of birth, and they can also look after a sick child thirty days a year, paid by the social welfare system. Most preschool children are involved in some kind of early childhood education program because around 90% of the parents of preschool children work outside the home. Of the three year olds, 42% attend day-care centers. However, Swedish early childhood education, which means both day care and kindergarten, is viewed as full-day or part-time *preschool*. This implies that we have the same official state guidelines (Socialstyrelsen, 1987) for both kinds of settings and that the same level of education should be provided by the staff working there. Both nursery assistants (with an upper-secondary-school education) and preschool teachers (with a university degree) work in these settings.

In Sweden, as in the rest of the world, early childhood education programs are developed mainly with older preschool children, aged four to six years, in mind (Johansson, 1992) and there is only limited knowledge of how to care for younger infants and toddlers. Sweden is one of the European countries in which the birthrate is increasing most rapidly (Kommissionen for de Europaeiske Faelbsskaber, 1990), which in combination with the acceptance of day care as a developmentally appropriate place to bring up a child, has resulted in an increasing number of younger children in preschool. The lack of knowledge and methods for good education and care for children in this youngest age group has led to some problems in recruiting preschool teachers to work specifically with them. During the last ten to fifteen years, different ways of solving this recruitment problem have been attempted. One attempt, and the most prevalent, has been to start sibling groups (age one to seven years) or extended sibling groups (into which school children are also integrated). Groupings of this type have decreased in popularity in recent years for various reasons, including the overrepresentation of younger children in the groups, the difficulties faced by staff in finding an appropriate program for every age group, and the partial change in ideology—from socialization during the 1970s to education today.

THE PROJECT

Having studied different intervention programs, a developmental psychologist, Kerstin Palmerus and myself, decided to apply the MISC (More Intelligent and Sensitive Child) program in Swedish toddler groups. Klein's (1989) program seemed appropriate for developing the staff's competence in mediation and communication with young children. One of the questions we had to face immediately was how to introduce the objective of the program. We could never present the MISC program to preschool staff as a way to develop the child's sensitivity and intelligence within early childhood education; intelligence tests of all kinds are very rarely used in Sweden, nor is the notion of intelligence. The philosophy in Swedish preschools is that education and care are closely related; the focus in preschool is on the child as a whole, which is to say, socially, emotionally, physically, and cognitively. Play and creativity are viewed as important aspects of the preschool curriculum, whereas academic subjects are viewed more often as related to school content. Work in preschool is generally more child-centered in contrast to school activities that are often teacher-centered (Pramling, 1991). Thus, it was expected that Swedish educators would be suspicious of any program designed to enhance the intelligence of young children.

With this background in mind, we tried to develop the first three categories in the MISC program into six, so that teacher-centered and child-centered intervention became distinguishable. We also separated the last two categories into four. Thus the categories of mediation were as follows (Palmerus, Pramling, & Lindahl, 1991):

1a   Intentionality and reciprocity—the adult initiates or leads the interaction.

1t   Intentionality and reciprocity—the toddler leads or initiates the interaction.

2n   Meaning by naming

2q   Meaning by questioning

3a   Transcendence—provided by the adult

3c   Transcendence—provided by the child

4	Feeling of competence—praising the toddler
4e	Feeling of competence—explaining, motivating
5c	Regulation of behavior—commanding
5e	Regulation of behavior—explaining why

Our basic assumption was that the more an adult is able to understand a child's intentions and feelings, the better she/he will be able to meet the child's needs through an appropriate interaction. Thus, we emphasized throughout the project the significance of the child's initiative and the need to interpret the child's intentions; that is, we constantly try to take the child's perspective.

AIMS

The aim of this intervention study was to improve the quality of mediation in the day care of young children, to increase the psychological and educational knowledge of day-care staff regarding the quality of mediation, and to develop the content and methods appropriate for mediational interactions with toddlers in day care. We intended to *increase the staff's awareness of young children's development and needs, as well as their awareness of their own behavior.*

SUBJECTS AND SETTINGS

The three day-care centers we worked with were all situated in a suburb of Sweden's second largest city, Gothenburg. The population of this city consists mainly of workers and immigrants, most of whom live in apartments in high-rise buildings. The proportion of people living on social welfare in these areas is high as compared with other areas of the city. Two groups of children that participated in the intervention, Group A and Group V, belong to rather large day-care centers with a total of four or five groups; the third group, J, was situated in a separate location in the grounds of an apartment building. Group J started operating at the onset of the project, whereas the other two groups were already well established. Table 10.1 shows the numbers of children and staff in the groups.

TABLE 10.1: DURATION OF PARTICIPATION IN THE GROUPS

Groups	Number of children	Age (years)	Preschool teachers	Nursery assistants
A	14	1–4	2	2
V	14	1–3	0	4
J	16	1–4	2	3

All staff members were interviewed individually at the beginning of the project and nineteen months later, at the end of the project. The interview dealt with their earlier experience of working with toddlers, their expectations of the project, their knowledge of child development, their tasks as caregivers and educators, and their attitudes toward their work.

As an introduction to the project, the staff attended a one-week "condensed" course that covered theories and empirical findings concerning children's perceptual, cognitive, emotional and social development, and information about the Swedish "preschool program" (Socialstyrelsen, 1987). Finally, the intervention program MISC was introduced (Klein, 1989).

Every fourth week the interaction between children and every staff member was video recorded and analyzed later in group meetings conducted for every group of workers in their own educational settings. The analysis was made in relation to the criteria of MISC and to the content and organization of the recorded interactions. When the video recordings were discussed with the staff, positive mediational behaviors were identified, explained, and reinforced. We also discussed different possible ways of mediating in the situations seen and how to meet the children's intentions even better. Throughout this entire process of video analysis, we focused both on the adults' interaction with an individual child and on their interaction with a group of children.

This presentation does not focus on the question of how children develop, but rather on how the adults who work with the children develop.

RESULTS

The results were analyzed in terms of the staff's awareness and attitudes, expressed in the interviews, and in their observed behavior. These results were also compared with a later study (Larsson, 1993) in which comparable day-care groups were video recorded and studied using the same observation methods as in the present study. The preschool staff studied in the later investigation was not exposed to the MISC program.

The Staff's Awareness and Attitudes

There were differences between the staff members with regard to their awareness of children's behavior, their attitudes toward them, and their own role as caregivers; however, their general educational views were similar.

CHARACTERISTIC OPINIONS AND ATTITUDES OF THE STAFF PRIOR TO MISC TRAINING

- They had high expectations that they would become better able to care for young children following the MISC training.

- Care and routines are the main tasks in dealing with young children.
- It is necessary to compensate young children for the stimulation and affection they cannot get at home.
- The main objective of child care is to help the children feel safe and adjust well to the day-care center.
- It is more important to help children form positive social relations than to teach them any other skills.
- Care is the most important task and if there is any time left, it can be used for education.
- 50% of the staff found it difficult to vary their behavior in relation to individual needs of different children (Palmerus & Pramling, 1991).

These opinions represent the general attitudes and thoughts of staff members working with young children in the country as a whole. I must also emphasize that the views expressed here do not represent the official guidelines, in which care and education are of equal importance. When the staff members think about education, they probably think of the more teacher-centered activities used in working with older children, and because of this they emphasize "care" in working with younger children. They also emphasize social relationships, which have been shown to be among the behaviors most affected by day care (Matlock & Green, 1990). The staff's view reflects their problems in dealing with individuals within a group and their need for a program appropriate for this age group.

ATTITUDES EXPRESSED BY THE STAFF FOLLOWING THE PROJECT

When the staff members were interviewed following termination of the MISC intervention, they expressed the following attitudes and thoughts:

- The observation and guidance period was a positive experience that has given the staff a broader scope for looking at toddlers' needs and skills.
- It became easier to cooperate with other staff members, because their ways of thinking about the program for younger children became more consistent and synchronized.
- Routine activities were used in a more stimulating way, which meant that education and care became more integrated.
- Staff and parents fulfilled different roles. It is well known among early childhood educators that staff members have problems in distinguishing between their role as mothers and their role as caregivers in a day-care setting (Caldwell, 1989). Following the intervention, parents became more

emotionally attached to their children, whereas staff members felt more free to enhance the cognitive or social development of the children and followed more specific objectives of interaction with them. The contribution of the staff to children's emotional development remained important, but they recognized now their role as educators of the young child.

- Following the intervention, staff members expressed their wish to influence development and learning in a positive way, and felt they had gained some knowledge about ways to do it.
- Staff members perceived themselves as mediators, enhancing the development of the children and helping to "open their eyes" to their surroundings.
- The relationship between care and education was perceived now as a function of the quality of interaction with the children throughout the day. *Everything could be done in an educational way.* This conclusion meant that the staff now, to a large extent, let the children do things in their own way, that is, arrange the table, dress, tidy up the toys before lunch, and follow their activities with enriching mediation.
- All staff members became more aware of the reasons for their behavior. They also stressed how they started to organize things differently in order to individualize, namely, to be able to meet the needs of individual toddlers, more adequately. They found themselves generally more involved.
- All staff members expressed the benefits of watching themselves in video recorded films, and how the opportunity of reexperiencing educational situations gave them a wider view of what was happening (Palmerus & Pramling, 1991).

In summary, the staff members expressed a marked change in thoughts and attitudes following the intervention. They felt that they had become more involved and had acquired the ability to utilize routines and everyday situations in order to enhance their mediation. They also seemed more satisfied, because the conflict between working on a group level and with the individual children had to a certain extent been resolved. In addition, they expressed something that we have been able to observe, namely, that groups of children were reorganized into smaller groups with their own staff. The staff felt the need to structure the children's day in a way that gave them opportunities to interact continuously with every child, which meant that throughout most of the day they kept children in smaller groups, with one adult, instead of all children together with the entire staff.

Effects on the Staff's Behavior
The video recordings of the interactions between the children and the staff

were coded according to the MISC criteria (Klein, 1989) by an independent observer who was not involved in the project. A note was made of each minute in which a certain category appeared on the film. The percentage of coded minutes in a sequence was calculated for each category. The analysis included comparisons between staff members with regard to mean frequencies of appearance of mediational behaviors. In addition, the mean of the first third of the observations was compared with the mean of the last third of the observations because some staff members had been absent on some occasions (one-third could include three to four observations). The general overall finding was that *the children in the three groups were involved to a far greater extent in interaction with adults at the end of the project than at the beginning. The general trend for the staff was to become more able to take the child's perspective and get the child to think, reflect, and verbalize.*

Significant variations were found between the individual teachers with regard to the frequencies of interaction in the different mediational categories, and with regard to mediation provided to different groups of children.

Intentionality and Reciprocity

Let us begin to look at the variation in the staff's capacity to follow the children's initiative as evaluated by the observational category of "intentionality and reciprocity" (see Figure 10.1). J, A, and V represent the different groups, and the numbers 1–5 represent the different adults in the groups. The adults differed with regard to the frequency with which they followed the children's initiative prior to the MISC intervention. Variations remained following the intervention. One can see, however, changes in both directions, toward more or fewer responses to the child's initiatives. A group trend in the direction of these differences can be noted in Figure 10.1 and more clearly in Figure 10.2a.

We can see in Figure 10.2a that following the intervention, children

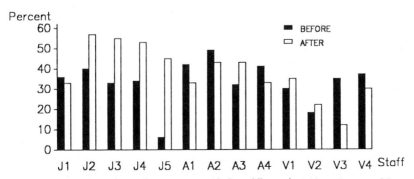

Figure 10.1. "Intentionality and reciprocity," with the toddler as the initiator (category 1t)

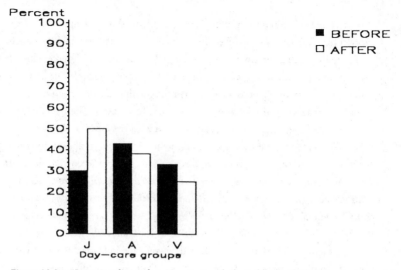

Percent

Figure 10.2a. "Intentionality and reciprocity," with the toddler as the initiator (category 1t)

in Group J are involved in more child-initiated communication as compared to children in Groups A and V. The differences between the groups appear to be greater at the end than at the beginning of the project.

When the number of instances of "Intentionality and Reciprocity" with the adult taking the initiative is analyzed, a trend opposite to that found in relation to the child-initiated interactions is noted. Group V has the highest percentage (91%), whereas Group J has the lowest (70%) of staff-initiated interactions at the end of the project. There are many possible explanations for this finding. The staff in Group V has worked together for ten years, while group A started working together only at the onset of the project. The staff members in Group V were all nursery assistants who did their best to "teach" children. Teaching to them meant initiating rather than following children's initiations. A third explanation could be related to the fact that when the staff became better able to listen to the children, they decreased their own initiative taking.

Mediating Meaning

Based on the analysis of the video recorded adult–child interactions, it became obvious that adults talk a lot with young children—it seems as if they constantly name and label things. Differences between the groups with regard to the category of "Mediating Meaning" through naming (category 1n) ranged between 80% and 90%, and the observed change following the intervention was minor. Group A changed the most, almost 10%, which is

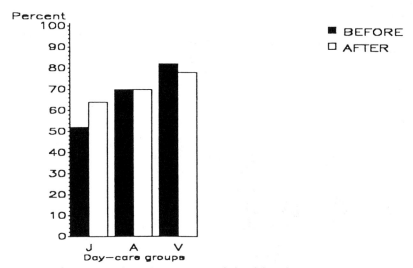

Percent

■ BEFORE
□ AFTER

Figure 10.2b. "Intentionality and reciprocity," with the adult as the initiator (category 1t)

probably due to their particular situation as a newly organized group with more children and adults than the other groups, and their initial lower level of mediation.

It seems that adults not only talk a lot with the children, but they also present them with many questions that invite them to be active and give meaning to objects, situations, relations, and so on.

Transcendence

Expanding communication beyond the situation "here and now" was one of the categories for which the largest differences between individual staff members were found prior to the MISC project, both for the adults and the children as the ones initiating the transcendence. For J5 it was practically zero, at the onset of the project as compared with V2, for whom it appeared in about 54% of the interactions with children. Staff members J3, V2, and V4 showed more extended interactions with the children as the transcenders at the beginning of the project than at the end of it. This is interesting, because if we look at this category but focus on the adults as the ones who expand, explain, or generalize from the situation "here and now" (category 3a), all these three teachers are the most active and tell the children a lot. These three staff members have taken the role of being teacher.

In general, we can see from Figures 10.3a, and 10.3b that transcendence increases, both with staff being the ones who expand and with children doing it in response to questions posed by adults. The only exception

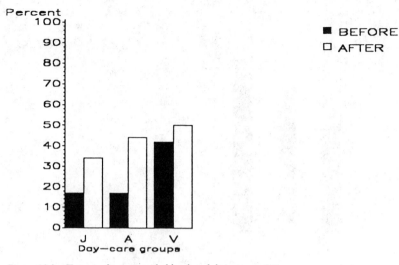

Figure 10.3a. Transcendence provided by the adult (category 3a).

to this general trend was found for Group V. In this group the frequency of adults' transcendence increases while the children initiate transcendence less frequently.

The extent to which it is possible to invite the children to be transcenders depends partly on the children's age and ability. But at each age level, adults can take a reflective approach in their communication with in-

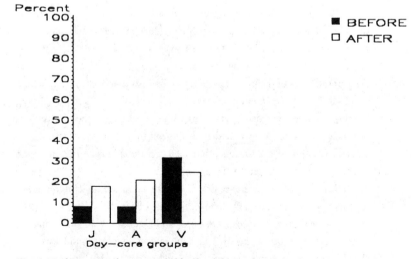

Figure 10.3b. Transcendence provided by the child (category 3r).

fants and toddlers. This means that for very young children, the staff can both ask and answer age-appropriate questions.

I believe that the category of "Transcendence" is the most important in the MISC program. It is by thinking and reflecting in cooperation that the foundations for later metacognitive awareness are developed (Pramling, 1989). To give children opportunities to think and reflect about themselves and the world around them is probably the best educational investment that can be made.

It is also with regard to this category that the staff's competence can be evaluated. It takes a lot of knowledge, affect, and skill to continue a dialogue and transcend with young children. It is definitely not only a question of verbal communication, but also communication at all levels. To keep the reciprocity in an interaction, transcendence takes all the adults' attention and psychological engagement. *One has to be totally there in the situation to go beyond it!* It also demands high levels of matching between adults' intentions and children's abilities, needs, and immediate intentions.

Mediating Feelings of Competence

Praising children seems to be very unusual in Swedish day-care centers, as we can see in Figure 10.4a. Praise may be given in many different ways, but in our analysis we have differentiated between a mechanical response, like saying: "Good boy," and the more expanded category in which adults explain the reason for praise or motivate the children by going into a dia-

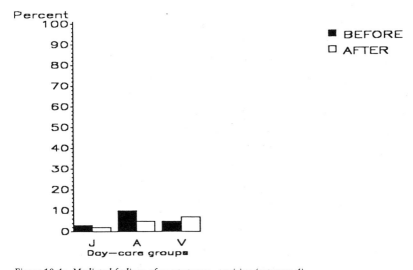

Figure 10.4a. Mediated feelings of competence—praising (category 4).

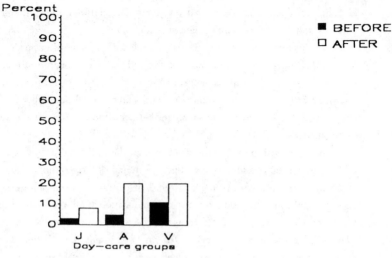

Figure 10.4b. Mediated feelings of competence with explanations (category 4e).

logue with them. Praise increased following the project, not the mechanical praise, but rather providing explanations or motivating the children (see Figure 10.4b).

It is important to explain what children do well and praise them in order to reinforce specific behaviors. But in our study, this category was noted only when adults verbalized praise. There is, however, nonverbal feedback and praise that is as important (i.e., to engage in the children's world, to cooperate, to smile, to widen your eyes, to clap your hands). Such endorsement was not picked up as "Mediating Feelings of Competence" in our observations; it was difficult to observe in the video recordings as it demands that the camera focus on the adult's face. It is easier to hear if an adult says: "Now you did a really good job, Peter," than to notice that an adult smiles and winks at a child in secret understanding.

The finding that we, in Sweden, do not praise our children may be viewed as an expression of a cultural characteristic. Reinforcement is frequently perceived by adults as a means of encouraging children to seek appreciation rather than to function because of interest in the task. I also think that the basic ideology in Swedish day care is that children must be allowed to try out their capacities on their own before any adult intervention is allowed.

Regulation of Behavior

"Regulation of Behavior" is another category of interaction that was infrequently observed in our sample of Swedish day-care groups; however, it in-

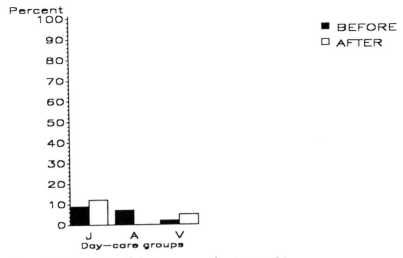

Figure 10.5a. Regulation of behavior—commanding (category 5c)

creased following the intervention, particularly regulation with explanation (see Figure 10.5b). As shown in Figure 10.5a, regulation of behavior by command was not seen in Group A by the end of the project.

The category of "Regulating Behavior with Explanation" was observed infrequently, but following the intervention, adults increased the frequency of explaining their behavioral regulations to the children. This cat-

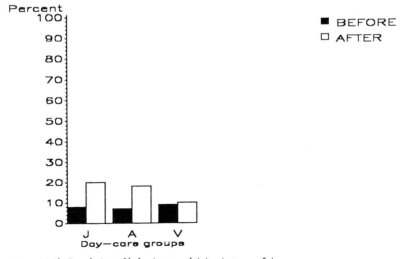

Figure 10.5b. Regulation of behavior—explaining (category 5e)

egory may be seen in qualitatively different ways. Sometimes, regulation of a young child's behavior needs neither command nor explanation; for example, motor regulation alone is sufficient when an adult just puts his/her own hand over a boy's hand and helps him cut his potatoes, to make it possible for him to continue eating. Eye contact or a smile could at times be equally efficient in regulating a child's behavior.

The MISC program is said to be culturally independent (Klein, 1989). However, the utilization of the mediational criteria is an expression of the culture. We have seen examples of it in this study. The child-centered approach and transcendence were the categories that were most valued by the Swedish project leaders, and these were the categories in which the staff demonstrated most progress.

A Comparison Study

Larsson (1993) video recorded three groups of children and their day-care staff. She video recorded every staff member three times for about twenty minutes each, with one week between the observations. Her observations were coded in the same way as those in the study described before.

Her results show the same pattern of individual differences as presented earlier. It is interesting to note that there was no significant difference between the groups from the MISC intervention study and the groups in Larsson's study with regard to the category "intentionality and reciprocity." The variations between the groups, however, were larger in Larsson's study than in the intervention study.

For the "Mediating Meaning," there was a small difference in favor of the intervention group. Two of Larsson's groups were age-integrated, and in these there was a lower frequency of mediating meaning than in the rest of the groups. The fact that young children in the sibling groups got less communication with adults than older children was noticed by Lindahl (personal communication), who reports that adults talk to the older children but hug the younger ones.

The most significant differences between the groups in Larsson's study and the group in our intervention study were for the categories of transcendence, both with regard to the adults' initiating and expanding the communication and to the children's initiating or responding to such initiations. This finding is in agreement with the fact that the categories related to transcendence were the ones that changed most following the intervention.

With regard to the category of "Mediated Feelings of Competence without Explanation," the frequencies reported were low for all groups, both before and after the mediation, and the variation between the groups was small. However, with regard to adults' explaining their praise, higher frequencies were found in our intervention groups. This was also one of the categories that changed most following the intervention.

The frequency of "Regulation of Behavior without Explanation," was slightly different for the groups observed by us as compared with the ones observed by Larsson. All three groups in Larsson's study demonstrated a higher frequency of "Mediated Regulation of Behavior" than the intervention groups. Although this category increased following the intervention, Larsson's staff used this mediational category more frequently than our groups.

In another evaluation of the MISC program carried out in Norway, the "Regulation" category was reported more frequently than in our study (Aamlid, 1992). The only explanation I can suggest for this finding is that in our study, we focused mainly on the children, and on their intentions; it could very well be that the adults interpreted this as a signal not to regulate the children's behavior or, in other words, not to be "pushy" or regulate the children's behavior.

Although the pedagogy in Swedish early childhood education is extensively child centered, our experience is that child centering is not based on a genuine knowledge and understanding of the children's "life-world," on what children intend to do or express based on their experience; rather, it is more an expression of withholding oneself as an adult.

DISCUSSION

It may be generally stated that in Sweden young children are involved in a lot of interactions with adults in day-care centers. All the same, one has to be aware of the variation in quality of interaction in Nordic day-care centers (Aamlid, 1991; Diderichsen, 1992) as elsewhere in the world.

The staff in our study became both more aware of children's intentions and needs, and acted accordingly by allowing the children to take a major role in the interactions. The children, in other words, became more active in the communication. One has to bear in mind that there is a slight tendency for the less-educated nursery assistants to use the more mechanical aspect of the mediational categories, and become "teachers" who want to teach children, contrary to the better-educated preschool teachers who are less likely to do so (Palmerus & Pramling, 1991). To *mediate mechanically* means to label and talk just for the sake of doing so, without really trying to find out what is occupying the children's minds. This means that the better educated child-care workers are, the more they will learn from working with the MISC program, at least if they have the intention of involving the children as the most active partners in the process of mediation (Pramling, 1989).

By focusing on the fine differentiation of mediational categories, the staff became better able to observe children and understand their intentions and needs. Their observations of children and their own reactions led to educational implications, such as reorganizing their work in time and space to make it possible to reach every child through interaction. We also noticed that some of the staff members were able simultaneously to use different mediational categories in an interaction with a group of children, whereas others could only cope with one child at a time.

Our day-care staff has learned to take greater responsibility for their own behavior and to provide children with more opportunities to develop.

When analyzing video recordings, staff members have learned a lot about the need to use appropriate materials in their interactions with the younger children. They also learned about the importance of children's play. It was easy to see in the videotapes that children's play developed both quantitatively and qualitatively when the adults, guided by the children, participated in the play. Similar findings were reported earlier by Vedeler (1987). The video recordings and their analyses were a very powerful educational tool. To observe oneself in cooperation with one's colleagues is thrilling and demanding. The staff members almost always recognized their own "mistakes" on the video. In the beginning they were ashamed to see their "mistakes," but as time went by, they learned to laugh at them and discuss alternatives.

If we look at the largest changes in frequencies of the mediational categories that occurred during the project and compare those with Larsson's findings, it becomes clear that the largest gain following the intervention was found in relation to category 3, when either the child or the adult expands the situation beyond the one at hand. In other words, the staff became better able to carry out a dialogue in communication with toddlers.

The change in organization—to smaller working groups in which one staff member is responsible for "her children"—is a very important result of the MISC intervention. This can be seen in light of Larsson's study, in which the younger children in her age-integrated groups received less communication with one adult than did those in our sample. In other words, to work with the MISC program presupposes an organization in which the staff gets opportunities to communicate with every single child. Roupp, Travers, Glantz, and Corlen (1979) showed that staff cooperated and communicated less with children in a larger group than in a smaller group, although the child–adult ratio was the same in both of these groups.

In the sibling groups there is a lot of interaction with mediational potential going on between children. This mediation should also be recognized in the MISC program. Piaget (1973) described two different socialization processes in a child's life. The socialization process occurring between an adult and a child always represents a hierarchical order, whereas socialization between peers represents equality. One process cannot replace the other.

CONCLUSIONS

Young children learn about people and things by observing, listening, imagining, experimenting, turning things back and forth, throwing, tasting, and so on. All these aspects should be recognized when a program for young children is planned. However, the most important aspect of such education must be the emotional and verbal communication between the adult and the children. It is also important for the adult to learn how all everyday activities can be utilized in interaction with children. I am even more convinced, after this project, that staff members working with infants and toddlers need to learn to understand "the child's world," as it appears in the day-care setting (Lindahl & Pramling, 1992). The more an adult knows about every child's specific situation in day care, the lower the risk of applying the MISC program mechanically, with the adults using the mediational categories without a genuine involvement in the child's world.

When one interacts with a child, one influences the child's feelings, thoughts, and social relations. It is important to look at education for young children not only as a process for making them both sensitive and intelligent, but also as giving them opportunities to be creative and develop different kinds of skills.

Quality education for young children must include quality mediation. But the interaction must also have a content that can be of help in the child's social, emotional, and cognitive development. The MISC program can serve as a fertile ground for the development of programs for young children. I am sure that staff members will learn a lot, both about their children and their own roles by analyzing video recordings in line with this program.

What is typical of the Swedish culture and of the way Swedes bring up their children? Sweden is the only country in the world with a law forbidding parents to spank their own children. This has probably led to a kind of respect for the child as an individual with his/her own rights. From this perspective, however, there is a risk of becoming too vague as an adult in bringing up children. But there is also a greater potential for letting children be somebody in their own right, from the very beginning. A Nordic approach to enhance children's development is to emphasize independence (Hundeide,

1991). To become an independent person often means giving children opportunities to try things out by themselves. Adults are expected to be there and be supportive but not to push the child in any direction. I think the results of the mediation in the groups of young children that I have presented here represent these values of our culture and possible ways for both cultural transmission and enhancement of child development.

11 RAISING CARING AND COMPETENT CHILDREN IN THE UNITED STATES: FLORIDA

Martha L. Coulter

Despite impressive gains in technological advances in recent years, the United States lags behind most developed countries in almost every indicator of maternal and child health and family well-being. Although some national data are not directly comparable between the United States and individual countries, the conclusions of all comparative studies indicate that outcomes in Europe and other developed nations are generally better. Each year approximately 3.7 million women—about 7% of all U.S. women of childbearing age—have a baby. About four in ten of these women are unemployed or work only part-time and more than one-fourth of them are poor: that is, they have a family income below the federal poverty level. This results in about 12 million children in poverty. New census data indicate that almost one in ten persons are now receiving food stamps, a national program to assist poor families in purchasing food. Crime rates are increasing, especially related to drug traffic and use. Homicide is now the most frequent cause of death among black teenage boys.

National infant mortality rates remain high. The U.S. rate per 1,000 births declined only slightly, from 12.6% in 1980 to 10.0% in 1988. A comparison of 1984 rates with European data indicates that fifteen European nations had better rates at that time (Miller, 1987). Disparities between blacks and whites and between poor and nonpoor persist. Low birth-weight rates, a second critical indicator, describe the number of babies who are born weighing less than 5¹/₂ pounds or 2,500 grams (out of every 1,000 live births). About 7% of all newborns weigh less than 2,500 grams. Low birth weight is the major factor associated with infant mortality. The prevalence of low birth weight has not declined during the 1980s. The disparity between black and white birth-weight rates remains striking. Although reliable predictors of low birth weight are complicated, some factors are clearly associated. Poverty increases the risk of poor birth outcomes, especially if accompanied by other factors that are associated with a health disadvantage. Inadequate prenatal care is one of those factors. A 1987 study by the Guttmacher Institute estimated that about one-third of U.S. women are getting insufficient prenatal care (1.3 million). The percentage of women getting insufficient prenatal care in the first trimester is highest among the unmarried (58%), teenagers (56%), the least educated (53%), blacks (51%), Hispanics (47%), and the poor (47%). The number of teens who do not obtain sufficient prenatal care are about twice as likely to have a low birth-weight baby (10% vs. 5%). Drug exposure during pregnancy may additionally result in a range of prenatal morbidities, including HIV-positive status leading to pediatric AIDS, and these exposures continue to rise. Child-maltreatment reports across the nation continue to rise steadily, as does homelessness, with mothers and children increasingly represented. Nine percent of the homeless are women with children accompanying them and of these, 88% were the single-parent heads of their households (Burt, 1992).

Florida, a large, urban, southern state in the United States, known best for its beaches and tourist attractions, has some of the highest rates of societal and health problems of any state in the nation. Many of Florida's children carry the burdens of poverty, deprivation, abuse, and the social and psychological stresses that accompany these conditions (Center for the Study of Social Policy, 1991; Children's Defense Fund, 1991). Many of the children in Florida do not acquire the skills necessary to cope adequately with the demands of society. Estimates of the percentage of children who do not complete high school range from 15% to 40%. Often their parents are unsupported in their parenting roles, suffer from multiple stresses, lack knowledge about sound health and nutrition practices, parenting skills, and child development. There were 119,374 reports of child maltreatment in Florida in 1989–1990 alone (Florida Protective Services System Annual Report, 1989–1990). Of those cases that were verified, 10% were in the category of drug-dependent newborns. Florida children were more likely to become victims of abuse and neglect and/or die young than youngsters in more than half the United States (Coulter, 1991). Twelve percent of the overall childhood population in the United States suffers from hunger, and Florida data support the (at least) equal percentage in Florida (Taren, 1991).

As in other parts of the nation, out-of-home child care in Florida is a major influence on Florida's children. Florida has enough formal child-care arrangements to serve roughly half of its preschool population. Furthermore, even these statistics do not include many of the 57,000 preschool children estimated to be enrolled in nonpublic school and church-related child-care and early education programs, which are not required to be licensed in

Florida. Concern about the low mandatory standards of child care in Florida stems from research indicating that, whereas quality child care may be helpful to children, enhancing their future learning and achievement, poor-quality programs can undermine children's later school performance and overall development (Muenchow, 1991).

Hillsborough County, a large west-central county near the Gulf of Mexico, where the University of South Florida is located, ranks fifty-eighth out of sixty-seven Florida counties in combined low birth-weight and very low birth-weight rates (84.9 per one thousand births). A high percentage of these babies are born to low socioeconomic-status mothers. These infants are subject to the risks associated with both low birth weight and with poverty. These factors contribute to a pattern of poor physical, cognitive, and emotional development for the children raised in such high-stress environments (Schorr, 1989). Several intensive studies conducted in the Hillsborough area and around the state have identified further problems that handicap the ability of parents and caretakers to support their children's development. One study that involved in-depth interviews with pregnant low-income women, identified numerous barriers to accessing prenatal care and further identified extreme social isolation. Less than half of the women reported having a family member to whom they could talk, who would provide emotional support and encouragement. There was an overwhelming request by the women for help on issues related to children's health, prenatal care, pregnancy, and parenting skills (Coulter & Innis, 1990).

A second, large study conducted in five counties, including Hillsborough, involved a combination of intensive focus-group interviews, and structured individual interviews with both providers of early intervention services and parents of children with handicaps, developmental delays, and children at risk for developmental delay. The focus of the interviews was on the adequacy of the present service-delivery system to meet the early intervention needs of parents and their children. Although providers were somewhat more satisfied than parents with the existing system, both indicated that lack of access to the system was a major problem, as was information about what services were needed. Providers found parents unknowledgeable about their children's needs. Parents found little support in their efforts both to understand their children's problems and to learn the best ways to help them, and found many service providers cold, disparaging, and lacking in respect for parental knowledge and abilities. Both agreed that many needy families were not receiving services. Many parents reported extreme negative treatment while attempting to access information and services, but this experience was even more frequent in poor families (Coulter & Innis, 1990; Coulter, Wallace, & Laude, 1989).

These interviews with providers and families support the findings of almost every group, study, or even speculation about maternal and child health and early intervention services in the United States. The system is chaotic, hard to access, much more accessible to the wealthy and insured, and is slanted toward provision of acute care rather than preventive and primary care. Family support, parenting education, and case-management services are desperately needed and are usually unavailable for those who most need them.

Policy shifts in the United States, most recently the federal and state Healthy Start efforts and Public Law 99-457 Part H (a bill supporting the development of services for children from birth to age three; the concentration on primary care service delivery; and the blending of efforts of education and health) have the potential to make changes in the fundamental nature of the system. Costs are a significant barrier to this change. However, new efforts at service provision with less costly price tags include the use of paraprofessional service providers, better parent involvement, and particularly a major shift toward a concentration on preventive rather than expensive curative treatment.

SELECTION OF THE MISC PROGRAM

It was with these data in mind that efforts to find an effective intervention that could be utilized in many programs and settings across the state were initiated. The characteristics of the needed intervention included the following:

1.   *Empowering.* Often poor parents, especially in the urban inner cities, do not feel empowered to adequately fulfill their role as parents. Living with systematic disadvantages and limitations to their individual growth often combined with pejorative and negative treatment by professionals results in the powerlessness experienced by poor and minority parents, especially women. Women report that they fear that social workers will take their children away from them for doing things they did not realize were abuse. Some women report past errors in responding to the health needs of their children, out of ignorance or confusion (such as improperly understanding labels or directions). Racism and inadequate support for individual cultural backgrounds have led some parents to feel that they have little to offer their children.

The usual methods to teach parenting and caretaking has been with the use of curricula, carefully constructed sets of activities and guidelines that may or may not fit the parents' natural style of interaction with their children. Any further disruption of parental abilities to interact with their children could be disastrous. Feelings of powerlessness and isolation may be exacerbated by any failures, particularly because some of these feelings may stem in part from the parents' difficulty in forming stable, interactive relationships with their children. It was necessary to find a model that was parent-supportive while it improved parent–child interaction.

2.   *Preventive.* A model was sought that had the potential to prevent problems covering a fairly broad spectrum, including child maltreatment, poor cognitive development, poor emotional development, and the lack of development of prosocial values. Because research shows that parents who lack the knowledge and skills to interact with their children are more likely to be abusive or neglectful toward their children, and less likely to stimulate their cognitive development and learning skills, an interactive model was sought.

An intervention was sought that could be combined with other sources of care, such as maternal and child health care, to be used as a broad-scale, primary prevention tool. It was necessary for reasons of cost and implementation to find an intervention that was not dependent on in-depth individual diagnostics to determine which parents and children needed it, but was appropriate for all parents and children as a fundamental part of basic early intervention and child-care services. Since the intent was to imbed this intervention in every primary and child-care setting possible, including health settings, child-care settings, early intervention programs for children with delays or handicaps, and others, the intervention needed to be useful and applicable in all of them. A critical factor was the usefulness of the model across a variety of cultures and racial backgrounds, and in Florida, ease of translation into Spanish.

3.   *Inexpensive.* The use of expensive professionals to deliver direct individual services was financially prohibitive. A model allowing for supervisor training that could then be implemented by direct service professionals, paraprofessionals, or parents, was sought. The intervention needed, additionally, to be inexpensive to participate in, using materials that parents or caretakers had at hand, not requiring or even suggesting the purchase of new or expensive toys or items. An appropriate model for either group or individual implementation was sought.

4.   *Theory-based.* The model chosen needed to have sufficient theoretical grounding and empirical examination to be trustworthy. The author was familiar with the theoretical framework of Feuerstein and found his work to be well grounded theoretically, optimistic, and with reasonable empiri-

cal support. The linkage of his theory to the importance of culture and the focus on the critical nature of interaction made his work appealing.

When I became aware of the work of Pnina Klein and the development of the MISC program, a model that could be used as a primary prevention intervention, it had strong appeal. Of special importance was the focus on empowering parents through support of their natural parenting styles and on positive reinforcement of identified parent–child interactions, recognition of and support for the importance of cultural variations in childrearing, and its potential for influencing positively the development of parent–child attachment and the development of prosocial values. After training in Israel, I was convinced of the merit of the program and its ability to be implemented. Empirical data provided clear support for the positive influence of the program in affecting cognitive development, and although the effect on attachment and child maltreatment has yet to be demonstrated empirically, clinical data and early reports of ongoing research support the impact of the program on attachment. The model includes much potential for the provision of social support, especially when implemented through a home-visiting model, and this support has wide acceptance in the literature and in clinical practice for its positive influences. The growing body of empirical evidence suggests that social support may mediate environmental stress and personality deficits to enhance parent–child attachment, increase parental self-esteem and coping skills, foster healthy child development, and prevent family breakdown (Miller, 1987).

Program Implementation

The Florida program is a multifaceted approach that includes specific project training, graduate-student education, statewide policy development, and statewide parenting and programmatic efforts. Each of these efforts is in a different stage of development and implementation. The efforts originate out of the University of South Florida, College of Public Health, Department of Community and Family Health in conjunction with the State Office of Maternal and Child Health, through its Healthy Start program. The following description presents the overall framework of the Florida program, delineates each of the efforts, and provides information about the expected direction and the experiences encountered so far in each setting.

Program Framework

The driving policy of the Florida effort is that children of every woman (or man) in the state will have access to comprehensive, supportive health care from pregnancy through early childhood. This health care will include not only access to primary maternal and child health care, but will also include parenting support, information, and services that focus on building healthy interactive relationships between parents and children. It is also the hope that child-care programs will provide focused interactive programs that not only utilize mediated learning techniques, but also reach out to parents to include and support them in their childrearing efforts. The program, in conjunction with the state's Healthy Start efforts (which work to assure the provision of maternal and child health services), will include education and training for policy makers, preparation of materials for use statewide, specific training of individual health and child-care project personnel, implementation of selected intensive research projects, and establishment of an ongoing training site.

Preparation of Materials

The preparation of materials to be used in training occupied the first phase of the Florida program. Because no programmatic funds were available for any of the Florida model's, implementation support had to be sought for each phase of the program. Original support for training-materials preparation was received from the March of Dimes, a private foundation that has as its goal early intervention and the prevention of birth defects. Training tapes were prepared with mothers and toddlers who lived in the Hillsborough area. The tapes included white, black, and Hispanic mothers. A training manual, as well as a training guide, were produced. Major changes were not made in the MISC, and parts of the manual were identical to the MISC manual, but additional child-development materials were included in the manual, and examples and descriptions were changed or added to make the program more relevant to Florida families. Later, in other settings, examples that were more appropriate for group-care settings were utilized. At present, a new set of training materials is being developed as part of a statewide parenting initiative described later. The projects and efforts presented in this chapter are delineated in order of implementation, with the recognition that these efforts are all part of an overall plan for enhancing the focus and comprehensiveness of state efforts to give each baby and child a "Healthy Start."

Program Directions

RESOURCE MOTHERS' PROGRAMS

The State of Florida has implemented several programs around the state that are designated as Resource Mothers' Programs. These resource mothers (or fathers) are paraprofessionals who have been employed as support persons in a variety of differing tasks, depending on the setting. Examples of their foci include support and assistance to pregnant teenagers, and outreach, support, and treatment for drug-using pregnant women or young mothers. The responsibilities of the resource mothers and fathers include case management, provision of social support, assistance in development of parenting skills, and referral for needed services.

Training in the MISC program was provided to both state program managers and supervisors of the Resource Mothers' Projects. Each of the program managers and supervisors utilized this information in training their resource mothers. Although video training was utilized in supervisor training, video equipment was not available to the supervisors in training their employees. Observation and identification of examples of positive, parental mediated-learning experience were used instead. A model was developed by which resource mothers would discuss the principles of the MISC intervention, (e.g., explanations of intentionality and reciprocity, mediation of meaning, transcendence, regulation of behavior, and mediation of competence) with women (often single, pregnant teens) while they were pregnant, as part of the support for their upcoming roles as parents. After the babies were born, more focused observation and training could be made available to them as they learned to interact with and parent their babies. A particular focus with this group was the development of confidence and self-esteem in the young mothers, with heavy emphasis on their own culture, ideas, and feelings as the source of their expertise in raising their children. Their deep value to their infants, along with the development of reasonable expectations as to what a baby could do at each developmental age, was stressed. Further training for other Resource Mothers' Programs around the state will proceed over time as budget constraints allow.

HOSPITAL-BASED DEVELOPMENTAL CENTERS
Most regional hospitals in the state have developmental centers that provide specific child-development programs for hospital patients and community referrals. These centers often provide intensive services to parents and children who are graduates of the neonatal intensive-care units, children with specific syndromes, such as Down's syndrome, and assistance to parents who are at risk or have been reported for child maltreatment, often because of a substance-exposed newborn. Training has been provided to the professional staff of one regional hospital center in order that they may incorporate the program into their work with their clients. Due to the special nature of the setting, discussion in this group focused, in addition to the basic MISC program, on the special problems of premature infants and their parents, the

needs of children with special handicaps or delays, and the special needs of substance-using mothers. Copies of the training tape were provided to this group, with assistance in developing their own training tape for other staff members, and the use of videos with individual mothers, fathers, and children. The facilities at this center permitted such videos, making video reinforcement of developing skills a powerful tool for use with parents.

In order to facilitate the specific training of professionals in the state who work with early intervention programs and handicapped children, both at the child development centers and in clinics around the state, a graduate course of study is being designed that incorporates early childhood special education (M.Ed.) and maternal and child health (M.P.H.). Professionals with these dual master's degrees will have the ability to provide statewide program management in multifocus, comprehensive intervention, with a strong grounding in the principles of mediated learning.

CHILD-CARE CONSORTIUM
A model program funded through the local Children's Services Council in Hillsborough County has been developed that provides technical assistance, consultation, training, and evaluation to a consortium of child-care directors. The child-care centers involved include a range of types of centers including private centers, church-related centers, Head Start centers for poor children, and other publicly funded centers. As part of the training and technical assistance to the directors of the centers, all of the directors were trained in the MISC program. In this model, the training was provided over a period of six weeks. Each training session was followed by directors' sessions to train their staff. Problems in understanding and communication were discussed at the following session.

For purposes of this training, the examples in the MISC materials were modified to be applicable to group child-care settings. Intensive discussions were held on how the racial and cultural background differences of the child-care staff and their children in care could be used to facilitate rather than create difficulties in interacting with the children. Efforts were made to include parents in the understanding of the principles of mediated learning and to support their pride in their own family and culture. Examples of efforts made by child-care directors to bring the families into the program included their asking parents to send their children in costumes that represented the family background, such as Hispanic dress from specific regions, dress from African nations, or European typical dress. Items that had meaning for mothers and fathers were solicited, as were stories that represented family history.

The interaction skills of many of the child-care directors were outstanding, and their grasp of the principles of the MISC program was immediate. The use of existing materials in the child-care setting was stressed, and role playing with items that the directors had with them was exciting. It was of particular interest to find that the personalities and interests of the directors began to emerge strongly, in a clearly supported way, through the interactions, and this process was discussed as it happened. Some directors chose "high-tech" items such as pocket computers as items for discussion; others chose "natural" items, such as Florida seashells. All participants found the program beneficial, helping them to clarify the nature of their interactions with the children in their care, and develop a framework around which to train staff that was interaction based, rather than material based.

RESIDENTIAL PROGRAM FOR SUBSTANCE-ABUSING MOTHERS
Substance-abusing mothers are often court-ordered into residential treatment both for addiction treatment and for parenting skill development. Most have had their children removed from them in the past while undergoing treatment. A new program, however, has been initiated that allows the mothers to bring their infants and children with them while they are in treatment. The overall goals of this project are to see if bringing the children encourages the women to stay in treatment and facilitates their treatment. These mothers are now being trained in the MISC program, in their treatment setting.

Because of the intense schedule of the mothers in treatment, and the fact that they spend little time with their children during the day, modifications in the usual training program were made. The trainer provides group training and discussion, although with individual parent–child videos. These mothers often have special problems in interacting with their infants, and it is expected that the training program will be lengthy. However, since a great fear of many of these women is that their children will be removed from them, their motivation is expected to be high. Many extreme family problems are part of the environment of these mothers, and this interactional focus has benefits in assisting them to adopt new and improved communication styles with their children as well as with the adults around them. Whether new and modified materials need to be developed to focus on responding to the special target population of substance-using parents is a question to be examined in this project.

STATEWIDE PARENTING PROGRAM
The expansion of the use of mediated learning interventions as part of pro-

grams throughout the state is the overall intent of this project. In order to accomplish this goal, a joint effort of the state Healthy Start program and the University of South Florida has been initiated. This effort includes the development of a new package of training materials in parenting, which includes training in the MISC program; information about child health, nutrition, and development; information about issues such as child care and discipline; and activities that can be developed to support parents' and children's self-esteem. This training package will be used to train regional representatives who are already working in various programs and capacities around the state. Examples of the types of personnel who will be trained are agricultural extension agents (child-development specialists who work in rural communities), regional nursing consultants and social workers, and regional child-care consultants. They will be an ongoing training resource for local health nurses, paraprofessionals, child-care workers, and early intervention specialists. Special funding from a county child-care services board has been obtained to support the development of this training package. Once developed, funding for the actual training will be provided through state and federal resources. It is hoped that extensive funding will be obtained through private foundation money to evaluate in an ongoing way the impact of this program.

Preliminary to the initiation of this program, a large qualitative research effort is presently being conducted. This research will interview parents and providers around the state about their parenting needs and preferences. Focus-group research is being used to elicit extensive information on issues and feelings of parents about the topics to be included in the parenting training, as well as the best ways to offer the training in their communities. Data will also be collected on parental beliefs about child development and attitudes toward parenting and values. These group data will then be used to develop structured (qualitative), supported questionnaires (e.g., parents will answer the questions themselves, but with an interviewer present to answer questions regarding the questionnaire, or translate, if needed).

Part of the research effort will focus on the development of a marketing strategy; that is, based on the information gathered from parents, a plan will be developed to best ensure that the services offered are utilized. This plan will include special attention to the needs of special populations, such as migrant workers, teens, or rural mothers and fathers.

Support for an intensive expansion of a new approach to early intervention requires efforts on a variety of fronts. Extensive lecturing, presentations, and training have been conducted throughout the state at schools, professional conferences, state early-intervention council meetings, and in academic settings. A conference on mediated learning interventions, including the MISC program and other mediated learning programs, such as the Cognitive Enrichment Network (COGNET) program (a classroom-based program for school-age children) was conducted. A network of interested persons has been established then, with development of training and support systems for interested persons.

Although training and program development, of necessity, have been the major foci of the university's efforts, plans are being developed for intensive research efforts that, in a controlled setting, can evaluate the effects of the program as designed. A location has been identified, two sites in low-income housing projects, where a Home Instruction Program for Preschool Youngsters (HIPPY) for four-year-olds is already located. The expanded MISC and home-visit health and parenting program will be initiated in one site for parents of newborns, with the other site providing social support and health education only, in a home-visit format. Parents will be used as trainers, and because these parents are uneducated, unemployed, and have no experience with this type of work, extensive preliminary training will be provided in work habits, social skills, and relationship building, long before the actual program content is taught. The outcome indicators to be measured include not only child variables such as cognitive development, but also parent-empowerment variables and measures of child maltreatment. Due to the presence of the HIPPY program and other school-based tutoring programs, it will be possible to follow the children's progress through high school.

DISCUSSION

The implementation of a small project in a controlled setting can be a difficult task. The efforts to expand a whole series of programs ranging from prenatal care to child day-care settings to include mediated learning approaches is an even more formidable task. It is my belief, however, that the serious and multitudinous problems suffered by the children of Florida and by their parents, can be alleviated best by a strong, constant, supportive set of programs that facilitate interaction and relationship-building between parent and child or caretaker and child. If each of the many problem outcomes is examined independently, such as maltreatment, poor preschool cognitive development, or insecure attachment, then the same type of early experience can lead to a reduction in the outcome, and all of these experiences are interactive experiences. It is true, of course, that in these difficult circumstances parents also need other things: They need good prenatal care; information about child health, nutrition, and development; good quality day care, housing, and income to live on. But even with the provision of these other supports, they need assistance in developing good interactions with their children. The wide prevalence of factors that Feuerstein calls "distal" factors, those things that prevent parents from providing good mediated learning experiences, make the situation a critical one. It is necessary for parents to focus on interaction despite poverty, hunger, homelessness, racism, lack of transportation, lack of access to health care, and often lack of love and support from family or friends. For these parents to be able to do so, they need specific assistance and focused reinforcement. It may be that some parents, such as drug-using mothers, may not be able, at least in the present, to satisfactorily develop good interactive relationships. In these cases it is also critical that the child-care workers be available to provide some substitute mediation.

Children in the United States often live in extraordinarily complex situations. They may have lives characterized by much chaos and many competing messages and stresses. It is essential that someone be available to mediate this world for them, to help them focus, develop their minds and their values, and grow up to be caring and competent adults. The Florida efforts are a beginning in that direction.

12 CONCLUSION

One of the basic features of the MISC intervention is its relative independence of the specific contents, materials, and contexts in which it can be applied. Rather than providing caregivers with structured instructions or materials, the program presents a means of sensitizing caregivers in the following three domains:

1. Their own conceptions of their children, themselves, their power to affect children's development, and their objectives in childrearing.

2. The need for "emotional literacy" in order to establish and maintain an expressive communicative cycle of interaction with the children.

3. An awareness of basic patterns or criteria of adult–child interaction that constitute a mediated learning experience for young children and consequently create in them "needs" predispositions that promote flexibility of mind and enable them to learn from future experiences.

These three aspects of the sensitization were introduced in training the trainers or mediators in each of the six cultures/countries represented in this book.

Despite relative uniformity in the general outline of the basic training, the intervention itself was applied differently in various countries. Each team that went through the training was expected to modify and design the actual intervention in line with its own cultural orientation and the living conditions of the population with which it was planning to work. It was not merely a process of translating, or even of choosing examples from everyday life within their community; rather it was a process of analyzing one's own cultural philosophy of education; resources of stories, songs, music, regional customs, values, and so on; and building the intervention on the basis of this understanding.

Several interesting philosophical questions became apparent in comparing, for example, Hundeide's chapter on the MISC intervention in Indonesia and Fuglesang and Chandler's chapter on the intervention in Sri Lanka. Whereas Hundeide passionately stresses the need to return to storytelling and other cultural means of mediation contrary to introducing "modernity" or Western analytical types of mediation, Fuglesang and Chandler advocate the need to integrate both as a necessary goal growing out of the people's own needs for cultural transmission and for survival and adjustment to this rapidly changing "modern" world.

It is most interesting to note that cultural variability in the interpretation of the intervention was apparent even in the definitions of the intervention objectives. Premling discusses the objective of promoting individualization as well as following the child's initiative as primary objectives in the Swedish MISC intervention. She found that the program had a different effect on experienced as compared to inexperienced early education workers. The experienced teachers became more child-oriented and followed more of the children's initiatives following the intervention. The Swedish caregivers feel that it is acceptable to "teach" young children, which was a change from their initial orientation, that their role was to offer an accepting, affective social–emotional environment for the children. The caregivers in Sri Lanka and Ethiopia, for example, felt that the intervention helped them realize that they can "teach" children through simple everyday types of activities rather than the limited technical types of structural activities related to the teaching of reading and writing in their country. Although the MISC presents a model of an unstructured intervention, the level of structure in its implementation varied in different countries. These variations may have been caused by culturally determined philosophies of education and/or living conditions. For example, the war conditions in Sri Lanka limited mobility of mediators and led to the creation of mailed mediation exercises.

The different chapters in this book reflect differences concerning conceptualization of the need for intervention. In Sri Lanka, for example, the intervention was introduced by an aid organization. The complex social and political considerations presented in Fuglesang and Chandler's chapter highlight issues that must be taken into consideration prior to any intervention in poor communities within a Third World context. Coulter's chapter describing the need for intervention with high-risk teenage mothers with problems of drug or alcohol addiction and McNight and Gold's chapter on the use of the MISC in teachers' training for special education teachers, present different needs for this form of intervention within the United States.

The chapters differ with regard to the form and type of research presented. Cross-cultural research can be designed in a structured manner with similar standardized measures applied across different populations. Because of the diversity discussed earlier, I felt that more could be learned by allowing each of the contributors to report on their efforts to implement the intervention and reflect on issues that seemed significant within their cultural context and real living conditions of the populations with which they had worked. This choice resulted in variability that reflects the richness and complexity of the issues related to cross-cultural research on early childhood intervention.

Beyond variability in the interpretation and adaptation of the program, in some cases there were deviations in the implementation that did not coincide with the general orientation and philosophy of the MISC intervention. For example, as described in Hundeide's chapter on the intervention in Indonesia, the mediators (kaders) were health workers who used an authoritative style of interaction and gave the mothers directions rather than follow the MISC orientation, in order to observe mothers' behavior and strengthen existing behaviors that were mediational in nature. Despite this central problem, positive results of the intervention were found even for this population. Hundeide presents suggestions for enhancing sustainability of the effects of early intervention within this context as well.

It appears that the MISC mediational approach allowed a variety of interpretations and adaptations to needs of people in different cultures as well as populations with special needs across cultures. Despite the belief in the universality of the basic criteria of mediation, these were ranked differently in terms of their perceived importance in various countries. Despite this variability it may be concluded that the mediational approach to early intervention was generally accepted across different cultures and implemented in different settings with promising results. Sensitizing caregivers, providing them with "emotional literacy" as well as giving them tools for observing the children and their own interaction with them, was found to be an effective means of intervention with infants, young children, their families, caregivers, and educators. Indonesian mothers resisted the use of expansion (explaining; associating between events in the past, present, and future, etc.). They felt that this is how "teachers speak," whereas Sri Lankan preschool teachers felt relieved to learn that children could learn even when they spoke "like a mother." The mediational intervention is a step forward toward an integrated "educare" rather than separate entities of education and care.

PART 3
APPENDICES

Appendix I

Observation for Mediational Interaction (OMI)

The OMI is an observation method for the assessment of mothers' (or other caregivers') mediational interaction with their infants and young children. The OMI is used within the MISC intervention as one of the basic measures of mediation. It can be applied to videotaped mother–child interactions at any health or day-care center or to observations carried out at home. There are several variations of the OMI (Klein, 1988, 1992; Klein & Alony, 1993; Klein, Weider, & Greenspan, 1987b). The OMI involves counting the frequency of behaviors defined as factors of mediation.

The observation requires noting only those *in situ* behaviors that fit within the defined criteria of mediation. Behaviors of either a parent or an infant are coded in relation to the respective behaviors and the meaning conveyed through these behaviors. For example, observing a parent hand an object to a child was coded as reflecting intentionality and reciprocity only if it was met by a response suggesting reciprocity on the part of the child. Several additional categories of nonmediational behavior are coded in the OMI (these are marked by stars on the sample observation coding page; see Table IA). For example, maternal behavior that is intentional but not met by the child's reciprocity reflects the mother's motivation to act but may not reach the child. Similarly, a mother's expressions of affection, love, acceptance, or excitement that are not related to anything specific in the environment or to the child's behavior are not mediating anything specific to the child, but may reflect a mother's active affective involvement with the child. Demands are noted as separate from regulation of behavior, and are behaviors that may lead the child to act in a way that is desirable to the parent but do not assure that any learning has occurred.

The OMI enables researchers to rate the frequency of mediational interactions initiated by the child as compared to those initiated by the mother, as well as the frequency and types of response to those initiations.

There are two basic methods of coding the OMI. One method calls for coding the frequency of behaviors in the various categories, whereas the other requires coding these behaviors as they occur, in a sequential order. The first method of coding yields the sum of mediational behaviors in the different categories; the other yields a more detailed account of the flow of interaction. The latter method is particularly suitable for preremediation assessment or clinical intervention programs with populations of children with special needs.

TABLE IA PARTIAL SAMPLE OF OBSERVATION SHEET FOR THE ASSESSMENT OF MLE WITH INFANTS AND TODDLERS

	Provision of MLE by		Request for MLE by		Total	
	Mother	Child	Mother	Child	Mother	Child
MLE criteria						
Intentionality and reciprocity						
Verbal						
Nonverbal						
Combined verbal and nonverbal						
Intentionality without reciprocity						
Mediation of meaning						
Expression of affect (nonverbal)						
Naming						
Naming and affect						
Relating to past or future						
Acceptance and affect (unrelated to infants' behavior or to anything in the environment)						
Transcendence in relation to content of specific experience						
Clarifying processes (insight)						
General rules						
Other						
Clearly above child's capacity to grasp						
Mediated feelings of competence						
"Good," "Great," "Fine" (statement only) but with good timing						
Reinforcement + explanation						
Modification of situation to allow success						
Undifferentiated encouragement						
Mediated regulation of behavior						
In relation to time						
In relation to space						
Sequencing of steps						
Matching ability and task requirements						
Other						
Commands						
*Nonmediational behaviors (no teaching involved)						

Appendix II

Basic Elements in the Pedagogy of Mediation to Young Children
(A Sample from MISC in Kindergarten and School)

Horizontal and Vertical Processes

Horizontal processes in mediation, as defined in the MISC approach, relate to repeated application of learned models of behavior, including thinking strategies and modes of expression that have been acquired in previous experiences of learning. In other words, horizontal mediation involves practice and repetition, preferably through the use of a variety of different situations and materials. The adult may invite the child to cope with seemingly different situations that require application of what he/she already knows. For example, if the child can count, enabling him/her to count various objects in different situations is considered a horizontal process.

Vertical processes in mediation relate to mediation that is designed to help the child solve progressively more complex problems or to apply progressively more developed thinking strategies to existing social and other situations. For example, if the child can add single digits, attempts to teach him/her addition of a two-digit number and a one-digit number constitute a vertical process of mediation.

Surface Objectives and Deep Objectives

Surface objectives are the objectives that are immediate, concretely related to the actions of the adult in his/her interaction with the child (i.e., teaching a new word, a new skill, or a problem-solving technique). The deep objective is more general; it relates to more distant objectives, such as wanting the child to be able to communicate well with others, to be a moral individual, to enjoy life, to be a leader, and so on. Good mediators are aware of *both* types of objectives and try to regulate the immediate surface objectives in line with the deep objectives. Parents are in a position to be more flexible in this process as compared with teachers, who have a fixed curriculum that they have to follow and whose "deep" objective is to achieve the objectives defined by that specific curriculum.

Natural, Worthwhile, and Meaningful

Mediation is based on the understanding of what is *natural* for the child. If a six-month-old child is presented with an object, it is likely that he/she will place it in his/her mouth. It would be unnatural to attempt to train the child not to place objects in his/her mouth, however. A good mediator would select objects that may enhance the child's experience of learning "using" what is natural to him/her (different tastes, textures, etc.). Mediation that is matched to the ability of infants who have learned to bang may involve presentation of various objects that will produce different sounds if banged on or banged with.

In line with cognitive developmental theory, children have an innate need to activate, to practice what they are capable of doing, and to apply their budding abilities in their experiences with the environment. In this sense there is no need for external rewards and encouragement, or for external guidance. Cultural transmission and the development of higher cognitive and social–emotional skills involve adult mediation to the young child. This mediation should be *meaningful* and *worthwhile* to the child if the deep objective of the mediation, that is, helping the child to develop as a member of a specific culture and as an active learner, is to be achieved. *Worthwhile* relates to the extent to which an invited action is favorable and desirable to a child. *Meaningful* relates to the extent to which the mediated experience is associated with or endowed with meaning or excitement (as perceived by the child).

Appendix III

Basic MISC Training Materials Used in Different Countries

Training 1: How Does It Feel to Mediate?

This training exercise leads one to imitate the behaviors that are considered as typical of some basic forms of mediation. Modeling may be useful with families who show very poor mediation.

Enhancing Mediation through Focusing, Exciting, and Expanding

The main functions of mediation are focusing, exciting, and expanding. Read the following and act them out as though you are mediating to a child:

1. a. Focusing behavior

For toddler or older child inquiries may be added as part of focusing, for example:

- "Look, look at that."
- "See? Right here."

- "Listen . . ."
- "Can you hear it?"   "Look, what is it?"

- "Taste it."
- "Do you taste it?"   "Listen, can you recognize it?"

- "Touch it."
- "Do you feel it?"

- "Smell it."
- "Do you smell it?"

We can clearly see that focusing as demonstrated above has two components: 1. Directing the child's attention and 2. Trying to find out whether reciprocity has been established, in other words, whether the child has paid attention.

1.b. *Focusing non-verbally*

Focusing can also be done non-verbally in many different ways, for example:

- Behaviors that make some things stand out against the background (covering confusing surroundings, repeating stimuli, making a stimulus stronger or bigger exaggeration.
- Controlling the *distance* from the stimulus (bringing the child closer to a stimulus or the stimulus closer to the child).

If the adult wishes to focus the child's attention on something big (on the whole rather than on its parts), then taking the child away from the stimulus may be appropriate for focusing.

(Focusing as part of good mediation will be done in accordance with the child's needs, abilities and interests at a particular moment, and in line with the adult's general educational plan for the child.)

2. *Energizing, adding affect and meaning*

Verbal examples:

- Changing the rate of speech, speaking suddenly at a faster speed or at an exaggerated slower speed.
- Spacing the verbal expressions: L . . o . . o . . k, a b . . a . . b . . y!
- Repeating expressions, especially adjectives or adverbs, "It is beautiful, beautiful"; "You ran well, very well."
- Identifying by relating to past or future experiences: "It is a doggie like Dan's doggie."

3. *Expanding*

Showing relations between things, comparing, contrasting. Demonstrating cause and effect relations.

Examples:

"Look at this flower, it looks just like a butterfly. Why is it not a butterfly?"
"My shirt smells of smoke; it's because I sat too close to the fire, and my clothes absorbed the smoke."
"Your shoulders are wet but your hair is dry. Your hat protects your head from the rain but you had nothing to cover your shoulders, so they got wet. If you cover something, it stays dry in the rain."
"You have so many balls, let's see how many, let's *count:* one, two, three . . ."

THE FOLLOWING ARE EXAMPLES OF MISC TRAINING MATE-
RIALS PREPARED BY THE AUTHOR FOR USE IN SRI LANKA.

TRAINING 2.

1.a. Activating your understanding of the criteria by producing your own examples.

Give your own example for:

Focusing _____

_____

_____

_____

_____

Energizing _____

_____

_____

_____

_____

Expanding _____

_____

_____

_____

_____

1.b. Make your own dramatization or role playing of the three criteria as presented in the examples above.
(Alternate roles of child and caregiver)

Enhancing the Quality of Mediation:
Feeding

<u>With mediation</u>

Focus the child's attention on the food

Point out the kinds of food on the plate
(before mixing them, for example, rice,
vegetables, meat)

Focus the child's attention on perceptions
through all senses.
Let the child *taste* the food
touch it
smell it
Tell him/her what he is tasting,
touching or smelling.

Provide *meaning* through *naming* of things
on the plate and *their qualities, e.g., soft,*
hard, hot, cold, smooth, small, big.

Express your own excitement and likes
about the food, "Oh, I love peas", "I love
the smell of tomatoes."

<u>Without mediation</u>

Feeding the child with little or
no activity beyond placing the
food in the child's mouth.
"Open your mouth"

"Come on, eat quickly"

"Don't spit it out"

Expand, go beyond the immediate experience. "Yes, the rice is hot. I cooked it in hot water so it would become soft." (Pointing out cause and effect.) "Look, this is how rice looks before it is cooked." (Pointing out the "before" and "after" sequence.) "The pineapple is sweet, a banana is sweet, but the fish is salty." (Comparing and contrasting)

Praise the child, mediate competence: "Yes, that's good, you put the rice into your mouth, nothing fell onto the table." "You almost finished all your meat." "You can hold it all by yourself now."

Regulating Behavior. Mediate planning: "Let's taste the noodles first, they are soft and not too hot, and later you can eat the meat, it is still hot," or "mix these two so it won't be so dry." "Eat slowly, slowly," or "chew harder so it will be easier to swallow, it will become softer ... like this."

Bathing

With mediation	Without mediation
Focus the child's attention on various components of the situation, e.g., the bath, the water, the soap, the bubbles, the towel etc.	Undressing and dressing the child, washing the child with little or no communication other than commands or instructions directly related to the situation
Mediate meaning by naming the objects or parts of them.	
Share excitement with the child, "MM ... it smells so good," "The water feels warm and comfortable," "This towel is beautiful, it has lovely designs on it."	e.g., "Lift your arm," "That's enough, out now," "Don't cry."

Expand (i.e., introduce associations from the past: "This soap smells like a flower," "Remember the time you didn't hold on to the bath and you slipped into the water?" "We must wash your hands well, you have touched all those dirty poles on the street."

Form connections with the future, "Soon we'll take you out and cuddle you in the soft towel."

Dripping water into the bath ... "Here, look, it's raining." "Look how many different colors the soap bubbles have, red, green, yellow, purple ... What else is red ...? Green ...? There are small, tiny ones like these, and big ones here ..."

Praise, mediate competence (e.g., "Very good, you are holding on so you won't slip." "You know how to save the soap from falling into the water." "That's nice, you have made a boat from this plate." "Good, you have washed your face very nicely, it is clean now."

Regulating and planning behavior: "Here, first we wash your arms, then your hands and fingers ... otherwise your fingers will get dirty when we wash your arms." "Let's take your clothes off - we have to unbutton the shirt before we try to take it off, otherwise it won't come off." "Try to wash your feet, like that ... harder, the dirt won't come off it you do it so softly."

TRAINING 4.

Activities for the Identification of the MLE Criteria
(The activities listed below relate to pictures 1-5.

Step 1: General questions:
Which of the basic criteria of MLE is best represented by each of
the following pictures?

Pictures nos. 1 _____ 2 _____
3 _____ 4 _____ 5 _____
Is there intentionality in each picture? How can you tell?
1 _____
2 _____
3 _____
Is there reciprocity? How can you see it?
1 _____
2 _____
3 _____
4 _____

Step 2: Exercising Mediation
Suppose the mother in each picture would say the sentences listed
below for each picture, what criteria of MLE would you then identify
in the interaction?
Picture 1
a)   L..o..o..k ... a ball! ....
b)   Back and forth, back and forth ... back and forth ....
....

Picture 2

a) That's great, you built it all by yourself ....

b) How many blocks do you think there are in here? ....
    ....

c) Carefully, slowly now, if you put another block on it may fall
    ....

d) You built a tall tower ....

Picture 3

a) Very nice, you put them all in place ....

b) You did it carefully, first this one, then this, then that
    ....

c) It looks like a boat, a beautiful boat ....

d) Let's see how many different colors we have here ....
    ....

Picture 4

a) I am pouring cold water, feel the water now, it's comfortable
    ....

b) See, when the water is too hot, we can put some cold water
    in to cool it down ....

c) Here is your rubber ducky ....

d) Slowly, sit down, first try putting your hand into the water,
    then sit down ....

Picture 5

a) Do you want to touch it? ....

b) This little chick is small and soft ....

c) It has hatched out of the egg just a little while ago, it is still
    a baby ....

d) Touch it gently, yes ... like that, with your fingers ....
    ....

e) You are a good boy, you care for little animals ....
    ....

1

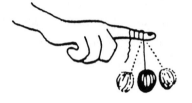

TRAINING 6.

<u>Test your mediational skills</u> (analysis of verbally presented episodes of interaction).
The following suggested situations present possible episodes in everyday life in a family with an infant or young child. Imagine yourself as the adult caring for the child, how could you make the following situations into experiences of Mediated Learning?

1) Mother is pouring water into the bath or wash basin. The baby is standing near her. He/she is beginning to pull of his/her shirt in anticipation.

What do you intend to mediate? ....
....

How can you achieve reciprocity from the child? ....
....

How would you introduce meaning into this situation? ....
....

How would you introduce transcendence? ....
....

How would you introduce mediated feelings of competence? ....
....

Is it appropriate to introduce mediated regulation of behavior here? How?..
....

2) Father or mother is taking the child to collect firewood (or vegetables and/or fruit from the garden or field). The child is walking alongside the parent trying to keep pace.

What do you intend to mediate? ....

....

How can you achieve reciprocity from the child? ....

....

How would you introduce meaning into this situation? ....

....

How would you introduce transcendence? ....

....

How would you introduce mediated feelings of competence? ....

....

Is it appropriate to introduce mediated regulation of behavior here? How? ....

....

What should we look for in a good place for young children?

<u>A look at the caregivers</u>

They smile frequently.

They express interest and excitement about things the children experience.

Their voices sound relaxed, quiet.

They provide information about things that interest children.

They provide encouragement.

They give specific, individualized praise.

They give children individual attention.

They respond to children's demands and interests.

Identification of Good Caregivers for Young Children

The MISC Program

The following points may be of help in the process of choosing caregivers for young children.

What should we look for?

<u>Personality</u>

---- Enjoys the beginning of each new day, shows enthusiasm about something or someone. (How can one mediate excitement if one is not excited oneself?)

---- Is aware of her own feelings and can verbalize them. Can recognize the feelings of others. Can identify and share children's feelings.

---- Believes in her capacity to affect children's growth and development. (If such a belief is lacking, why should one invest one's energy in mediating to children?)

---- Loves to listen and talk to children (remembers what they have said or wanted and responds to it).

---- Likes to be close to the children, likes to maintain physical contact or eye to eye contact with one or more of the children most of the time.

---- Accepts and respects individual differences in children's rate of development and behavior.

---- Is capable of attending to and focusing on detail as well as on the global picture or situation. (E.g., Can see and point out to the children the feathers as well as the bird, the leaf as well as the tree.)

<u>Knowledge</u>

---- Has a good understanding of the criteria of mediation. Can say all 5 basic criteria and explain them, with examples.

---- Has a good basic knowledge of the environment (names of trees, birds, places, and stories about them).

---- Has a good knowledge of the culture and the people around her (including songs, dances, art).

---- Recognizes basic landmarks and basic processes in the development of young children.

---- Knows how to construct an educational sequence for a child (i.e., how to choose a starting point in terms of level of difficulty, and how to proceed to more difficult levels suitable for a particular child).

---- Understands basic landmarks in cognitive and social emotional development of young children.

Although one can learn to become a good mediator and caregiver, it is easier to achieve good mediation with individuals who are naturally enthusiastic, optimistic, talkative and sociable.

A good caregiver is a good mediator

1. Someone who can match her intentions to teach with the children's needs, interests, and capacities in various situations of everyday living, using those situations to enrich the child's understanding of the world around him and to increase his "appetite" to learn more.

2. Someone who can express enthusiasm and excitement over different things.

3. Someone who can and is willing to label (name), expand, explain, relate, compare, contrast, classify (group) and analyse things for the children.

4. Someone who can see the accomplishments in children's behavior and is willing to praise children and explain why they deserve praise.

5. Someone who is aware of the need to plan or regulate one's own behavior and can mediate it to young children.

Basic Requirements for Good Care of Infants and Young Children

---- Is the general atmosphere one of acceptance and love?
Do caregivers smile at the children?
Hug or kiss them?
Hold them close?
Tell them they love them?

---- Is there any indication that someone thought of the children's interests,
e.g., chose toys or objects they might like to play with?
Pictures they may be interested to look at?
Music they may like to hear or produce?

The caregiver should be able to answer the question: Why is any object around?
How can it be used for the child's benefit?

What do you want the child to focus on today? I.e.,
to see
to hear
to feel
to smell

Did you do anything to make it possible for the child to focus on anything you think
is interesting for him/her?

---- Did anyone think of the children's comfort? E.g., carpeting or other floor
covering, low chairs, tables, appropriate toilets, water faucets?

---- Is the environment responsive?
Does any behavior on the child's part initiate a response?
People who come and talk to him/her?
Toys that move or make a sound in response to the child's movement?
Are toys available and displayed so the child can benefit from them?

---- Can the child reach out by himself for any kind of food or drink if he so desires?-

---- Can he go to the toilet by him/herself?

---- Does someone praise or encourage the children's activity verbally?
Are any of the children's drawings publicly displayed?

---- Does someone share *excitement* with them over things around them?
"Look how beautiful this is", "I love flowers", or "I love music".

---- Is there any expression of perceptions and ideas beyond that which is necessary
to satisfy any existing need?
E.g., Speaking to the child about the food while feeding, playing and speaking
to the child while bathing or while changing his/her diaper.
Speaking to the child about things one uses on the way to places

---- Is there any attempt to mediate to the children concepts of time and space,
of relations, of cause and effect?

- Is there *stability* in the care given to children?
Do most caregivers stay at least one year with the children?
Do the children have a stable "home base"?

---- Are the children taken out for brief field trips every day (weather permitting?

---- Is there *something new* introduced to the children every day? (Focusing their
attention on something they have not seen before or have not known about.)

Space Is there an average of 2 square meters space for each child in the center?

Materials and Toys Are there enough materials for the child *to choose* and age
appropriate task to get involves in?

Parental participation Are parents consulted or asked to participate in any of the
activities ongoing in the center (other than being invited to shows and parties)?

Safety Are there any safety hazards in or around the center?

General Notes _____

_____

_____

THE FOLLOWING ARE EXAMPLES OF MISC TRAINING MATERIALS PREPARED BY REDD BARNA FOR USE IN ZIMBABWE.

MEDIATED LEARNING EXPERIENCES

YES, THAT IS MY
EAR
SAY: EAR...

MY EAR
AND <u>YOUR</u> EAR
EEARR !!

MEDIATION OF MEANING

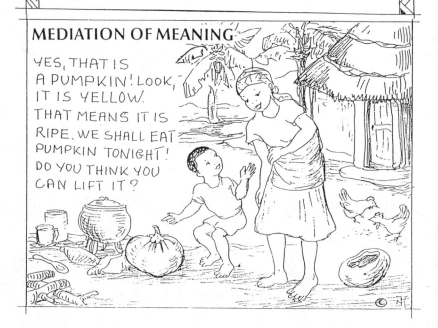

YES, THAT IS
A PUMPKIN! LOOK,
IT IS YELLOW.
THAT MEANS IT IS
RIPE. WE SHALL EAT
PUMPKIN TONIGHT!
DO YOU THINK YOU
CAN LIFT IT?

MEDIATION OF EXPANDED MEANING

TASTE THE PUMPKIN! IT IS A LITTLE SWEET. LOOK, THIS IS ANOTHER PUMPKIN. THE SKIN IS DRY AND HARD. WE CAN USE THE PUMPKIN AS A BOWL. THIS PUMPKIN IS CALLED A GOURD.

MEDIATION OF EXPANDED MEANING

OH, HERE IS ANOTHER PUMPKIN WE CALL GOURD. LISTEN TO THE MUSIC! THE MAN PLAYS A FINGER PIANO INSIDE THE GOURD. IT SOUNDS MUCH BETTER. HE HAS TWO FINGER PIANOS - ONE INSIDE AND ONE OUTSIDE

THE FOLLOWING IS AN EXAMPLE OF MISC TRAINING MATERIALS PREPARED FOR USE IN ISRAEL.

Comparing Mediational Styles of High and Low Mediators
(Mothers of 8–12-Month-Old Infants) in Israel

(High Mediators)	**(Low Mediators)**
Mothers use frequent verbalization to mediate their thinking about the child. It sounds almost like reporting to another adult. "You are too busy, you don't know what to choose."	Almost no "reporting" behavior. Little verbalization. Frequent substitution of sounds, i.e., "oh oh" for words to express disagreement, anger, concern. No differentiation.
If one form of calling an infant's attention does not bring about the desired response, mother tends to combine a number of techniques, e.g., calling infant's name, making sounds with a toy, movement, changing body position to improve possibility of eye contact.	Tends to repeat same form of calling child's attention (also true for attempts to get the child to comply).
Only 10% of the mothers engaged in encouraging motor activity, e.g., walking, during the play session rather than exploring the offered toys.	70% of the mothers encouraged their infants' gross motor activities.
Mothers sat on the carpet with the baby attempting to achieve eye contact or at least to see the infant's face.	30% of the mothers did not attempt to achieve eye contact with the infant and remained seated on the couch throughout the entire play session.
Most intentional acts are met by reciprocity. Intentionality without reciprocity is primarily of a verbal nature, e.g., many rhetorical questions building expectations for need to reply.	Intentionality without reciprocity primarily of motor and visual perceptual nature.
Many of the mothers' behaviors are organized in sequences of behaviors, each expanding the previous ones, e.g., starting with calling the infant's attention followed by manipulating and naming objects, repeating actions or pointing out salient characteristics of the target behavior.	Many fragmented behaviors, i.e., mothers call the infant by name or use other methods to capture his/her attention, but when they have that attention they do not proceed to use it. Any reciprocity that is achieved is short-lived.
Mothers rarely label objects or actions using one single word. Labelling frequently appears with an age appropriate expansion of information, not necessarily verbal, related to the labelled object or action.	Most frequently, labelling occurs with labels, stated only once.

Mothers verbally expressed their own learning from the play sessions at the center (spontaneously), e.g., "I see you like that toy more than the others, we'll have to get you one like that".	No expression of learning from the play session.
Mothers repeat expectations for meaning, e.g., "What is in there?", "What is that?", or opening up boxes, pots, containers, putting things inside. Mothers answer the questions as they arise.	No systematic repeated experience of request for mediation. In several cases when questions were posed by mothers, e.g., "what is in there?", these were left unanswered or answered in a manner unsynchronized with child's attention.
Many verbal statements of praise expressed together with nonverbal indications of excitement and positive effect, e.g., smiles, clapping hands, changes in tone of voice.	Show almost no clear expression of praise following infant's behavior.
Few and brief episodes of rough physical play or tickling.	Many rather prolonged tickling episodes and rough physical play. The use of tickling as a means of calming the baby.

Few commands. Any instructions given, e.g., "get the ball" are preceded by attempts to ensure that the infant focuses and by repeated attempts to model the desired behavior, and to reinforce approximation of it.

Many commands stated with no or little nonverbal elaboration, direction or attempt to model the desired behavior. Hardly any reinforcement for approximations of the target behavior.

Demonstrate little physical rough and tumble play but express physical pleasure in the relationship.

Demonstrate much physical pleasure in the relationship and much rough and tumble play. Repeated request for the infant to kiss or hug the mother.

Goal setting behavior is present but there is a reinforcing episode of goal reaching following infant's efforts to reach it.

"Teasing" the child in order to teach goal reaching, i.e., showing the child a desired object then moving it away out of reach repeatedly following infant's attempts to reach it.

Cause and effect sequences are intentionally modified by mothers to bring about more dramatic effects, e.g., when the infant bangs on the carpet with a set of metal measuring spoons she moves it up to meet the child's arm. Repeated.

Few sequences of cause and effect are repeated or modified to mediate the cause and effect relationship.

Mediated competitive behavior present in combination with mediated feelings of competence, e.g., mother makes the ball roll slightly and crawls together with the baby to get it.

What appears to be mediated competitive behavior most frequently turns to episodes of teasing the child.

Samples of MISC training materials used in Florida

EXPLAINING

MISC

TALK ABOUT THINGS AROUND YOU AND EXPLAIN THEM TO YOUR CHILD.

Explain *what* you do,
   how you do it,
      why you do it,
         what *your ideas* are about things, and
            what *you believe* to be true.

Develop in your child the need to go beyond the present experience.

Communicate your beliefs and values, your own view of the world, and your likes and dislikes.

PRAISING

SHOW YOUR CHILD THAT YOU ARE PLEASED WITH HIS OR HER BEHAVIOR.

Let your baby know *why* you think she or he did something well.

Give your child simple things to do, and show that you are pleased.

Tell your child exactly what she or he did well.

Showing you approve and are pleased with your child's behavior will make your child want to do more of what led to his or her success.

This will begin to happen without having to constantly praise your child and will help your child to feel more capable to learn and do new things.

References

Aamlid, K. (1991). 0-3 arranger i gene grouper Ellen soskengrupper? [0 to 3 years old children in sibling groups or in toddler groups?]*Debattserien for barnehagefolk*, Nr 2.

———. (1992). Noen aspekter ved voksen–barn samspill i barnehager for barn under tre ar. [Some aspects of adult–child interaction in day-care settings.] I *Forskning om smabarn*. Centrum for kunskap om barn. Goteborg, Sweden: Goteborgs universitet.

Abroms, K., & Gollin J. (1980). Developmental study of gifted preschool children and measures of psychological giftedness. *Exceptional Children, 46,* 334–343.

Ainsworth, M., Blehar, M., Waters, E., & Wall, S. (1978). *Patterns of attachment: A psychological study of the strange situation.* Hillsdale, NJ: Erlbaum.

Alinsky, S. (1972a). *Reveille for radicals.* New York: Vintage Books, Random House.

———. (1972b). *Rules for radicals: A pragmatic primer for realistic radicals.* New York: Vintage Books, Random House.

Bayley, N. (1969). *Manual for the Bayley Scales of Infant Development.* New York: Psychological Corporation.

Bell, R.Q. (1979). Parent, child and reciprocal influences. *American Psychologist, 34,* 821–826.

Belsky, J. (1984). The determinants of parenting: A process model. *Child Development, 55,* 83–96.

Berenstein, B. (1970). *Class, code and control* (Vol. 1.) Henley on Thames, UK: Routledge & Kegan Paul.

Berne, E. (1964). *Games people play.* New York: Grove Press.

Berry, J.W., & Bennett, J.A. (1992). Cree conception of cognitive competence. *International Journal of Psychology, 27,* 73–88.

Bjerre, L., & Hansen, E. (1976). Psychomotor development and school adjustment of 7-year-old children with low-birth-weight. *Acta Paediatrica Scandinavia, 65,* 25–30.

Bowlby, J. (1969). *Attachment and loss, Vol. 1: Attachment.* London: Hogarth Press.

———. (1980). *Attachment and loss, Vol. 1: Attachment.* 2nd edition. New York: Basic Books.

———. (1988). *A secure base.* New York: Basic Books.

Braaten, E. (1991). *Mediated learning experiences (MLE) and development: Western concepts and Sundanese reality.* Unpublished manuscript, Institute of Anthropology, University of Bergen, Norway.

Broch, D., & Beyer, H. (1990). *Growing up agreeably.* Honolulu: Hawaii University Press.

Bromwich, R. (1981). *Working with parents and infants: An interactional approach.* Austin, TX: PRO-Education.

Bronfenbrenner, U. (1975). *The ecology of human development.* Cambridge, MA: Harvard University Press.

Bruner, J. (1988). *Actual minds, possible worlds.* Cambridge, MA: Harvard University Press.

————. (1990) *Acts of meaning.* Cambridge, MA: Harvard University Press.

Bryant, D.M., & Ramey, C.T. (1987). An analysis of the effectiveness of early intervention programs for environmentally at-risk children. In M.J. Guralnick & F.C. Bennett (Eds.), *The effectiveness of early intervention for at-risk and handicapped children* (pp. 33–78). New York: Academic Press.

Burke, K. (1945). *A grammar of motives.* NewYork: Prentice-Hall.

Burt, M. (1992). *Over the edge.* New York: Sage.

Caldwell, B. (1989, September). *You have come a long way baby, but you still have a long way to go!* Invited address at the Australian Early Childhood Education Association, Canberra, Australia.

Carew, J.V. (1980). Experience in the development of intelligence in young children at home and in daycare. *Monograph of the Society for Research in Child Development, 45* (6–7, Serial No. 153).

Center for the Study of Social Policy. (1991). Kids count data book: State profiles of child well-being. Washington, DC: Author.

Chambers, R. (1983). *Rural development, putting the last first.* London: Longman.

Children's Defense Fund. (1991). *The state of America's children.* Washington, DC: Author.

Chomsky, N. (1964). *Current issues in linguistic theory.* The Hague: Mouton.

Clarke-Stewart, K.A., & Fein, G. (1983). Early childhood programs. In M.M. Haith & J.J. Campos (Vol. Eds.) & P.H. Mussen (Ser. Ed.), *Handbook of child psychology: Vol. 2. Infancy and developmental psychobiology* (pp. 917–1000). New York: Wiley.

Cole, M., & Scribner, S. (1974). *Culture and thought.* New York: Wiley.

Collins, W.A. (1984). Commentary: Family interaction and child development. In M. Perlmutter (Ed.), *Parent–child interaction and parent–child relations in child development* (pp. 241–258). The Minnesota Symposia on Child Psychology, Vol. 17. Hillsdale, NJ: Erlbaum.

Consortium for Development Research and Services. (1989, June). *Study of traditional child rearing practices in Sri Lanka.* Colombo, Sri Lanka: Redd Barna.

Coulter, M.L. (1991). Child abuse and neglect. In C.D. Herrington (Dir.), *Condition of children in Florida* (pp. 32–41). Tallahassee, FL: Florida State University, Center for Policy Studies in Education.

Coulter, M.L., & Innis, V.L. (1990). *Perinatal community outreach project.* University of South Florida, Tampa, FL. Unpublished manuscript.

Coulter, M.L., Wallace, T., & Laude, M. (1989). *Early intervention service: Selected Florida counties* (Contract No. A-14933). Tampa, FL: University of South Florida, College of Public Health.

Crowell, J.A., & Feldman, S.S. (1988). Mothers' internal models of relationships and children's behavioral and developmental status: A study of mother–child interaction. *Child Development, 59,* 1273–1285.

Diderichsen, A. (1992). *Omsorg for kunskpa om barn.* [Care for young children in day-care centers.] Goteborg, Sweden: Goteborgs universitet.

Donaldson, M. (1978). *Children's minds.* London: Fontana Books.

Dunn, L.M., & Dunn, L.M. (1981). *Peabody Picture Vocabulary Test—Revised.* Circle Pines, MN: American Guidance Service, Inc.

Dunst, C.J., & Trivette, C.M. (1988). A family systems model of early intervention with handicapped and developmentally at-risk children. In D.R. Powell (Ed.), *Parent education as early childhood intervention: Emerging directions in theory, research, and practice* (pp. 131–150). Norwood, NJ: Ablex.

Edwards, C.P. (1986). Another style of competence: The caregiving child. In A. Fogel

& G.D. Melson (Eds.), *Origins of nurturance*. Hillsdale, NJ: Erlbaum.

Edwards, D., & Mercer, N. (1987). *Common knowledge*. London: Routledge.

Elkind, D. (1987). *Miseducation*. New York: Knopf.

Ellis, A. (1962). *Reason and emotion in psychotherapy*. New York: Lyle Stuart.

Esman, M.J., & Uphoff, N.T. (1984). *Local organizations: Intermediaries in rural development*. Ithaca, NY: Cornell University Press.

Feldman, R.D. (1982). *Whatever happened to the quiz kids?* Chicago: Chicago Review Press.

Ferdinando, M. (1991, July). *The impact of Mediated Learning Experience approach to early childhood development in Redd Barna Sri Lanka pre-schools: A general evaluation*. Report on Phase I in Community Development Projects, Hanguranketa, Ginigathena, Matale, and Kekirawa RB Project. Unpublished report. Colombo, Sri Lanka: Redd Barna.

Feuerstein, R. (1979). *The dynamic assessment of retarded performers*. New York: University Park Press.

———. (1980). *Instrumental enrichment: Redevelopment of cognitive functions of retarded performers*. New York: University Park Press.

Field, T.M. (1983). Early interactions and interaction coaching of high-risk infants and parents. In M. Perlmutter (Ed.), *Development and policy concerning children with special needs*, (pp. 1–34). Minnesota Symposia on Child Psychology. Hillsdale, NJ: Erlbaum.

Field, T.M., Walden, T., Widmayer, S., & Greenberg, R. (1982). The early development of preterm discordant twin pairs: Bigger is not always better. In L.P. Lipsett & T.M. Field (Eds.), *Infant behavior and development: Prenatal risk and newborn behavior* (pp. 153–163). Norwood, NJ: Ablex.

Florida Protective Service System Annual Report (1989–1990). Tallahassee, FL: Department of Health and Rehabilitative Services.

Fraiberg, S. (1977). Blind infants and the mothers: An explanation of the sign system. In M. Bullowa (Ed.), *Before speech: The beginning of interpersonal communication* (pp. 149–169). Cambridge, UK: Cambridge University Press.

Freeberg, N.E., & Payne, D.T. (1967). Parental influence on cognitive development in early childhood: A review. *Child Development, 38*, 65–87.

Freire, P. (1970). *Pedagogy of the oppressed*. New York: Seabury Press.

———. (1973). *Education for critical consciousness*. New York: Seabury Press.

———. (1978). *Pedagogy in process*. New York: Seabury Press.

Fuglesang, A., & Chandler, D. (1986). *Search for process. Vol. I: Report from a project on community participation, Vol. II: Case studies, Vol. III: Selected bibliography*. Unpublished manuscripts. Study sponsored by The Dag Hammarskjöld Foundation, Uppsala, Sweden.

———. (1989). *Talkshops—Learning to talk with the young*. Colombo, Sri Lanka: Redd Barna.

———. (1993). *Participation as process —Process as growth: What we can learn from Grameen Bank, Bangladesh*. Dhaka, Bangladesh: Grameen Bank. In press.

Gardner, H. (1986). *Frames of mind*. New York: Routledge & Kegan Paul.

Geertz, C. (1983). *Local knowledge: Further essays in interpretive anthropology*. New York: Basic Books.

Geertz, H. (1959). The vocabulary of emotions: A study of Javanese socialization processes. *Psychiatry, 22*, 225–237.

Gezelius, H., & Millwood, D. (1988). *NGOs in development and participation in practice: An initial inquiry*. Working Paper No. 3, Popular Participation Program, Department of Social Anthropology, University of Stockholm, Sweden.

Giddens, A. (1991). *Modernity and self-identity: Self and society in the late modern age*. London: Polity Press.

Ginsburg, H. (1972). *The myth of the deprived child: Poor children's intellectual development and education*. Englewood Cliffs, NJ: Prentice-Hall.

Goodnow, J.J. (1977). *Children's drawings*. London: Open Books.

Goodnow, J.J., Cashmore, J., Cotton, S., & Knight, R. (1984). Mothers' developmental timetables in two cultural groups. *International Journal of Psychology*, 19, 193–205.

Gran, G. (1983). *Development by people: Citizen construction of a just world*. New York: Praeger.

Greenfield, P. (1989). A theory of the teacher in the learning activities of everyday life. In B. Rogoff & J. Lave (Eds.), *Everyday cognition*, (pp. 75–102). Cambridge, MA: Harvard University Press.

Greenspan, S.I. (1989). Intelligence and adaptation. *Psychological Issues*, 12, (3–4), Monograph 47/48. International Universities Press.

Guidano, U.F., & Liotti, G. (1983). *Cognitive processes and emotional disorders*. New York: Guilford Press.

Haywood, H.C., Brooks, P., & Burns, S. (1990). *Cognitive curriculum for young children (experimental version)*. Watertown, MA: Charlesbridge.

Hess, R.E., Kaskigawa, K., Azuma, H., Price, G.G., & Dickson, W.P. (1980). Maternal expectations for the mastery of developmental tasks in Japan and the United States. *International Journal of Psychology*, 15, 259–271.

Hundeide, K. (1986, August) *An indigenous approach to early intervention*. Paper presented at UNICEF Symposium, New York.

———. (1988). *Differential development in Third-World countries*. Paper presented at the International Conference on Individual Differences, Tel-Aviv, Israel.

———. (1991). *Helping disadvantaged children: Psycho-social intervention and aid to disadvantaged children in Third World countries*. London: Jessica Kingsley.

———. (1992). *Natural forms of mediation in culture*. Unpublished manuscript. University of Oslo, Norway.

Hundeide, K., & Naeshagen, R. (1988). *The use of drama in teaching language to immigrant children*. Unpublished manuscript in Norwegian. University of Oslo, Norway.

Johansson, J.E. (1992). *Metodikamnet i forskollaratutbildningen*. [Pre-school methods in pre-school teacher education.] Goteborg, Sweden: Acta Universitatis Gothoburgensis.

Kellog, R. (1970). Understanding children's art. In P. Cramer (Ed.) *Readings in developmental psychology today* (pp. 31–39). Del Mar, CA: CRM Books.

Kilbride, P.L., & Capriotti Kilbride, J. (1990). *Changing family life in East Africa*. University Park, PA & London: Pennsylvania State University Press.

Kirk, S.I., McCarthy, J.J., & Kirk, W.D. (1968). *Illinois test of psycholinguistic abilities*. Urbana, IL: University of Illinois Press.

Klein, P.S. (1984). Behavior of Israeli mothers toward infants in relation to infants' perceived temperament. *Child Development*, 55, 1212–1218.

———. (1985a). *More intelligent child*. Ramat Gan, Israel: Bar Ilan University Press.

———. (1985b). A more intelligent and sensitive child. Ramat-Gan: Bar-Ilan University Press (In Hebrew).

———. (1985c). *Promoting flexibility of mind in young children*. Ramat Gan, Israel: Bar-Ilan University Press. (In Hebrew).

———. (1988). Stability and change in interaction of Israeli mothers and infants. *Infant Behavior and Development*, 11, 55–70.

———. (1989). *Formidlet learning*. [Mediated learning experience.] Oslo: Universitetsforlaget.

———. (1990). The more intelligent and sensitive child (MISC) program for DS children. In E. Chigier (Ed.), *Looking up at Down syndrome* (pp. 181–192). London: Freund.

———. (1991). Improving the quality of parental interaction with very low birth weight children: A longitudinal study using a mediated learning experience model. *Infant Mental Health Journal*, 12(4), 321–337.

————. (1992). Assessing cognitive modifiability of infants and toddlers: Observations based on mediated learning experience. In H.C. Haywood, & D. Tzuriel (Eds.), Interactive assessment (pp. 233–250). New York: Springer-Verlag.

Klein, P.S., & Alony, S. (1993). Immediate and sustained effects of maternal mediation behaviors in infancy. *Journal of Early Intervention*, 71(2), 177–193.

Klein, P.S., & Feuerstein, R. (1984). Environmental variables and cognitive development: Identification of potent factors in adult–child interaction. In S. Harel & W.N. Anastasio (Eds.), *The at-risk infant: Psycho-socio-medical aspects* (pp. 369–377). Baltimore: Paul H. Brookes.

Klein, P.S., & Hundeide, K. (1989). *Training manual for the MISC (More Intelligent and Sensitive Child) program.* Sri Lanka: UNICEF.

Klein, P.S., Mogilner, B.M., & Mogilner, C. (1982). The relationship between maternal visiting patterns and the development of premature infants. *Journal of Psychosomatic Obstetrics and Gynaecology*, 13(4), 124–127.

Klein, P.S., & Nir Gal, O. (1992). Effects of computerized mediation of analogical thinking in kindergartens. *Journal of Computer Assisted Learning*, 8, 244–254.

Klein, P.S., Raziel, P., Brish, M., & Birenbaum, E. (1987). Cognitive performance of 3 year old born at very low birth weight. *Journal of Psychosomatic Obstetrics and Gynacology*, 7, 117–129.

Klein, P.S., & Tannenbaum, A.J. (1992).*To be young and gifted.* Norwood, NJ.

Klein, P.S., Weider, S., & Greenspan, S.L. (1987b). A theoretical overview and empirical study of mediated learning experience: Prediction of preschool performance from mother–infant interaction patterns. *Infant Mental Health Journal*, 8(2), 110–129.

Kommissionen for de Europaeiske Faelbsskaber. (1990). *Bornepasning i den Europaeiske Faelbasskaber 1985–1990.* [Early childhood education in the European Community.] Nr 31. Rue de la Loi, 200, 1049 Bruxelles.

Korbin, J.E. (Ed.). (1983). *Child abuse and neglect: Cross-cultural perspectives.* Berkeley: University of California Press.

Labov, W. (1979). The logic of non-standard English. In J. Lee (Ed.), *Language development*, (pp. 97–110). New York: Wiley.

Lakoff, G., & Johnson, M. (1980). *The metaphors we live by.* Chicago: University of Chicago Press.

Lally, J.R., Mangione, P.L., & Honig, A.S. (1988). The Syracuse University Family Development Research Program: Long-range impact of an early intervention with low-income children and their families. In D.R. Powell (Ed.), *Parent education as early childhood intervention: Emerging directions in theory, research, and practice* (pp. 131–180). Norwood, NJ: Ablex.

Larsson, M. (1993)."*MISC-programmet" pa Svenska daghem.* [The MISC-categories in Swedish day-care centers.] D-uppsats. Institutionen för pedagogik. Goteborg, Sweden: Goteborgs universitet.

Lazar, I., Darlington, R., Murray, H., Royce, J., & Snipper, A. (1982). The lasting effects of early education: A report from the Consortium for Longitudinal Studies. *Monographs of the Society for Research in Child Development*, 47 (2, Serial No. 195).

Lepper, M.R. (1981). Intrinsic and extrinsic motivation in children: Detrimental effects of superfluous social controls. Aspects of development of competence. *Minnesota Symposia on Child Psychology*, 14, 155–214.

Lerner, R. (1982). Children and adolescents as producers of their own development. *Developmental Review*, 2, 342–370.

LeVine, R.A. (1980). Anthropology and child development. *New Directions for Child Development*, 8, 71–86.

LeVine, R.A., & White, M.I. (1986). *Human conditions.* London: Routledge & Kegan Paul.

Lieberman, A., Weston, D., & Pawl, J. (1991). Preventive intervention and outcome with anxiously attached dyads. *Child Development, 62,* 199–210.

Lindahl, M., & Pramling, I. (1992). Att gora daghemmet till sin livsvarld. [To make the day-care one's own world.] I *Forskning om smabarn.* Centrum for kunskap om barn. Goteburg, Sweden: Goteborgs universitet.

Luria, A.R. (1977). *Cognitive development.* Oxford, UK: Oxford University Press.

Lyons-Ruth, K., Connell, D., Grunebaum, H., & Botein, S. (1990). Infants at social risk: Maternal depression and family support services as mediators of infant development and security of attachment. *Child Development, 61,* 85–99.

MacIntyre, A. (1981). *After virtue.* Notre Dame, France: University of Notre Dame Press.

Matlock, J., & Green, V. (1990). The effects of day-care on the social and emotional development of infants, toddlers and pre-schoolers. *Early Child Development and Care, 64,* 55–59.

Meadows, S., & Cashdan, A. (1988). *Helping children learn.* London: David Fulton.

Miller, C.A. (1987). *Maternal health and infant survival.* Washington, DC: National Center for Clinical Infant Programs.

Muenchow, S. (1991). Child care. In C.D. Herrington (Dir.), *Condition of children in Florida.* Tallahassee, FL: Florida State University, Center for Policy Studies in Education.

Nowrojee, S. (1991). Two Book Reviews. *Childwatch* Nos. 2 and 3. Nairobi: The African Network for the Prevention & Protection Against Child Abuse and Neglect.

Oudenhoven, N.V. (1992). *About children, policy considerations: A comparative assessment.* The Hague, Netherlands: Bernhard van Leer Foundation.

Palmerus, K., & Pramling, I. (1991, September). *Increasing the competence of staff dealing with young children.* Paper presented at the Fifth International Early Childhood Education Convention, Dunedin, New Zealand.

Palmerus, K., Pramling, I., & Lindahl, M. (1991). *Daghem for smabarn.* [Day-care for young children.] Rapport fran Institutionen for metodik i lararuthbildningen. Goteburg, Sweden: Goteborgs universitet.

Papousek, H., Papousek, M., & Koester, L.S. (1989). Sharing emotionality and sharing knowledge: A microanalytic approach to parent–infant communication. In C.E. Izard & P.B. Read (Eds.), *Measuring emotions in infants and children* (pp. 93–123). London: Cambridge University Press.

Papousek, M., Papousek H., & Bornstein, M.H. (1985). The naturalistic vocal environment of young infants: On the significance of homogeneity and variability in parental speech. In T.M. Field & N. Fox (Eds.), *Social perception in infants* (pp. 269–297). Norwood, NJ: Ablex.

Piaget, J. (1973). *Sprak och tanke hos barnet.* [The child's language and thought.] Lund, Sweden: Gleerups.

Pramling, I. (1989). *Learning to learn: A study of Swedish pre-school children.* New York: Springer-Verlag.

———. (1991, September). *To develop the child's understanding of the surrounding world.* Paper presented at the Fifth International Early Childhood Education Convention, Dunedin, New Zealand.

Ramey, C.T., Bryant, D.M., & Suarez, T.M. (1985). Preschool compensatory education and the modifiability of intelligence: A critical review. In D. Detterman (Ed.), *Current topics in human intelligence* (pp. 247–296). Norwood, NJ: Ablex.

Ricks, M.H. (1985). The social transmission of parental behavior: Attachment across generations. *Monograph of the Society for Research in Child Development, 50*(1–2, Serial No. 209), 211–227.

Rogoff, B. (1990). *Apprenticeship in learning.* Cambridge, MA: Harvard University Press.

Rommetveit, R. (1974). *On message structure.* London: Academic Press.

Rosenthal, D. (1985, July). *Child-rearing and cultural values: A study of Greek and Australian mothers*. Paper presented at the meeting of the International Society for the Study of Behavioral Development, Tours, France.

Roupp, R., Travers, J., Glantz, F., & Corlen, C. (1979). *Children at the center.* Cambridge, MA: ABT Associates.

Rutter, M. (1981). *Maternal deprivation reassessed.* London: Penguin Group.

Rutter, M., & Mittler, P. (1972). Environmental influences on language development. In M. Rutter & J.A.M. Nartin (Eds.), *The child with delayed speech.* (pp. 89–120). London: Heinemann/SIMP.

Sarbin, T. (1986). *Narrative psychology: The storied nature of human conduct.* New York: Praeger.

Scarr, S., & McCartney, K. (1988). Far from home: An experimental evaluation of the mother–child program in Bermuda. *Child Development, 59,* 531–543.

Scarr, S., & Weinberg, R.A. (1986). The early childhood enterprise: Care and education of the young. *American Psychologist, 41*(10), 1140–1146.

Schaffer, H.R., & Emerson, P.E. (1964). The development of social attachments in infancy. *Monograph of the Society of Research in Child Development, 29,* 94.

Scheper-Hughes, N. (1990). Mother love and child death in Northeast Brazil. In J.W. Stigler, R.A. Schweder, & G.H. Herdt, (Eds.), *Cultural psychology 6*(19), 542–565. Cambridge, MA: Harvard University Press.

Schorr, L.B., & Schorr, D. (1989). *Within our reach: Breaking the cycle of disadvantage.* New York: Doubleday.

Schweder, R.A. (1982). Beyond self-constructed knowledge: The study of culture and morality. *Merrill-Palmer Quarterly, 28,* 41–69.

———. (1991). Cultural psychology: What is it? In R.A. Schweder (Ed.), *Thinking through cultures.* (pp. 21–48). Cambridge, MA: Harvard University Press.

Setiono, K. (1992). *A preliminary report on the Bandung project.* Unpublished project report. Padjanjaran University, Bandung, Indonesia.

Shani, M., Cohen, A., & Klein, P.S. (1993). *The effects of computer use on the cognitive performance of kindergarten children.* Unpublished manuscript. School of Education, Bar-Ilan University, Ramat Gan, Israel.

Shanmugam, G. (1991). *A preliminary study on the behavior symptoms of the Redd Barna pre-school children in the north eastern-Mullaitivu project and eastern-Vellavely project of Sri Lanka.* Unpublished report. Colombo, Sri Lanka: Redd Barna.

Shibles, W. (1971). *Emotion: The method of philosophical therapy.* Whitewater, WI: Language Press.

Shotter, J. (1984). *Social accountability and selfhood.* Oxford, UK: Blackwell.

Skeels, H.M. (1966). Adult status of children with contrasting early life experiences. *Monographs of the Society for Research in Child Development, 31* (3, Serial No. 105), 1–65.

Smedslund, J. (1984). The invisible obvious. In K. Niem (Ed.), *Psychology of the 1990's* (pp. 114–137). New York: Elsevier.

Socialstyrelsen. (1987). *Pedagogiskt program for forskolan.* [Educational program for pre-school.] Allmanna Rad, p. 4, Stockholm: Allmanna Förlaget.

Spitz, R. (1946). Anaclitic depression. *Psychoanalytic Study of the Child, 2,* 313–342.

State Education Department of the University of the State of New York. (1987–1989). New York State plan for educating children with handicapping conditions. Albany, NY: Author.

Stern, D. (1977a). *The first relationships: Infant and mother.* London: Open Books.

———. (1977b). *The interpersonal world of the infant.* New York: Basic Books.

———. (1985). *The interpersonal world of the infant.* 2nd edition. New York: Basic Books.

———. (1989). *The interpersonal world of the infant.* Reprint. New York: Basic Books.

Sutton-Smith, B. (1986). Children's faction making. In T. Sarbin, (Ed.), *Narrative psy-*

chology: The storied nature of human conduct (pp. 67–89). New York: Praeger.

Tal, C., & Klein, P.S. (1994). *Effects of the MISC on mother–infant attachment.* Paper presented at the 4th Conference of the International Association of Cognitive Education, Ginosar, Israel.

Taren, D. (1991). Hunger. In C.D. Herrington (Dir.), *Condition of children in Florida.* Tallahassee, FL: Florida State University, Center for Policy Studies in Education.

Tendler, J. (1982). *Turning private voluntary organizations into development agencies: Questions for evaluation.* USAID.

Thomas, A., & Chess, S. (1977). *Temperament and development.* New York: Brunner/Mazel.

Timor, B. (1993). Personal communication.

Trevarthen, C. (1992). The self born in intersubjectivity: The psychology of infant communicating. In U. Neisser (Ed.), *Ecological and interpersonal knowledge of the self,* (pp. 94–121). New York: Cambridge University Press.

Vedeler, L. (1987). *Barns kommunikasjon i rollek.* [Children's communication in role-play.] Oslo: Universitetsforlaget.

Vygotsky, L.S. (1978). *Mind in society: The development of higher psychological processes.* Cambridge, MA: Harvard University Press.

Walkerdine, V. (1988). *The mastery of reason.* London: Routledge.

Wallace, J. (1984, April). *Indicators of cognitive functioning in school-aged low-birth-weight children.* Paper presented at the International Conference on Infancy Studies, New York, NY.

Welbourn, A. (1991). *RRA and the analysis of difference.* Unpublished paper. University of Oslo, Norway.

Wertsch, J. (1985). *Vygotsky and the social formation of the mind.* Cambridge, MA: Harvard University Press.

White, B.S., Kaban, B.T., & Attanucci, J.S. (1979). *The origins of human competence.* Lexington, MA: Lexington Books.

Whiting, B., & Edwards, C. (1988). *Children of different worlds.* Cambridge, MA: Harvard University Press.

Williams, B.C., & Miller, C.A. (1991). *Preventive health care for young children: Findings from a 10-county study and directions for United States policy.* Arlington, VA: National Center for Clinical Infant Programs.

Wilson, J. (1986). Assessing aesthetic appreciation: A review. In M. Ross (Ed.), *Assessment in education* (pp. 95–111). New York: Pergamon Press.

Woodhead, M. (1988). When psychology informs public policy: The case of early childhood intervention. *American Psychologist, 43,* 443–454.

Zahn-Waxler, C., Radke-Yarrow, M., & King, R. (1979). Child-rearing and children's pro-social initiations towards victims of distress. *Child Development, 50,* 319–330.

Author Index

Subject Index

aesthetics 66, 67, 68, 69, 70, 83, 84
affecting behavior ix, 11, 12, 18, 25, 28, 33, 39, 40, 41, 43, 64, 89
altruism 144
approval ix
attachment 14, 22, 33, 34, 35, 38, 48, 122, 202, 208
attunement 39, 90

Bayley Mental Development Scales 28, 38
Beery and Bucktanika test 29
brainstorming 31, 35, 38, 99

child development network 152
Cognitive Curriculum for Young Children (CCYC) 85
cognitive modifiability 10
competence (of MISC) 14, 15, 19, 25, 27, 30, 32, 33, 37, 38, 43, 44, 45, 47, 49, 55–57, 59, 60, 64, 67, 75, 76, 78, 84, 90, 93, 97, 100, 105, 106, 108, 110, 118, 126, 128, 131, 132, 140, 175, 176, 180, 181, 189, 190, 192, 204, 218, 228, 234, 244, 235
conscientization 151
cultural translation 126, 127, 135
cultural transmitting 4, 5, 17, 137, 138, 196, 212, 222

Developmental Test of Visual Motor Integration 51, 53

empowerment 20, 31, 114, 135, 146, 149, 151, 200, 202, 208
enhance cognitive development 20, 109, 184
enhancement of literacy 73
enhancing children's development 136
enhancing learning potential 17, 38, 199
enhancing mediation 95

enhancing social values 139
enrichment ix, 4, 64, 66, 68, 71, 76, 109, 114
enthusiasm 6
erosion 144
excitement, 13
expansion ix, 3, 13, 25, 26, 28, 29, 36, 39, 40, 41, 45, 49, 55, 56, 58, 61, 67, 70, 76, 86, 105, 106, 126, 128, 131, 132, 133, 138, 140, 146, 166, 175, 176, 187, 194, 206, 213, 223, 224, 226, 245

Family Development Research Program (FDRP) 20
flexibility of mind ix, 3, 4, 7, 8, 9, 10, 21, 73, 78, 113, 136, 137, 159, 211
focusing ix, 4, 10, 11, 12, 19, 25, 26, 28, 29, 30, 36, 44, 46, 49, 55, 56, 58, 60, 61, 66, 67, 70, 75, 76, 85, 86, 99, 104, 105, 123, 126, 132, 140, 155, 166, 173, 194, 224, 226, 237
fragmentation 6

hyperactivity 7

Illinois Tests of Psycholinguistic Abilities (ITPA) 29, 51, 53
immunization 136
inclusion 80
inferiority 137
intervention ix, 17–24, 26, 28, 30, 31, 33, 35, 43–59, 63, 64, 65, 73, 82–100, 104–112, 114, 117, 122, 123, 126, 127, 128, 130, 135, 136, 139, 152, 180–185, 190–194, 201–207, 211, 212, 213, 217, 218

kaders 123, 127, 213

SOURCE BOOKS ON EDUCATION

SCHOOL PLAY
A Source Book
by James H. Block
and Nancy R. King

ADULT LITERACY
A Source Book and Guide
by Joyce French

BLACK CHILDREN AND
AMERICAN INSTITUTIONS
*An Ecological Review and
Resource Guide*
by Valora Washington
and Velma LaPoint

SEXUALITY EDUCATION
A Resource Book
by Carol Cassell
and Pamela M. Wilson

REFORMING TEACHER
EDUCATION
Issues and New Directions
edited by Joseph A. Braun, Jr.

CRITICAL ISSUES IN FOREIGN
LANGUAGE INSTRUCTION
edited by Ellen S. Silber

THE EDUCATION OF WOMEN
IN THE UNITED STATES
*A Guide to Theory, Teaching,
and Research*
by Averil Evans McClelland

MATERIALS AND STRATEGIES FOR
THE EDUCATION
OF TRAINABLE MENTALLY
RETARDED LEARNERS
by James P. White

EDUCATIONAL TESTING
Issues and Applications
by Kathy E. Green

TEACHING THINKING SKILLS
Theory and Practice
by Joyce N. French
and Carol Rhoder

TEACHING SOCIAL STUDIES TO THE
YOUNG CHILD
A Research and Resource Guide
by Blythe S. Farb Hinitz

TELECOMMUNICATIONS
A Handbook for Educators
by Reza Azarmsa

CATHOLIC SCHOOL EDUCATION
IN THE UNITED STATES
Development and Current Concerns
by Mary A. Grant
and Thomas C. Hunt

SECONDARY SCHOOLS
AND COOPERATIVE LEARNING
Theories, Models, and Strategies
edited by Jon E. Pederson
and Annette D. Digby

SCHOOL PRINCIPALS AND CHANGE
by Michael D. Richardson,
Paula M. Short,
and Robert L. Prickett

PLAY IN PRACTICE
*A Systems Approach to Making
Good Play Happen*
edited by Karen VanderVen,
Paul Niemiec,
and Roberta Schomburg

TEACHING SCIENCE TO
CHILDREN
Second Edition
by Mary D. Iatridis with a
contribution by Miriam Maracek

KITS, GAMES AND MANIPULATIVES
FOR THE ELEMENTARY SCHOOL
CLASSROOM
A Source Book
by Andrea Hoffman
and Ann Glannon

PARENTS AND SCHOOLS
A Source Book
by Angela Carrasquillo
and Clement B. G. London

PROJECT HEAD START
Models and Strategies for the Twenty-First Century
by Valora Washington
and Ura Jean Oyemade Bailey

EARLY INTERVENTION
Cross-Cultural Experiences with a Mediational Approach
by Pnina S. Klein

EDUCATING YOUNG ADOLESCENTS
Life in the Middle
edited by Michael J. Wavering

INSTRUMENTATION IN EDUCATION
An Anthology
by Lloyd Bishop
and Paula E. Lester

TEACHING ENGLISH AS A SECOND LANGUAGE
A Resource Guide
by Angela L. Carrasquillo

THE FOREIGN LANGUAGE CLASSROOM
Bridging Theory and Practice
edited by
Margaret A. Haggstrom,
Leslie Z. Morgan,
and Joseph A. Wieczorek

READING AND LEARNING DISABILITIES
Research and Practice
by Joyce N. French,
Nancy J. Ellsworth,
and Marie Z. Amoruso

MULTICULTURAL EDUCATION
A Source Book
by Patricia G. Ramsey,
Edwina B. Vold,
and Leslie R. Williams

RELIGIOUS HIGHER EDUCATION IN THE UNITED STATES
A Source Book
edited by Thomas C. Hunt
and James C. Carper

TEACHERS AND MENTORS
Profiles of Distinguished Twentieth-Century Professors of Education
edited by Craig Kridel,
Robert V. Bullough, Jr.,
and Paul Shaker

MULTICULTURALISM IN ACADEME
A Source Book
by Libby V. Morris
and Sammy Parker